MARSHAL NEY AT QUATRE BRAS
New Perspectives on the Opening Battle of the Waterloo Campaign

MARSHAL NEY AT QUATRE BRAS
New Perspectives on the Opening Battle of the Waterloo Campaign

Paul L Dawson

Frontline Books

MARSHAL NEY AT QUATRE BRAS
New Perspectives on the Opening Battle of the Waterloo Campaign

This edition published in 2017 by Frontline Books,
an imprint of Pen & Sword Books Ltd,
47 Church Street, Barnsley, S. Yorkshire, S70 2AS

Copyright © Paul L Dawson

The right of Paul L Dawson to be identified as the author of this work has been asserted by him in accordance with the Copyright, Designs and Patents Act 1988.

ISBN: 978-1-52670-071-1

All rights reserved. No part of this publication may be reproduced, stored in or introduced into a retrieval system, or transmitted, in any form, or by any means (electronic, mechanical, photocopying, recording or otherwise) without the prior written permission of the publisher. Any person who does any unauthorized act in relation to this publication may be liable to criminal prosecution and civil claims for damages.

CIP data records for this title are available from the British Library

For more information on our books, please visit
www.frontline-books.com
email info@frontline-books.com
or write to us at the above address.

Printed and bound in the UK by TJ International Ltd.
Typeset in 10.5/12.5 point Palatino

Contents

Introduction		vii
Acknowledgements		xi
Chapter 1	Invasion : 15 June	1
Chapter 2	Quatre-Bras	12
Chapter 3	Bachelu's Attack	43
Chapter 4	Foy's Attack	55
Chapter 5	Hurber's Charge	63
Chapter 6	Jérôme's Division	95
Chapter 7	Kellermann's Charge	109
Chapter 8	Movement of 1st Corps	142
Chapter 9	17 June	163
Chapter 10	Charge of the 7th Hussars	183
Chapter 11	Waterloo	206
Chapter 12	Conclusion	219
Appendix	D-Erlon's Communication of 15 June	226
Bibliography		227
Index		237

Introduction

Marshal Ney was a French soldier. He served during both the French Revolutionary and Napoléonic Wars. Created Marshal of the Empire by Napoléon in 1804, he was known as *'Le Rougeaud'* ('red faced' or 'ruddy') by his men. Following the Russian campaign, he became known as *'le Brave des Braves'* ('the bravest of the brave') by Napoléon. His career is well known by many historians and wargamers. Today, he is perhaps best remembered as the rearguard commander in Russia, and for leading the massed ranks of glittering cuirassiers to death and glory at Waterloo.

Many have sought to find reasons for why Napoléon lost the Battle of Waterloo, as if to shift the blame from the emperor to other factors. Marshal Ney, Marshal Grouchy and Marshal Soult have all been blamed for the defeat. The truth is, however, that the British army was better fed, better equipped and better trained, and Napoléon was outgeneraled by the Duke of Wellington. The uncomfortable truth is that the Armée du Nord fought well, but it was bettered by Wellington's infantry; British, Dutch-Belgian, Nassau, Hanoverian and Prussian. There was no great conspiracy theory for the defeat of Napoléon on the part of the French. Napoléon had lost battles and campaigns before (Leipzig being a case in point) and had had the time to regenerate a new army and renew the fighting. In 1815, the Allies had learned that the only way to stop Napoléon running back to Paris and building a new army (as he had done in 1812, and twice in 1813) was to harass his army to the point of exhaustion and not give Napoléon any breathing space. The pursuit of the defeated French after Waterloo cemented the Allied victory. It was a total defeat as the Prussians had suffered in 1806. Napoléon's grip on power in 1815 was already shaky, and news of the defeat resulted in political intrigue to remove him from power, as had occurred previously with the Malet Plot of 1812. What happened politically in 1815 had occurred in 1812 and 1814, and reflected Napoléon's own coup in 1799.

However, many still consider Ney, like Grouchy, to be a major factor in Napoléon being out-generaled, as it were, at Waterloo. This book seeks to evaluate Ney's actions in the Hundred Days campaigns, and assess if he was culpable for the defeat. Our study is based on two forms of evidence: personal testimony and empirical hard data. What follows is a discussion of these sources to enable the reader to understand the strengths and weaknesses of the material used in the creation of a narrative about Napoléon's last army. The material used has undergone a variety of processes before it was read by the author. Not all the archival paperwork prepared in 1815 has survived to the current day. Not all written memoirs of participants have survived. Those cited here are just those the author could identify—many more may exist in private collections, museums and libraries, and they may well tell a different narrative from that presented here. The narrative has been constructed from the sources available to the author.

In creating our narrative, we have endeavoured to let the primary sources speak for themselves without having to fit what they say into a superficial construct created by other authors. We must be aware, however, of the limitations and failings of these memoirs as a source of empirical data. The memoir, as Paul Fussell has established, occupies a place between fiction and autobiography.[1] Between 2004 and 2012, neuroscientist John Coates conducted research into memory. The study found that what is recalled from memory is what the mind believes happened rather than what actually happened. This effect is often referred to as 'false memory'.[2] Thus, a lot of the letters we use are partly real recollections from first-hand experience added to, and expanded with, what the writer has learned since the events took place.

One of the most cited works about Ney and the Hundred Days is Duc d'Elchingen's *Documents inedits sur la campagne de 1815*,[3] which was written to restore the reputation of Marshal Ney by his son. The Service Historique at Vincennes preserves the original manuscript copy of the book dated 1837. Of the documents presented, a good number can be cross-referenced to the register of orders issued by Marshal Soult and General Reille. Where the orders can be cross-referenced, the copies made by Ney's son are, in all cases, word-for-word copies of the originals, so we can have some degree of confidence in the material collected overall. However, a lot of the material cannot be cross-checked with documents written in 1815. The Service Historique also preserves a great number of documents written during the campaign. These documents, as well as Reille's and Soult's order registers, have never

INTRODUCTION

been translated and used in an English-language study of Quatre-Bras. In some cases, the documents have not even been published before in French. In some cases though, many letters and orders cited as being from 16 June are, in reality, perhaps forgeries as we shall see. Therefore, with a large corpus of archive material never used in the study of the battle before we can present a new narrative of Quatre-Bras from the French side. The two most recent studies of the battle by Andrew Fields and Mike Robinson are excellent introductions to the battle, but are both deeply flawed by not using original archive documents and instead are based, for the French forces, on easily accessible published texts. Thus, the study of the battle is not advanced as the same source material is used time and again without any thorough research being conducted on the French participants. With this book I have addressed this issue. These archive sources, coupled with using (for the first time) the actual day-by-day casualty figures from the campaign, have allowed me to write a new history of Quatre-Bras, to reveal the true story of Marshal Ney on 16 June.

We must note that in all correspondence written between 15 to 17 June that what we know as 'Quatre-Bras' was referred to as 'Trois-Bras' or 'Three-Arms'. But, for convenience, we use the incorrect term 'Quatre-Bras' to describe the locality as this term is ingrained in the history of the campaign.

Finally, we must also stress the role of the interpreter in the creation of the narrative. We all have preconceived ideas and personal biases about historical events based on political, economic, sociological and ideological grounds; these will all impact on the way the historian interprets the source material. No historian is free from bias. In summary, one must stress that the narrative of events of the Battle of Waterloo, and others of the 1815 campaign, can only be based on the memories of participants. What I present in the narrative of the events of Waterloo is an interpretation based upon the experiences of those involved. It should be seen as *a* version of events and not *the* version of events within the post-processual framework as espoused by Shanks and Hodder.[4] We will never fully understand the battle, nor be able to create a single credible narrative, as the sources are, in the main, neither empirical nor corroborative or free from bias. In recent years, the ever-increasing cacophony of voices from participants at Waterloo that have been printed are often taken at face value as true reflections of events, without any critical evaluation of the material in a historical manner. There is little to be gained purely from the study of eyewitness accounts, and the cited memoirs of various participants should only be seen as the author's recollection of the events at the time in which they were written.[5] These memoirs had a different 'credibility' from the hard empirical data recovered from the documentary sources held in various archives in Britain and across Europe.[6]

Time

In any discussion of the campaign we have to create a timeline of events. In 1815, time was not yet standardised; officers did have watches, but each watch would keep time differently to one another, so for one officer the time could be 16.00 and for another 16.10. Therefore, we cannot rely upon the time given by eyewitnesses, as it relates to the eyewitness and not the other participants of the campaign.

However, we can overcome this to some extent. The French government issued an almanac every year in which the time of sunrise and sunset was recorded in Paris.[7] If we turn to the almanac for June 1815 we find that on the 16th the sun rose at 3.58 and set at 23.21.[8] Therefore, it was but dusk until 22.00 and not dark until midnight. Thus, based upon the absolute timing for sunrise and sunset, the Battle of Quatre-Bras lasted far longer than most writers allow for. In this book the timings are based upon the known times for sunrise and sunset to provide a reliable and verifiable timeline for the day; the officers recorded times being largely ignored and their statements upon dawn, dusk, night, etc. being fitted to the absolute chronology created by the published sunrise and sunset times.

NOTES:
[1] Paul Fussell, *The Great War and Modern Memory*, Oxford University Press, Oxford, 1975, p. 311.
[2] John Coates, *The Hour Between Dog and Wolf*, Fourth Estate, London, 2012.
[3] Michel Louis Felix Ney, *Documents inédits sur la campagne de 1815*, Anselin, Paris, 1840
[4] Michael Shanks, Ian Hodder, *Processual, postprocessual and interpretive archaeologies* in Hodder et al, *Interpreting Archaeology*, Routledge, London and New York, 1995, p. 4.
[5] Paul L. Dawson, *Memoires: Fact or Fiction? The Campaign of 1814*, The Napoleon Series, December 2013, available at http://www.napoleon-series.org/research/eyewitness/c_memoires.html [accessed 28 February 2017].
[6] Anna Green, Kathleen Troup, *The Houses of History*, Manchester University Press, 1999, p. 236.
[7] Anon, *Almanach royal pour les années M.DCCC.XIV et M.DCCC.XV*, Asnard et Pochin, Paris, 1814
[8] Anon, *Almanach royal*.

Acknowledgements

In the preparation of this book I would like to thank all those who have offered advice and support, and all those who have helped me with my research. Furthermore, I would also like to thank M. Yves Martin, Mr Ian J. Smith, John Lubomski and Sally Fairweather for their assistance with, and photographing of, archival material at the Archives Nationales and Service Historique de la Défence Armée du Tére, in Paris. Erwin Muilwijk and John Franklin deserve a special word of praise—without their assistance in the provision of source material this book could never have come to fruition.

Lieutenant Colonel Timmermans must be thanked for illustrations. I heartily encourage readers to visit his excellent website: www.Napoléon-monuments.eu

Chapter 1

Invasion: 15 June

When Napoléon returned to France in spring 1815, Europe was put into turmoil. The Allies met at the Congress of Vienna and declared war on the returned emperor. With the Allies ranged in opposition to him, Napoléon's hand was forced into taking military action. To prevent an invasion of France, he made plans to attack the mobilised Allied troops under Wellington and Blücher in the Netherlands. Despite being outnumbered, Napoléon's modus operandi was to keep the two forces separate, over which he had a numerical advantage, and defeat each army in turn by rapid concentrations of the French army, just as he had so effectively done in 1814. While the emperor attacked the Netherlands with the Armée du Nord, the borders of France would be controlled by the Corps d'Observation:
1) General Jean Rapp's 23,000-strong Armée du Rhine was placed to stop the Austrians of Schwarzenberg once they started their advance;
2) General Lecourbe's 8,400-strong Armée du Jura faced the Swiss;
3) Marshal Suchet's 23,500-strong Armée des Alpes protected Lyons against the Austrian-Piedmonts army;
4) Marshal Brune's 5,500-strong Armée du Var faced Onasco and the Neapolitan army

The Department of the Vendée was once more in rebellion and General Lamarque was dispatched with 10,000 troops, including elements of the Young Guard. Furthermore, two armies were deployed against the Spanish-Portuguese threat: the Armée des Pyrénées Orientales, of General Decaen at Toulouse, and the Armée des Pyrénées Occidentales, commanded by General de Clausel at Bordeaux. The minister of war, Marshal Davout, had 20,000 troops to protect Paris.

On 3 June, Napoléon informed Marshals Soult and Davout that Marshal Grouchy had been named commander-in-chief of the cavalry of the Armée du Nord. Grouchy joined the Imperial Headquarters at

Laon on the 5th, and began to work with Soult on establishing the movement orders for the forthcoming campaign.

The Imperial Guard left Paris on 8 June 1815. On 12 June, Napoléon left Paris and headed for Soissons, where the headquarters for the coming campaign were established. Arrayed along the Belgian border were two Allied armies: Field Marshal Gebhard Leberecht von Blücher commanded a force of 116,000 Prussians and Saxons, centered at Namur. The second comprised 93,000 British, Dutch, and German troops based at Brussels. These men were commanded by the Duke of Wellington. Leading elements of both Allied armies were at Charleroi and Gilly on the evening of 14 June 1815.

In the early hours of 15 June, the French army began to move across the frontier. Napoléon was confident of the expected outcome, so much so that the order of the day, issued the previous day, proclaimed:[1]

> Soldiers, today is the anniversary of Marengo and Friedland, places where the destiny of Europe was decided on two occasions. Accordingly, like after Austerlitz and Wagram, we believed the arguments and the oaths of the princes that we left on their thrones! Today, however, in their coalition against us they take offense at the independence and at the most sacred rights of France. They started their aggressions on in a precise manner: let us therefore march to meet them; they and we, are we not the same men?
>
> Soldiers, at Jena, against those same Prussians, who are today so arrogant, you were one against three, and at Montmirail, one against six.
>
> That those of you who were prisoners of the English tell you their stories of their Pontoons and of the horrible evils that they suffered.
>
> The Saxons, the Belgians, the Hanoverians, the soldiers of the Rhine Confederation, groan at their obligations to help the cause of the princes who are enemies of the justice and the rights of all people. They know that this coalition is insatiable. After destroying twelve million Italians, one million Saxons, six million Belgians, she will devour the smaller States of Germany.
>
> The fools! One moment of good fortune blinds them. The oppression and the humiliation of the French people are above their power! If they move into France, they will find their graves.
>
> Soldiers! We have to make forced marches, give battles, take risks; but, with steadiness, victory will be ours: the rights, the honour and the welfare of our country will be retaken.
>
> For each Frenchman who has the courage, the moment has come to win or to die!

Napoléon's plans called for a concentric advance of three columns onto Charleroi. Reille's 2nd Corps and d'Erlon's 1st Corps formed the left wing of the army, and were to march from Solre-sur-Sambre, via Thuin, to Marchienne-au-Pont, a short distance outside of Charleroi. Pajol's cavalry in the centre, supported by Domon's cavalry, was to advance from Beaumont to Charleroi, with General Vandamme's 3rd Corps to follow under the protective screen cavalry. At the rear were Lobau's 6th Corps and the Imperial Guard. The right wing comprised General Gérard's 4th Corps protected by one of Milhaud's cuirassier divisions.

Napoléon's plan was that if the army left its positions at 3.00, some 60,000 men would be at Charleroi by midday. But this carefully timetabled plan soon started to unravel. At 7.00, General-of-Division de Bourmont deserted to the Prussians, which flung his division into chaos. He was the first, but not the last officer who deserted the army. Vandamme did not get his marching orders as the courier carrying them, we are told, broke his leg, so he only moved off at 7.00—over two hours late.

Movements of 1st and 2nd Corps
Placed in command of 2nd Corps was Honoré Reille, who had volunteered as a grenadier in the 2nd Battalion of Var in September 1791, beginning a military career of over 25 years.

General Reille's 2nd Corps marched out at dawn, and occupied Thuin, Lobbes and Montignies-le-Tilleul, pushing back Prussian outposts at they did so. At Lobbes, the 1st Chasseurs à Cheval attacked pickets from the 2nd Battalion 1st Westphalian Landwehr Regiment and a squadron from the 6th Uhlans. A detachment of Bachelu's division was sent the Lobbes, with the bulk of the division heading off to Maladrie and Thuin.[2]

Reille did not reach Marchienne-au-Pont until 10.00, and quickly ordered Bachelu to storm the town and gain possession of the vital bridge over the River Sambre. The Prussian garrison at Marchienne-au-Pont comprised the 2nd Battalion 6th Prussian Infantry Regiment supported by two artillery pieces.[3] The Prussian garrison was no easy push over, and Bachelu was not across the Sambre until, it seems, 13.00. Jacques Martin, an officer in the 45th Regiment of Line Infantry (part of 1st Corps), narrates that:[4]

> In the morning, we came across our first body of enemy troops, who tried to resist us. They killed several hundred men, but they were driven off by the sword somewhere betwixt Marchiennes and Charleroi. There, they gathered in greater numbers, and wanted to

prevent our passage of the Sambre and expected the bulk of their army there, but the 2nd Corps, who preceded us, in no time after just a few shots, carried the bridges with their bayonets and gained the opposite bank.

Reille, with the leading elements of 2nd Corps, was at Jumet by 15.00, and from there began his movement to Gosselies. He ordered Piré's cavalry to sweep the countryside in front of the infantry and to pass to the left of the Monceaux Wood, through which his infantry marched. This movement was, in theory, to be supported by 1st Corps. Marie Jean Baptiste Lemonnier-Delafosse, aide-de-camp to General Foy (commanding part of 2nd Corps), notes:[5]

> June 15, at dawn, we attacked the enemy at Thuin, who were positioned on high ground, a position which was half-fortified by nature, who put up a stubborn resistance. However, the enemy could not hold our infantry in check, thanks to our prompt and vigorous attack which routed them, driving them back outside Thuin, beyond the woods of Rome, and onto the plateau above Marchienne-au-Pont. The light cavalry supported our infantry. The Prussians formed several squares, near a windmill on the right of the road to Marchienne, but they were crushed by our cavalry charge.
>
> General Foy arrived, and as result, led his infantry over the bridge across the Sambre, which was defended by the Prussians, but through the rapid advance by our light infantry, in front of our columns of infantry, the enemy began their retirement, and our division gained Gosselies, without encountering any obstacles; our cavalry pushed up to Frasné.

Colonel Auguste Louis Petiet, of the French Imperial Headquarters, recalls:[6]

> On the 15th, at daybreak, the army began to move to enter Belgium. The 2nd Corps attacked the Prussian outposts at Marchienne-au-Pont and pursued them vigorously. The cavalry of this corps had the opportunity to charge multiple infantry squares, crushed them and took several hundred prisoners. The Prussians hastened to re-cross the Sambre.
>
> Many sharpshooters defended the approaches to the bridge of Charleroi, the engineers and sailors of the guard were there. I

entered with them into the city. These brave sailors captured a Belgian battalion. After reporting these results to the emperor, I carried orders to General Pajol who was entering Charleroi with his cavalry, to pursue the enemy along the road to Fleurus.

Marshal Ney Arrives
First aide-de-camp to Marshal Ney, Colonel Pierre-Agathe Heymès, recollected how Ney left Beaumont on that same morning:[7]

> Meanwhile, having learnt around ten o'clock in the morning that Marshal Mortier had remained sick in that town, Ney went to see him and brought two horses. Colonel Heymès was on his side and they left to go on the road, followed by a civilian, [and] the wagons remained at Beaumont. While passing the column, the Marshal was welcomed by the flattering acclaims of the old soldiers, who were rejoined by the red-haired one who had before led them to so many victories.
> At seven o'clock in the evening the Marshal joined the emperor outside of Charleroi, at the crossing of the routes to Brussels and Fleurus.
> 'Welcome, Ney,' the prince said, 'I am pleased to see you: you will take command of the 1st and 2nd Corps of infantry; General Reille marches with three divisions towards Gosselies. General d'Erlon will remain tonight at Marchienne-au-Pont; you will have with you the light cavalry division of Piré; I will also give you two regiments of chasseurs and lancers from my Guard, but you will not commit them. Tomorrow you will be joined with the reserve of the heavy cavalry under the command of Kellermann. Go and push back the enemy.'

Ney left his meeting with Napoléon and moved off with the Imperial Guard light cavalry division in the direction of Gosselies, where he arrived around 4.30 p.m. It was here that Colonel Jean Baptiste Lemonnier-Delafosse watched the marshal pass through:[8]

> The same day, 15 June, it was at Gosselies that Marshal Ney took command of the left wing of the army, formed by the 1st and 2nd Corps of d'Erlon and Reille. I saw him passing by in full gallop, followed by his aide-de-camp, directing themselves to Frasné; it was two o'clock and all we presumed was that our attack manoeuvre would continue.

Combat at Gosselies and Frasné

The French 1st Hussars advanced to attack Gosselies. Outnumbered by the Prussian 6th Uhlans and 24th Infantry Regiment, they had no option but to retreat, pursued vigorously by the Prussian Uhlans.[9]

Sometime later the light cavalry division of the Imperial Guard under the orders of General Lefèbvre-Desnoëttes, arrived, and an unknown infantry regiment of the Young Guard, supported by two field guns, was established midway between Charleroi and Gosselies as a reserve for Lefèbvre-Desnoëttes.[10]

The Guard light cavalry arrived at Frasné about 17.30, and came under an artillery fire. General Lefèbvre-Desnoëttes immediately sent a request for infantry support, and General Bachelu directed to Frasné a battalion of the 2nd Regiment of Light Infantry. Adjutant-Commandant Toussaint-Jean Trefcon, chief-of-staff to General Bachelu, writes:[11]

> June 15, about ten o'clock in the morning we met the enemy in front of Marchienne. The 5th Division was responsible for capturing this village and the bridge over the Sambre. After a fierce exchange of musketry, we attacked the enemy with the bayonet. They were compelled to retreat, and the bridge was taken by the 2nd Regiment of Light Infantry from the brigade of General Husson. Although this bridge was quite narrow, the corps crossed fairly quickly, and once passed the Sambre we continued our march forward. We were going in great haste in the direction of Brussels. A counter-order reached us, giving instructions to the division to take positions ahead of Mellet. When we reached this village, our vanguard, formed by a battalion from the 2nd Regiment of Light Infantry, attacked a Nassau infantry battalion. This battalion stood firm and it took the intervention of the cavalry to force them to retreat. I was struck by the courage of the Dutch who, harassed by our cavalry, retreated in perfect order.
>
> We then took our positions in front of Mellet. The cavalry division of General Piré was in our rear.

Regarding the operations of his regiment, the famed Red Lancers of the Imperial Guard, Colonel Edouard de Colbert reported to Marshal Ney that:[12]

> Arriving at Frasné we found it occupied by about 1,500 Nassau infantry with eight guns. When they saw we were manoeuvring to turn their flank, they made a sortie from the village, where we did in fact surround them. General Colbert advanced up the road to

within a musket-shot of Quatre-Bras; however, the terrain was difficult and the enemy, with the woods at their back, kept up a lively fire. The troops at Frasné were serving under Lord Wellington. The troops there were beaten this morning and none passed this way. The Belgian army is said to be at Mons. We took fifteen prisoners, and lost ten men killed and wounded.

About his own movements, Lefèbvre-Desnoëttes reported to Marshal Ney that:[13]

> Arriving at Frasné according to your orders, we found it occupied by a regiment of Nassau infantry numbering about 1,500 men and eight cannon. When they noticed that we were manoeuvring to outflank them, they left the village. There we had them, in effect surrounded by our squadrons; General Colbert was within musket-shot of Quatre-Bras on the main road. But the terrain was difficult; the enemy had retreated to Bossu Wood, and were delivering a very brisk fire with their eight cannon, and it was impossible for us to overrun them. The troops that we found at Frasné had not taken up positions in the morning, nor were those who had fought at Gosselies. They are under the orders of Lord Wellington, and seem to retreat towards Nivelles. They have lit a beacon at Quatre-Bras and have fired their cannon a great deal.
>
> None of the troops which were fighting at Gosselies this morning has passed through here; they have marched to Fleurus. The peasants are unable to tell me of any large troop concentrations in this vicinity, only of an artillery park at Tubise composed of one hundred caissons and twelve cannon. They say the Belgian army is in the vicinity of Mons and that the headquarters of the young Prince Frederick of Orange is located near Braine-le-Comte. We have taken fifteen prisoners and have suffered the loss or injury of ten men.
>
> At daybreak tomorrow, I will send out a reconnaissance patrol to occupy Quatre-Bras if possible, for I believe that the Nassau troops have left. I have just received an infantry battalion which I have put in front of the village. Since my artillery had yet to arrive with me, I have sent orders for them to bivouac with Bachelu's division; they will then join me tomorrow morning.
>
> I am not writing to the emperor having nothing important to report to him other than what I have told Your Excellency.
>
> I am sending a sergeant who will receive Your Excellency's orders. I have the honour to point out to Your Excellency, that the

enemy has not deployed any cavalry, but the artillery is horse artillery.

Reille's report to Soult
About the day's operations, General Reille notes to Marshal Soult that:[14]

> In accordance with the orders issued to the army, I left Leers Fosteau with the 2nd Corps at three o'clock in the morning. In front of Thuin, I met with an enemy vanguard of cavalry and infantry, and in the village a battalion of about 800 men. After a lively exchange of musketry and some cannon shots, we chased them from that position which was very difficult to access. The enemy left some dead and wounded and a number of prisoners, among whom were two officers. The bridges of Lobbes, Thuin and Aulnes have remained in good condition. Further along we encountered the enemy in the woods of Montigny-pres-Figuex. A very lively fusillade took place. We chased him from the village and he endeavoured to retreat upon Marchienne. However, they were hard pressed by our infantry and I ordered Generals Piré and Hubert to debouch with the 1st Regiment of Chasseurs à Cheval, and they charged the enemy with great vigour. A hundred of their number were cut down and more than 200 were made prisoners. After passing the bridge of Marchienne, I ordered the cavalry leaving the Moulaux Wood to move aside so it could be passed by the infantry. Upon arriving at Jumet, General Bachelu engaged an enemy column which had forced the 1st Regiment of Hussars to retreat. He killed some men and took some prisoners.
>
> The 2nd Corps moved forward after this and took position with the 5th and 9th Divisions on the right and left of Gosselies, and the 6th Division behind the Lombrie Wood. The 7th Division was in the second line an hour before nightfall, in accordance with His Majesty's order to take the road from Jumet to Fleurus and to pass from Wangenies to that village. The 2nd Regiment of Light Infantry, which formed the head of the column for the entire day, showed great vigour and had about eighty men killed or wounded. The 1st Regiment of Chasseurs à Cheval lost between twenty and twenty-five. The number of prisoners sent to the rear is 266 with five officers.

Amongst those killed in the 2nd Regiment of Light Infantry was Lieutenant Paul Esteve. Reille, from his own notes, adds more detail to the events in the official report cited above:[15]

The bridge at Marchiennes was occupied, and after having united all of his corps, Comte Reille marched on Jumet through the Moncaux Wood, along with his division of cavalry. On leaving the wood, the advanced guard of infantry found the Prussian rearguard and repulsed it, who were routed by the 1st Regiment of Hussars who came from the direction of Charleroi.

The divisions were then formed on the height of Jumet, on the right beyond the road, and marched into the Lombue Wood and onto Gosselies, it was in this moment that Marshal Ney, who had arrived from Paris, came to take command of the left wing of the army, composed of the 2nd Corps and the 1st Corps, and then marched forward, along with a cavalry corps.

The marshal pushed on towards Frasné a division of cavalry of the guard he had brought with him, and took the 2nd Corps position, the cavalry and the 5th Division in Mellet, the 6th and 7th Divisions behind the Lombue Wood, and the 9th in Gosselies. The Prussian rearguard had withdrawn on Heppignies a little before dark.

The emperor gave orders to push a vanguard in the direction of Fleurus, the 7th Division was directed to this point, and they halted at ten o'clock at night at Wagnée.

Evening of 15 June

Rather than commit to further action, Ney withdrew his troops back to Gosselies, and bivouacked for the night in an area of roughly forty miles north to south by twenty miles east to west. The cavalry of Lefèbvre-Desnoëttes was located around Frasné, with Reille's 2nd Corps between there and Gosselies. Girard's division was at Wangenies (between Heppignies and Fleurus), south of Mellet, while d'Erlon's 1st Corps was covering the ground from Thuin to Gosselies.[16] Jacques Martin, an officer in the 45th Regiment of Line Infantry (part of 1st Corps), narrates that:[17]

> The day was winding down and we had been up since two in the morning and we had done, without food, a march of eight leagues, made more painful by the stifling heat. We were ordered to bivouac on the road to Brussels, a league ahead of Charleroi. That night was better than the last. It did not rain, the soldiers went to find wood and straw, and as is usual, seeking wood in the roofs, they found the wine stores. This is an unavoidable evil; to go to forage, we must enter houses: we are pleased when it happens without serious repercussions. Among those who were in charge of this duty was

one of our soldiers who had fought in Spain. He went straight to the village priest and, as he knew the uses of these gentlemen, descended to the cellar and we brought a few bottles of excellent old wine, we drank to the health of the good priest.

Ney reported his positions to Marshal Soult at 23.00 that night:[18]

> Gosselies 15 June 1815. 23.00
> To His Excellency marshal major-general
> M. marshal, I have the honour to inform Your Excellency that in accordance to the emperor's orders, this afternoon I occupied Gosselies, from where the enemy was dislodged by the cavalry of General Piré and the infantry of General Bachelu. The enemy's resistance was most obstinate and a discharge of twenty-five to thirty rounds of artillery fire repulsed them in the direction of Heppignies via Fleurus. We have taken between 500 and 600 prisoners from the corps of General Zeithen.
> Here are the dispositions of my troops:
> General Lefèbvre-Desnoëttes with the lancers and chasseurs of the Guard at Frasné.
> General Bachelu and the 5th Division at Mellet.
> General Foy and the 9th Division at Gosselies.
> The light cavalry of General Piré at Heppignies.
> I do not know where to find General Reille.
> General d'Erlon occupies the terrain around Jumet with the majority of the corps, but he has not sent to him his exact dispositions, I will send them on when they get to me. I attach a report by General Lefèbvre-Desnoëttes.

NOTES:
[1] SHDDT: C15 5 *Correspondence Armée du Nord 11 Juin au 21 Juin 1815, dossier du 16 Juin.*
[2] SHDDT: C15 22 *registre correspondence 2e corps observation Armée du Nord*, p. 27. After-action report of 15 June 1815, 21.00, Reille to Soult.
[3] Toussaint-Jean Trefcon, *Carnet de la campagne du colonel Trefcon, 1793-1815*, E. Dubois, Paris, 1914, p. 179.
[4] Jacques François Martin, *Souvenirs d'un ex-officier 1812-1815*, Paris, 1867, pp. 275-6.
[5] Jean Baptiste Lemonnier-Delafosse, *Campagnes de 1810 à 1815: souvenirs militaires faisant suite a ceux première et deuxième campagnes se St-Domingue de 1801 a 1809*, Alph. Lemale, Havre, 1850, p. 355.
[6] Auguste-Louis Pétiet, *Souvenirs militaires de l'histoire contemporaine*, Dumaine, Paris, 1844, pp.189-190.
[7] Colonel Heymès, *Relation de la campagne de 1815, dite de Waterloo*, Gaultier-Laguionie, Paris, 1829, pp.22-3.
[8] Lemonnier-Delafosse, p. 355.
[9] Maurice Fleury, *Souvenirs anecdotiques et militaires du colonel Biot*, Henri Vivien, Paris, 1901,

p.237.
10. Karl von Damitz, *Geschichte des Feldzuges von 1815 in den Niederlanden und Frankreich* (vol. 1), E. S. Mittler, Berlin, 1838, p. 84.
11. Trefcon.
12. Jean-Marc Largeaud, perssonal communication 10 August 2012, copy of letter dated 23 May 1829 from Colbert to Duc d'Elchingen held in the Archives Nationales.
13. SHDDT: C15 5, *15 Juin 1815*. Lefèbvre-Desnoëttes to Ney timed at 21.00. Copy of the now lost original order made on 20 February 1890.
14. Two original copies of this dispatch exist. SHDDT: C15 5, *Dossier 15 Juin 1815*. Reille to Soult. This is the original document sent to Soult. See also: SHDDT: C15 22, p. 27, after-action report of 15 June 1815, 21.00, Reille to Soult. This is the same dispatch copied into Reille's own register of correspondence.
15. Michel Louis Felix Ney, pp. 55-60.
16. August Wagner, *Plane der Schlachten und Treffen, welche von der Preussischen Armee in den Feldzügen der Jahre 1813, 14 und 15 geliefert worden*, Reimer, Berlin, 1825, p. 17.
17. Martin, pp. 275-6.
18. SHDDT: C15 5, *dossier 15 June 1815*, Ney to Soult at 23.00. Copy of the now lost original document made on 20 February 1890.

Chapter 2

Quatre-Bras

Napoléon and Ney met at the Imperial headquarters at Charleroi sometime after midnight on 15 June. Following, we presume, a long discussion with the emperor about the plan of operations for the 16th, Ney rode back to his headquarters. We like to think that he had been informed of the whereabouts of his troops, but, as we shall see, this may be an argument too far. As it was, in the early hours of 16 June Ney's command was spread across Belgium, covering an area of around forty miles. The 1st Corps was strung out over a distance of perhaps thirty miles, with the 3rd Division being placed at Marchienne-au-Pont. According to Heymès, Marshal Ney's aide-de-camp, Ney knew all this. He writes:[1]

> On the 16th, at two in the morning, the marshal returned to Gosselies where he remained for some time in order to communicate with General Reille; he ordered him to march as soon as possible with his two divisions and his artillery, and to assemble at Frasné, where the marshal would join him almost immediately. Once again, the marshal found himself at the head of his troops in the presence of the enemy. He collected the reports which the generals and various other officers had been able to procure, during which time I traversed the line, visiting each of the regiments, noting the names of the colonels and the number of their corps. Shortly thereafter I presented these details to the marshal, along with the general state of his army.

In the afternoon of 15 June, d'Erlon wrote to Soult the following regarding his troop movements:[2]

> Conforming to the general orders, one of my cavalry brigades has passed through Solre and Bienne-sous-Thuin, and a division of

infantry at Thuin, Lobbes and Abbey d'Aulnas. My other troops continue to arrive at Marchiennes, following the 2nd Corps, and are yet to cross the Sambre. I will position a brigade on the road to Mons, and another brigade on the road at Marchienne, and the other division will head to Gosselies.

On the night of 15 June, d'Erlon reported his positions as:[3]

> Conforming to Your Excellency's order of three o'clock, I moved to Gosselies. Upon arriving, I found the place occupied by the 2nd Corps, so I placed the 4th Division to the rear of this village, and the 2nd Division at Jumay [sic] as well as a brigade of cavalry.
>
> The 3rd Division has remained at Marchienne-au-Pont, and the 1st at Thuin, with my other cavalry brigade at Solre and Bienne-sous-Thuin, so my troops are greatly dispersed; I request Your Excellency to let me know if I can recall those troops left in the rear.

Rather than sending the order to his direct commander, the order went to Soult, who replied as follows:[4]

> Comte d'Erlon, it is the emperor's intentions that you concentrate all of your corps on the left bank of the Sambre, and unite with 2nd Corps at Gosselies, in line with the orders that you will be given by the Prince of the Moskowa. Also, recall the troops you have left at Thuin, Solre and that area. You are always to send out numerous patrols to cover the road to Mons.

Adjutant-Commandant Durosnel, chief-of-staff of the 3rd Infantry Division, issued the following order to General Nogues:[5]

> Quartier-General at Marchienne-au-Pont 3.00 16 June
>
> Conforming to the orders of the General-in-Chef, you are charged to unite your brigade and half-battery of artillery and set in motion to arrive at six o'clock in the morning, or at the latest seven o'clock in the morning at Gosselies.
>
> The commander of the artillery is ordered to supply you with two guns for the completion of your half-battery.
>
> Adjutant-commandant,
> Chief-of-staff
> Ch. Durosnel
> PS—the 2nd Brigade has arrived with the 1st Division, and both are being sent to the same destination.

This placed 1st Corps, at 3.00, spread out in a long line starting twenty-six or more miles south of Quatre-Bras. It would take the rearmost units a minimum of five to six hours to march this distance. Based on this, Durosnel's estimated arrival time at Gosselies seems realistic, as Gosselies is 5.6 miles from Marchienne-au-Pont, and can be walked in about two hours, so five hours would seem plenty of time for Nogues to arrive with his brigade from 1st Corps. By 8.00, all except Donzelot's 2nd Division would be at Gosselies, assuming d'Erlon issued orders promptly, and there were no further delays to their march. However, the orders had to arrive with the brigade commanders, who had to organise their men. No doubt tired and hungry, one can easily imagine that the rate of marching was somewhat slower than was ideal. When Marcognet's men got to Gosselies, the men would have been far from fresh having walked a marathon in full field service marching order under a hot sun.

Sometime after first light, Soult sent the following order to Marshal Ney:[6]

> Charleroi, 16 June
> The emperor has sent orders to the Comte de Valmy, to unite his corps and to direct his movement to Gosselies, and to make it available to Marshal Ney.
>   It is the intention of the emperor that the cavalry of the Guard that went along the Brussels road is to move to the rear and to rejoin the main body of the Imperial Guard; to prevent them from making wrong moves they are to be placed a little behind the line. General Lefèbvre-Desnoëttes will send officers to take orders. You will inform me whether the corps had carried out this movement, and the positions this morning the 1st and 2nd Corps occupies along with the attached cavalry divisions, as well as making known to us what news you have and what troops are in front of you.

Following this order, Kellermann was ordered to march the 3rd Cavalry Corps to Gosselies and to operate under Ney's orders:[7]

> Order the Comte de Valmy to unite his 3rd Cavalry Corps and to move to Gosselies and to be placed at the disposal of Marshal Ney.

However, the emperor's plans for the day overlooked important issues; no one knew where Kellermann was.

6th Corps

The rear-most corps of the Armée du Nord was, in theory, to be 6th Corps commanded by Comte Lobau. Early on the morning of 16 June, Lobau with, we assume, his corps, was based around Charleroi. Sometime after the order to Ney had been sent, Lobau received orders from headquarters to garrison Charrison, to organise the movement of the wounded to Avesne, and to place his corps on the Charleroi to Fleurus road.[8]

Perhaps in response to this, Lobau ordered Adjutant-Commandant Jeanin to head north and link with Ney. Lobau reported Jeanin's intelligence to the emperor. He commented that:[9]

> Sire,
>
> In conforming to your orders that Your Majesty had given me, Adjutant-Commandant Jeanin has made contact with the corps commanded by M. Marshal Prince of the Moskowa. This officer informs me that the troops are in echelon in the environs of Gosselies and the village of Frasné. It is hard to tell with any precision if the enemy is there in force as the terrain is mostly forest. The colonel has spoken to numerous senior officers, some of whom have interrogated some deserters, to gain information about the enemy, which they say is about twenty thousand men. Due to the nature of the terrain, only a small number of sharpshooters are at present engaged.
>
> I am yet to take position in front of Charleroi. In accordance to Your Majesty's orders I have replaced the battalion in the town for police duties and also to protect the large number of wounded.
>
> Charleroi 16 June 1815
> Lieutenant-general aide-de-camp to the emperor,
> Commander-in-chief of 6th Corps
> Comte Lobau
>
> PS—Colonel Jeanin has reported that Colonel Tancarville, chief-of-staff to Comte de Valmy, and had been transmitted to him from Comte d'Erlon, that a large body of enemy troops has been seen marching from Mons towards Charleroi.

Lobau's dispatch is interesting on a number of accounts. Firstly, by the time that Jeanin had arrived, Ney had not yet began a major action, but small clashes of vedettes were taking place when Jeanin was at Frasné. Jeanin gives the strength of the Allies at 20,000, yet at 11.00 Ney gives the strength at 3,000—a very large difference. Did Jeanin factor into his figures the bulk of the Allied army which, as he was reporting back to

Napoléon, was already heading south and west? Perhaps so. One wonders if Jeanin transmitted this news to Ney, or did he assume Ney could judge the situation well enough himself? The troops seen on the Mons road were undoubtedly the 3rd Netherlands Division; they had been spotted on the previous day. It was common knowledge that troops were heading from Mons.

It seems that Kellermann and d'Erlon were in contact with each other, but it seems not with Ney, and, as we shall see, not with Grouchy or Soult. But, of course, the correspondence to Ney that may have existed in 1815 now can no longer be found. As we have seen, on 15 June and the early hours of 16 June, d'Erlon was reporting to Soult rather than Ney. Until Kellermann got his orders from Soult to report to Ney, he would have reported to Soult. It seems communications between corps commanders was a little hit and miss, a deplorable situation during a campaign, especially in the period of the build up to two battles.

We also must wonder why Lobau sent Jeanin forward to find Ney. Had Ney not reported back to Soult about his position? Did the emperor require a trusted officer to send back to him information on the enemy position? It seems to be the case. Ney, based on surviving paperwork, was tardy in sending news back to Soult. Ney's first dispatch to Soult was not until 11.00, and the information conflicted with Jeanin's much earlier report. Without news from Ney, Napoléon could not plan his troop dispositions for the day without knowing what was happening on the left wing. Starved of this information, the emperor sent orders to his former aide-de-camp, Lobau, to find out what Ney was up to, and what forces he faced. With the receipt of the dispatch, the emperor knew that a body of perhaps 20,000 was on his left wing, with the possibility of being reinforced. With this news, he issued new orders as we shall see later.

Corporal Martial-Joseph Delroeux writes the following about events in Charleroi that day:[10]

> My regiment was one which had three battalions, I was appointed to the third, which was to form the garrisons in Charleroi, it grieved me that many soldiers were children, who liked fighting. However, by considering the matter on the bright side it could only be a joy for us because, in the case of non-success, there was no progress to be made by the unnecessary spilling of our blood and if the war would have been of long enough duration they would have a chance to show their courage, since the foreign powers had allied themselves and formed a contingent to fight Napoléon.
>
> The mayor, who needed a hand to cater to the establishment of a hospital for the wounded, as we fought there already was a

continual and excessive increase in the number, and asked our commander to send him some sub-officers he trusted to help. He sent me there with several sergeants and corporals. The highlight of our work was to conduct searches and to remove anything that was suitable to be used in the hospital.

The 17th, by the afternoon five hospitals had been set up, at that moment there arrived new wounded, we were obliged to put them in some neighbouring houses. The surgeons lacked sufficient bandages as there were many arms and legs that had been mutilated.

Furthermore, with Charleroi garrisoned, a veritable road block would ensue when Marcognet's division arrived in the town to move north to Gosselies.

Kellermann

On the morning of 15 June, General Kellermann and the 3rd Cavalry Corps were at Vervins, a town in north-east France, some eighty miles from Quatre-Bras.[11] We suppose that during the day, the corps covered forty to sixty miles, making them still some twenty to forty miles south of Quatre-Bras. Little wonder that the cuirassiers only went into action in the evening, no doubt as they had literally just arrived on the field after a forced march. Kellermann's orders from Grouchy, dated 15 June, are very informative. He was ordered to move out at 6.00 with the division under his direct command, and move to Charleroi, passing through Bossus, Florieaux, and Vogennes. A key passage in the order tells us that Lhéritier was detached from the main body of the corps and was to march as fast as possible to Charleroi.[12] Why was the corps split? Where was Lhéritier? Why was Kellermann not with the leading element of the corps? We simply don't know for certain.

But, it is clear that Kellermann was with d'Hurbal's division. Why was he needed with d'Hurbal? Historian Ian James Smith, who has undertaken groundbreaking research into the two regiments of carabiniers during the First Empire, thinks he has the asnwer to this. In a forthcoming book on the carabiniers, which he has graciously allowed me to present his cogent argument about Kellermann's activities that day, he comments that with the defection of General de Bourmont, Kellermann faced the same challenge with the carabinier brigade.

Ian Smith quite rightly postulates that the event no doubt put the two regiments into somthing of a confusion, but this defection was not unexpected. He adroitly comments that Kellermann himself had inspected the two regiments earlier in the year. The two carabinier regiments in 1814 (as they would be in 1816) became directly associated with Monsieur, the king's brother and future King Charles X. During the First Restoration, elements of the officer corps rapidly became ardent royalist popinjays. My own research reveals, and Indeed Ian Smith's research shows, that the two regiments in a joint venture had published a declaration stating that the emperor was a usurper, and the document was signed by all the officers in the two regiments. As Ian Smith comments:[13]

> The hard truth is, the two regiments were far from loyal to the cause of the emperor, and Kellermann knew. His worst suspicions about the loyalty of the brigade were confirmed with two officers deserting on 15 June. What was he to do? Clearly, he had to give the brigade a pep talk and try to calm the nerves of the men and, we suppose, to sound out the loyalty of the officers. Of course, this all took time. It explains why Lhéritier got to Quatre-Bras before d'Hurbal, and why the carabinier brigade was kept out of harm's way on 15, 16 and 17 June, and why Kellermann endeavoured to keep them out of action on 18 June—the fear was that the entire brigade could gallop off and join the Allies.

My own research confirms this. On 26 May, two officers had been arrested. The police report states:[14]

> Dessoffy, major of the 9th Regiment of Chevau-Légers (*emigre*) on 26th of this month enaged with two captains from the 1st Regiment of Carabiniers and an adjutant-major from 1st Corps [illegible] were found to be recruiting volunteers since the 5th. [illegible] a servant of one of the captains of carabiniers and his wife, and three others were detained at Montmercy ... We recovered the following weapons from these indivduals:
>
> | | |
> |---|---|
> | Double-barrel muskets | 4 |
> | Single-barrel musket | 5 |
> | Rifle | 4 |
> | Pistols | 17 |
> | Sabres | 3 |
> | Epée | 2 |

Clearly, these three officers had been recruiting royalist sympathisers and were in the process of recruiting and arming a terrorist cell. The presence of two captains from the 1st Carabiniers shows that the regiment, in the last week before the campaign began, clearly had very divided loyalties.

History shows that Kellermann was right about the brigade's loyalty, as in total six officers defected. Desertion of officers and men was a major problem in 1815. For example, Squadron Commander Moriez, who had returned to France in 1814 and had fought for the royalists during the Revolution with the Armée des émigrés and, rather unsurprisingly, deserted from the 6th Lancers. In a letter to Marshal Davout, General Vandamme complained bitterly that Adjutant-Commandant Nillis (of the same regiment) was acting with great imprudence and great indecency towards the emperor. In the 4th Lancers, Vandamme singled out Second Lieutenant Desbuisserets as a bad influence, as he was not only encouraging sedition, but also for the men to desert. Vandamme recommended that the regiment be sent new officers to replace those under suspicion as traitors. Colonel Deschamps was replaced by Colonel Louis Bro and a wholesale removal of officers from the regiment took place in the first days of April 1815. This pattern was no doubt true in other regiments, whereby royalist appointees were replaced with officers called back to the army from half-pay as they had not been traitors (i.e. they had not served the king), and therefore could be considered more reliable in their dedication to Napoléon, but this is a vastly over-simplified version of the truth. The army of 1815 was a shaky formation, with little trust between men and sub-officers and their officers.

In returning to the narrative of 16 June, the reality was that headquarters had no real idea where Kellermann was. At 5.00 on 16 June, Marshal Grouchy reported to Soult about his cavalry force that:[15]

The 1st Cavalry Corps was placed at Lambusart on the road from Gilly to Fleurus;
The 2nd Corps was at Lambusart in the rear of the valley;
The 4th Corps was based around the village of St François;
  The location of the 3rd Corps was unknown, with a best guess between Charleroi and Gilly.

Grouchy comments that he could not confirm where Kellermann actually was and, moreover, had had no dispatches from him during the course of 15 June. Basically, Grouchy, with no reports from Kellermann, had no idea where he was.[16] What was Kellermann doing? Why had he sent in no reports to headquarters for twenty-four hours? This lack of communication between corps commands and headquarters staff was to have a major impact on the battle to follow.

Was Grouchy's information blackout part of a cover up? If the emperor found out that the morale of the carabinier brigade was highly suspect and officers had defected, then he would have flown into one of his characteristic rages, would no doubt have blamed Kellermann, and perhaps relieved him of command; perhaps it was best if he kept his head down and endeavoured to resolve the situation as best as he could. Had there been an orchestrated plan between royalists to cause as much confusion to the Imperial army as possible on the morning of 15 June? de Bourmont headed off at, it seems, the same time as the carabinier brigade watched two officers ride off to join the king. This defection was certainly not the last. The *Montieur* newspaper reported:[17]

> General Gérard reports that General-Lieutenant Bourmont, Colonel Clouet and Major Villoutreys passed to the enemy. A lieutenant of the 11th Chasseurs also passed to the enemy. The major-general ordered that these deserters be at once judged in accordance with their fates.

The 4th Corps was in a state of shock, the carabinier brigade was disorganised and the 11th Chasseurs clearly had the same issues. Indeed, two more officers from the 11th Chasseurs headed off to the king at Waterloo: Major Alexander Rigny and Captain Mathey.[18] Corporal Martial-Joseph Delroeux of the 11th Regiment of Line Infantry comments:[19]

> There never was an army that marched to face the enemy with greater courage and resolution than this; the influence of Napoléon was great on the spirit of the soldiers. Unfortunately, the same accord did not exist amongst our leaders. Whilst the presence of the emperor heightened the courage of the soldiers, treason entered our ranks: the newly appointed General Bourmont, Colonel Cloeut and Chief-of-Squadron Villoutreys had passed to the enemy with a copy of the attack plan; it created a kind of stupor among the officer corps. Discipline seemed to be no longer the same as before, the misunderstanding of relaxing discipline was brought about by our superiors.

Thus on the morning of 16 June, Kellermann's corps was still a hard day's ride away. We assume that they left for Gosselies at first light or when he received orders, which could have been at any point during the course of the day, as the message couriers had literally no idea where Kellermann was. When Kellermann's troopers did arrive around 15.00 they had marched for twenty to thirty miles, no doubt in a forced march which had taken about four hours. The men and horses would have been fatigued, the 'horses on their teeth' to use an expression from the period, meaning the horses were exhausted. Ney would have known this, and so would Kellermann. What Kellermann's troopers and horses needed when they got to Gosselies was rest and food, neither of which they got, as we shall see. This fatigue no doubt impacted upon battlefield performance. Ney, on the morning of 16 June, was told by Soult he had eight infantry divisions, and four cavalry divisions. Ultimately, given 1st Corps was detached to Ligny, Kellermann was forty miles away and Girard's division was also sent towards Ligny, Ney would ultimately have under his command the two regiments of Guard cavalry, just three infantry divisions and the four cavalry regiments under Piré. This must have come as a nasty shock to him, as we shall see.

Durutte

Kellermann was not the only field officer with command and control issues. At daybreak on 16 June, the staff of the 4th Infantry Division rode off over the horizon to join the Prussians. Chapuis, of the 85th Regiment of Line Infantry adroitly notes:[20]

> We learnt that on the next day, 17 June, Colonel Gordon, the chief-of-staff of 4th Division and Battalion Commander Gaugler, the first aide-de-camp to General Durutte, had passed to the enemy the previous morning and had been concealed from us for twenty-four hours . . . The desertion of these two men, in positions close to General Durutte, and his hesitation a few hours earlier to execute orders, which should have been done quickly, produced such a bad impression on the 85th that it took all the efforts of the officers to restore the morale of the men.

Louis Jean Baptiste Gaugler was born on 28 June 1782. He had volunteered as a cadet on 3 March 1799 in the Legion Helvique, and was promoted to sub-lieutenant on 21 November 1799. His unit was taken into the 3rd Demi-Brigade on 18 April 1803, and was transferred to the 1st Regiment of Line Infantry on 5 July 1805. He was named aide-de-camp to General Durutte on 15 June 1807, and would remain by his side until 16 June 1815. He states that he joined the king at Gand with the arrival of the usurper, and was under the orders of the Duke of Berry.[21]

Also disappearing over the horizon was Ferdinand Henri Joseph de Gordon,[22] chief-of-staff to Durutte, no doubt with the staff of the division in meltdown; little wonder it never headed off to Marbais as ordered, or was slow in responding to orders. Durutte, as with

Kellermann, kept this news for himself, and endeavoured to cover up the event. Morale and loyalty of the army was indeed suspect—at Waterloo, four carabinier officers went over to the Allies. An officer from the 5th Lancers (discounting one officer who had defected at the start of June), an officer from the 6th Lancers, two officers from the 1st Chasseurs à Cheval and two officers from the 11th Chasseurs à Cheval also all headed off never to be seen again. Indeed, the officer corps of some regiments had been replaced before the campaign began to try and stamp out pockets of royalists, but clearly this was not enough. With little trust between the officer corps, and little trust between the other ranks and their officers, it is hardly surprising that the Armée du Nord was a deeply compromised force, which fell apart at Waterloo when Grouchy's men turned out to be Prussians. de Brack, of the Red Lancers, even went so far as to suggest Grouchy had defected and was attacking the emperor—thus with the officers concerned about defection and the men not trusting or listening to their leaders, it is easy to see why the army literally fell apart at the seams.

Soult's order to Grouchy
Unbeknown to the headquarters staff, the emperor and Soult began making plans for the day's events. About the broader picture, Soult wrote to Grouchy about Ney's operations:[23]

> I have the honour to inform you that I ordered the Comte de Valmy, as soon as he received my order, to move to Gosselies with the 3rd Cavalry Corps, where he will be at Ney's disposal.
> The 1st Regiment of Hussars will return to the 1st Cavalry Corps, where they shall be placed under the orders of the emperor.
> I have the honour to inform you that the Marshal Prince of the Moskowa has received orders to move with the 1st and 2nd Corps of Infantry and the 3rd Cavalry Corps to the intersection of the roads, at Trois-Bras, on the Brussels road, and he will detach a strong corps to Marbais, which will be available to you to support your operations at Sombreffe.

Soult closed the order informing Grouchy to establish a line of communications with Ney. In the order, Ney was to detach a corps to aid Grouchy as needed; no word at all of sending Kellermann to Marbais. Here, Napoléon was beginning to form his plan of operations. Grouchy was to attack with 3rd and 4th Corps, and a corps from Ney's command along with Kellermann's cavalry corps were to stand *en potence* (ready to intervene at what would become the Battle of Ligny) in a flanking assault to take the Prussians in the rear. Napoléon was clearly developing his strategy, and Ney was under no illusion that part of his command was to be sent to Grouchy (and by inference to Napoléon). Ney must have realised that he would only have to hand Reille's 2nd Corps, Piré's cavalry, and the Guard light cavalry.

The emperor subsequently sent the following dispatch through his own aide-de-camp, cutting out Soult's staff:[24]

> My cousin,
>
> I'm sending you La Bédoyère, my aide-de-camp, who will present you this letter. The major-general will have made known to you my intentions, but because he has some badly mounted officers at his disposition, my aide-de-camp could arrive earlier. My intention is that you will command the right wing, and be in command of the 3rd Corps of General Vandamme, the 4th of General Gérard, the cavalry corps of the Generals Pajol, Milhaud and Excelmans, together around fifty thousand men.
>
> The rallying point of the right wing will be at Sombreffe. In consequence, you have to ensure that the corps of the Generals Pajol, Milhaud, Excelmans and Vandamme will start out immediately to continue your movement to Sombreffe. The 4th Corps, which is at Châtelet, will receive directly the order to go to Sombreffe, without passing through Fleurus. This is important because I will establish my general headquarters in Fleurus and we have to avoid any traffic jams.
>
> Send immediately an officer to General Gérard in order to let him know your movement and that he will execute his accordingly.
>
> It is my wish that the generals take their orders directly from you. They will take mine only when I am there. I will be at Fleurus between 10 and 11 a.m. Afterwards I will go to Sombreffe, leaving the infantry and the cavalry of the Guard at Fleurus, and I will take them only to Sombreffe in case of necessity. If the enemy is at Sombreffe, I want to attack him. I even want to attack him in Gembloux and take this position, because it is my intention to depart this night, after taking the two positions, and operate with my left wing, commanded by Marshal Ney, against the English. Do not lose a moment because I will be moving soon to continue the operations.
>
> I suppose that you are at Fleurus; you have to communicate on a permanent basis with General Gérard, so that he could help you in attacking Sombreffe when it is necessary. The division of Girard will be in the vicinity of Fleurus. Do not use them unless there is an absolute necessity to do so, because they had to march all night. Also, let my Young Guard and the attached artillery stay in Fleurus.

The Comte de Valmy, with his two divisions of cuirassiers, is marching on the road to Brussels; he will join Marshal Ney in order to contribute with the manoeuvring this evening on the left wing.

Like I said, I will be at Fleurus from 10 to 11 a.m. Send me your reports concerning all that you hear of; make sure that the road to Fleurus will be free from congestion. All the information I have says that the Prussians cannot oppose us with more than 40,000 men.

Napoléon.

Thus, Girard was passed to Grouchy's command from Ney without a word about this getting to Ney. But, the order poses some interesting issues. It informs us that on the morning of 16 June, the emperor had already decided to send off Grouchy to chase the Prussians. If this order is genuine, then why did the emperor dither on the morning of 17 June in putting his plan into action? It also makes it very clear that on the night of 16 June the emperor planned to head north with 1st and 2nd Corps to Brussels. Furthermore, the emperor did not consider any major obstacle to Ney in containing the English army. It is also very apparent that Grouchy's action was of more importance; the primary objective for 16 June was tackling the Prussian army, and then the English and Allies. Ney, as we shall see, never seems to have grasped this.

Soult's order to Ney
Upon receipt of Lobau's dispatch, a second and more comprehensive set of orders was generated for Ney by the emperor, and reads:[25]

Charleroi 16 June

Mr marshal, the emperor orders that you are to march with 1st and 2nd Army Corps as well as the 3rd Cavalry Corps, which is now at your disposal, and lead them to the intersection of so-called Trois-Bras of the Brussels roads, where you will take up position. You will undertake reconnaissance along the Brussels and Nivelles roads, along which the enemy probably withdrew. His Majesty desires, that despite any setbacks, you are to establish a division with cavalry at Genappes and he orders you to send another division to Marbais to cover the area between Sombreffe and Trois-Bras. You can place with this division the cavalry of the Imperial Guard commanded by General Lefèbvre-Desnoëttes as well as the 1st Regiment of Hussars which was seconded to you yesterday to stand at Gosselies.

The corps that is to be placed at Marbais may also be used to support Marshal Grouchy in his movements on Sombreffe, and also support the position of Trois-Bras, as it may become necessary. You are to instruct the general who will be at Marbais to scout in all directions, particularly to Gembloux and Wavre.

If, however the division of General Lefèbvre-Desnoëttes is not standing on the Brussels road, it is to be replaced at Marbais by the 3rd Cavalry Corps under the orders of Comte de Valmy, as well as the 1st Hussars.

I have the honour to notify you that the emperor will be moving onto Sombreffe, where Marshal Grouchy will debouch with the 3rd and 4th Corps of Infantry and the 1st, 2nd and 4th Corps of Cavalry. Marshal Grouchy will occupy Gembloux. Please send a report of your news and arrangements to the emperor, and execute the order I sent you.

His Majesty charges me to remind you to tell all generals commanding army corps to concentrate their men, and draw back in all isolated men, to maintain the most perfect order amongst the troops as well as to concentrate your artillery and ambulances which may be in the rear.

The order clearly defined Ney's mission objectives: he was to occupy Quatre-Bras, as well as Genappe, and move a division towards Sombreffe to support Grouchy at Ligny. However, the general concept of the situation (that Ligny was the primary objective and Quatre-Bras the secondary objective) was not explained clearly to Ney for him to understand the plan of operations for the day; although he did clearly tell Grouchy. It is obvious from the tone of the letter that Ligny and the Prussians were the primary objective. The order also makes it very clear that an entire army corps was to be sent to Marbais to aid Grouchy. Ney had known since early morning that part of his command was to be sent to aid Napoléon, yet he clearly forgot this (as we shall see later) with tragic consequences. Napoléon's plan was devastatingly simple: Grouchy with 3rd Corps was to head to Sombreffe and Gembloux and engage the Prussians. If needed, the Guard and 4th Corps could be ordered up. Depending on how the situation unfolded at Sombreffe, the entire corps placed at Marbais was ideally placed to sweep down behind the Prussians. This tactic is called *'manoeuvres sur les derrières'*. For reasons best known only to Ney, he didn't realise that the action at Quatre-Bras was of secondary importance to the *'manoeuvres sur les derrières'* that was outlined in this order. Ney had clear orders to concentrate his forces, yet he issued no such order until 11.00—a tragic mistake. He sent no corps to Marbais and spent the morning dithering and dallying, unlike Grouchy who set off in response to his orders to find and attack the Prussians.

In a second order to Grouchy, which is not to be found in Soult's order book and is stated as a verbal order, the emperor writes about Ney:[26]

> If the enemy are at Sombreffe, you will attack, I will attack at Gembloux, it is my intention that we take both positions ... the Comte de Valmy with two divisions of cuirassiers will march on the Brussels road. They will join Marshal Ney, and will contribute to the operations of the left wing.

Clearly, Kellermann was now to head to join Ney and not move to Marbais to be available to Grouchy.

Order and confusion?
In addition to the first two orders, Napoléon is said to have written the following:[27]

> I am sending you my aide-de-camp, General de Flahaut, who brings you the present letter. The major-general [Imperial Headquarters] should have given you my orders, but you will receive mine earlier because my officers have better mounts and ride faster than his. You will receive the movement orders of the day, but I want to write them to you in detail, because it is of the greatest importance. I'm sending Marshal Grouchy, with the 3rd and 4th Infantry Corps towards Sombreffe. I'm taking my Guard to Fleurus where I will be also before noon. I will attack the enemy if I meet him, I will scout the way to Gembloux. There, after what will have happened, I will make up my mind, maybe at three o'clock in the afternoon, maybe this evening. My intention is that you should be ready to move towards Brussels, immediately after I have made up my mind.
>
> I will support you with the Guard who will be at Fleurus, or at Sombreffe, and I want to arrive in Brussels tomorrow morning. You will have to move this evening after I have made my decision, early enough to be able to inform you, so that you can move three to four miles this evening, and be at Brussels tomorrow at seven o'clock. You should be able to dispose of your troops in the following way: one division at two miles in front of Quatre-Bras given there will be no inconvenience in doing do so; six divisions around Quatre-Bras and one division at Marbais, in order to be able to get it closer to Sombreffe if I should need it there. This division will not delay your movements. The corps of the Comte de Valmy, who has 3,000 elite cuirassiers, will be posted at the intersection of the roman road and

the road to Brussels, in order that I can move it towards my position, whenever I should need it. As soon as I have made up my mind, you will send him [the Comte de Valmy] the order to join you.

I would like to have with me the division of the Guard that is commanded by General Lefèbvre-Desnoëttes and I will send you the two divisions of the Comte de Valmy, so as to call him back, when I need him, and to prevent General Lefèbvre-Desnoëttes from making wrong moves, because it could be that I will decide this evening to move to Brussels with the Guard. Nevertheless, cover the division of Lefèbvre-Desnoëttes with the two cavalry divisions of d'Erlon and Reille in order to spare the Guard, because should there be a clash with the British, I prefer that this should happen to the Line, rather than to the Guard.

The order seemingly tells Ney that he has eight divisions at his disposal, plus Kellermann. He is told not to send a corps but a division to Marbais. What were these eight Divisions? Logically, they are the infantry divisions from 1st and 2nd Corps, but what of the divisions of Piré and Jacquinot? Surely that makes ten divisions? What were Piré and Jacquinot to do? Had the emperor forgotten these two divisions? Since early on the 16th, Kellermann had been ordered to join Ney, and Ney had been told this in the two earlier orders sent via Soult, so Napoléon telling Ney to order Kellermann to join him makes no sense, as this had already been done. Had this slipped from the emperor's mind? In the context of the other orders from the emperor to Ney and Grouchy, the order is rather contradictory in nature, and poses a lot of questions.

This order, like a lot of the material relating to Ney in 1815, has always been taken as 100 per cent authentic by all historians who have studied the campaign. At no stage has the evidence used been put under scrutiny or even questioned about its authenticity. We can prove an order was sent from the emperor to Ney (carried by Flahaut), but we have no idea of what the order actually said. Yet historians present the order as nothing other than 100 per cent authentic, written on 16 June 1815. This is simply not true.

In order to check the authenticity of the order, our first point of call in the investigation is in Marshal Soult's order book written down during the campaign. All written orders transmitted by Soult were copied into the book, with time and date and also the name of the courier who carried the order. Upon consulting the document at the Archives Nationales, it becomes very apparent that this order to Ney cannot be found amongst the pages of Marshal Soult's order book, and nor can the order be found in Reille's order book, which again suggests the order was sent via a different channel other than from Soult. Therefore, the order is either a forgery or it was not transmitted via Soult (which seems unlikely, although in the order the emperor says why this is). But is this reasoning too good to be true? It seems an order of such importance was sent via other channels because Soult's staff officers were badly mounted and that Soult, as chief-of-staff, was not informed of the order. If the emperor's couriers were better mounted than Soult's, why did the emperor allow this potentially dangerous situation? If the emperor knew Soult's couriers were badly mounted and ineffective, why did he not make his own couriers available, or allow the situation to exist at all? This does seem unlikely, yet we know an order was carried to Ney via Flahaut.

On looking at Soult's order book, no name for the courier who sent the first order to Ney is recorded, the second was carried by Leroux and the third by Waleski. Is it possible Flahaut carried the first order? Yes, but the time Flahaut gives is much later than we suppose it to have been sent. Of course it is not impossible that Flahaut set off with the first order and then Leroux headed off with the second, and both arrived with Ney at the same time. Ney, though, does state that he received orders from Soult and from the emperor directly, which implies that the first order may not have been taken by Flahaut, as the order is from Soult and not from the emperor directly.

If we assume the order carried by Flahaut and cited above is genuine, how has the document been transmitted to us in 2017? No long-lost original copy can be found either in the Archives Nationales or the French Army Archives. The copy that exists in the French Army Archives dates from 1837, and cannot be corroborated by original documents from 16 June 1815. This poses several possibilities: 1) it may be a forgery written by Ney's son; 2) it may be edited by Ney's son; 3) it may be a word-for-word copy of the now lost original. Its absence from Soult and Reille's order books is most worrying in the regard that it is not a genuine order from 1815, which, as we shall see with the so-called order by de la Salle for the movements of 1st Corps, has muddied the history of the battle at Quatre-Bras.

The document first appears in print in 1840 (published by Ney's son) and again a few years later in 1843 by the son of Marshal Grouchy, who states that the order was a verbal order transmitted via Bertrand.[28] Ney's son does not state this, and this comment has clearly been added after the fact by Grouchy's son. Furthermore, Ney's son tells us in an annotation to his 1837 document, clearly made after 1843, that Grouchy inserted the order into the published sequence of verbal orders sent to him that, crucially, were written down. Why would Grouchy publish this order? Simply, the order is of great importance to him. Grouchy, in his defence of his actions on 17 to 19 June, claims that Soult's orders took far longer to get to him than it took his couriers to arrive with headquarters. Grouchy senior asserts that Soult's 10.00 dispatch only arrived with him around 14.00, or later, because the couriers were badly mounted and had no grasp of map work to locate his forces. He further develops the argument that the 14.30 order, which sent him to Waterloo, did not arrive until 19.00 (if the order is genuine), and thus he could never have got to Waterloo. Therefore, by publishing the letter Grouchy's son had positive proof from the emperor himself that Soult's courier system was incompetent. Publishing the order greatly aided Grouchy's agenda.

Ney's son further notes that he copied the order from the work of his father's aide-de-camp, Heymès.[29] We need to now investigate Heymès and his motivation for publishing.[30] As with Grouchy being slandered by Napoléon, Gourgaud and Gérard, Heymès was publishing to rehabilitate Ney's reputation. He writes about 16 June to offer up evidence to his readers that Ney was not slow at attacking Quatre-Bras, and says the order did not arrive with Ney until 11.00 to 12.00. Therefore, in Heymès's reasoning, Ney was not to blame but the emperor. However, when we read Heymès's narration of 16 June, we find that it is very confused. In his writing about the order to move 1st Corps to Ligny, his account contains a serious contradiction: if Napoléon would have called for d'Erlon to move towards Saint-Amand, why was it considered to be an incorrect movement after all? This makes his account unreliable, so is the order an invention? Certainly, Flahaut says he carried an order to Ney and then returned to the emperor with a report, as the emperor clearly mentions Flahaut in his dispatch to Ney sent on the night of 16 June. General Reille also says that Flahaut carried an order to Ney, so we can be certain of this fact. Grouchy, citing Ney, who cites Heymès, states the order was verbal. So how come it exists in the written form? Is the document presented by Heymès the order as he remembered it in 1829, rather than being a word-for-word transcription of the lost verbal order? Or did Heymès write down the order during his interview with Soult?

Both situations are highly plausible. We have no other evidence to support either notion. However, given that Heymès is contradicted by Reille and Flahaut, we need to question the reliability of Heymès. If Flahaut left Charleroi at 9.00, Frasné was an hour's ride away to the north, so the order would be with Ney between 10.00 and 11.00 at the latest. In the published edition of the order by Grouchy, the document arrives with Ney between 11.00 and 12.00. Ney's son, quoting General Reille, states the order arrived between 10.15 and 11.00, which is exactly what Flahaut (the courier of the order) says, as we shall see. We know Ney issued orders at 11.00 (as we shall see later), so the order must have arrived by 11.00 as Ney says as much, further questioning the reliability of Heymès. The emperor's dispatch to Ney mostly repeats his own orders sent via Soult, and merely adds that Ney would have Kellermann's cuirassiers between himself and Napoléon, where a division was also to be placed at Marbais, and the Guard cavalry was not to be used. The dispatch's language is also of interest. Why does Napoléon state the cuirassiers were elite? Both he and Ney knew this. The letter talks of the roman road, which no other order issued on 15, 16 or 17 June mentions at all. The use of the phrase makes it clear that Heymès had in mind a specific location between Frasné and Quatre-Bras, which is a contradiction of his own order issued earlier in the day which stood Kellermann towards Marbais.

This seems a sudden change of plan, given Kellermann was to move to Marbais so as to be available to Ney and Napoléon, whereas the location given is far closer to Ney. Further evidence that the document is not from 1815 is the use of 'Quatre-Bras' to describe the battlefield. In *all* correspondence issued by Soult on 16 and 17 June 1815 the location is called 'Trois-Bras' or 'Three-Arms'. Quatre-Bras only became the name of the battle some time later. This suggests that Heymès was writing after the point of fact (i.e. not 16 June 1815), thus the order as we have it is only as accurate as Heymès's memory was fourteen years later.

Be that as it may, we know Flahaut carried an order to Ney from the emperor, as stated by Ney, Reille and Flahaut. However, we do not know what the order said, nor will we ever know. All we have to work with is the order as cited by Heymès. We feel that the gist and feel of the order was as Heymès recalled it in 1829, or at least implied. If we discount the order as Heymès recalls it, we have no idea at all as to the content of the order. We are trusting perhaps too much that Heymès's recollection is a true reflection of what the order said, and that he has not edited or invented the order to suit his own agenda, which is of course a distinct possibility. It is possible that Heymès, knowing the events of 16 June (that the emperor sent a verbal order to Ney, carried by Flahaut), invented the order, fitting it into the known facts of who carried it, to exonerate Marshal Ney. This of course means that Heymès was ignorant of the orders sent by Soult, which indeed he implies he was.

In his own narration, Heymès claims that Ney stood inactive at Quatre-Bras until he received the order from the emperor carried by Flahaut, thus showing for all the world that Ney was not to blame for the late start at Quatre-Bras, but that the fault lay with the emperor for not sending orders to Ney earlier in the day. The order, then, nicely suits his agenda, and here by sheer coincidence is the order that proves Ney was not guilty as charged. In a final analysis, Heymès's version of events totally contradicts what we actually know; that Soult sent three orders on the morning of 16 June. Therefore, we cannot be certain of what the order actually said, and the text of the order as it stands is likely to be forgery made by Heymès.

For fact, the order was handed to General Flahaut, who explained the order to Reille and then to Ney. He writes:[31]

> At Charleroi, the emperor, as you state, dictated to me between eight and nine o'clock in the morning, a letter for Marshal Ney, in which he let him know the manner in which he had distributed the army under his immediate orders and those of Marshal Grouchy, and informed him (as far as I can remember) of the operations he would undertake with the latter, being the corps of Comte Lobau and the Imperial Guard, against the Prussian army. But as for the orders relating to the various movements, I was charged with giving them verbally to Marshal Ney. I then gave him on behalf of the emperor, the order to advance upon Quatre-Bras, to strongly occupy this important place and (if the forces that he met would permit him) to support the movement being undertaking by the emperor against the Prussian army with all the troops he had available.
>
> Having given him [Ney] the order towards eleven o'clock, as I stated in the letter to the Duc d'Elchingen [Ney's son] which you cite, I rode ahead and met, quite close to Quatre-Bras, General Lefèbvre-Desnoëttes with his cavalry.

Ney's dispatch to Soult

The first order to Ney was sent at daybreak, so would have been with him by 6.00 at the latest. Soult ordered Ney to send information to him in direct reply to the order, yet Ney did not send any such reply until 11.00:[32]

> Frasné, 16 June 1815. 11.00
> To His Excellency Marshal Duc de Dalmatie
>   Major-general
>   I have received this instant your instructions for the movement of the 1st and 2nd Corps of Infantry and also the division of light cavalry of General Piré and the two divisions of cavalry from the 3rd Corps.

Those of the emperor have already been received.

Here are the dispositions I expect to make.

The 2nd Corps of General Reille will have a division below Genappe, another at Bantelet and the other at the entrance to Trois-Bras.

One division from the light cavalry of General Piré will march with the 2nd Corps.

The 1st Corps will be established as follows: one division at Marbais, and the two others at Frasné, one division of light cavalry at Marbais, the two divisions of the Comte de Valmy at Frasné and Liberchies.

The two divisions of the light cavalry of the Imperial Guard will be at Frasné, which is where I shall establish my headquarters.

For your information the enemy have about three thousand infantry at Quatre-Bras with a strong force of cavalry. I shall inform the emperor of my dispositions for the march into Brussels which will be executed without any major obstacles.

Marshal Prince of the Moskowa

Signed: Ney

Clearly, at 11.00 Ney was still at Frasné, some nine miles south of Quatre-Bras, perhaps at most three hours away on foot. He could never have started the action in the early hours of 16 June if he only received orders between 10.00 and 11.00 and did not issue orders until 11.00, which still left Kellermann's cavalry over twenty miles away, and 1st Corps perhaps ten miles away. Robbed of Girard, Ney had just three infantry divisions immediately to hand to oppose what would turn out to be the majority of Wellington's army.

Ney's report has some stark contradictions. In the early hours, despite the wooded nature of the battlefield, Adjutant-Commandant Jeanin, upon reconnoitring the area and speaking to officers who had questioned Allied deserters, gave the figure of Allied troops at 20,000, possibly more if the figure did not include the body of troops moving from Mons. With the receipt of the dispatch, headquarters could breathe a sigh of relief. Rather than 20,000-plus troops on the left, a mere 3,000 were present, which Ney assured would be swiftly pushed out of the way. Thus, Napoléon could progress with his plans to concentrate against the Prussians at Sombreffe and not have to worry about his left wing.

For Napoléon, Ney had at his disposal far more troops than needed to be able to execute his orders with a degree of celerity and be able to move to Brussels once the Prussians were contained. Based on this very low number of troops, when Napoléon needed more men at Ligny, and with no other news from Ney, he ordered Ney to swing around to Ligny. When he gave these orders in the early afternoon, Napoléon had no reason not to believe that his orders had not been carried out. Ney had not sent any dispatches to him informing of the state of play at Quatre-Bras. If Ney did not tell Napoléon what was going on at Quatre-Bras, then, without up-to-date information, Napoléon made plans accordingly on what information he did have. When he issued the order for Ney to wheel right, the most reliable information he had was that Ney was opposed by 3,000 troops, expected no resistance and by early afternoon he assumed Ney had achieved his objectives and thus had troops to spare to swing round to Ligny. Therefore, Napoléon, without any news since 11.00, was working with outdated information. Napoléon did not know that Ney was faced by a larger force, nor that he was encountering major difficulties in getting to Quatre-Bras, let alone Genappe as ordered—yet he told the emperor none of this. Ney's estimation of the troop numbers facing him was wrong by 17,000 men. Jeanin's estimate was far closer to the truth of what forces Ney would have to face at Quatre-Bras.

This was a major error on Ney's part. Yes, Jeanin observed that it was impossible, due to the heavily wooded area around Frasné, to give an accurate number of troops, but how did Ney get it so wrong? Or Jeanin? Jeanin clearly based his figures on what he could observe on the field, what he had learned from Allied prisoners of war, and also the news from d'Erlon. Ney seems totally unaware of the body of troops heading from Mons—why? I find it impossible that d'Erlon, Tancarville or Soult would not have reported this information to Ney; it was no good Napoléon knowing that a large body of troops was heading west from Mons and the field commander standing in the direct line of march of those soldiers was not informed of this. The French headquarters had known the Allied troops at Mons were moving west. I find it implausible that the officers Jeanin spoke with, who had questioned prisoners of war, did not pass the information onto Reille or Ney.

It is of course entirely possible that Ney did not know about the force heading from Mons, nor of the intelligence that had been gathered that morning, but we cannot be 100 per cent sure either way, as the archival paperwork that exists in 2017 is not the total documentation that existed on 16 June 1815. Ney's ignorance of information gathered by his subordinates, or gross underestimate of troops in front of him, was to have a major repercussion on the outcome of the battle.

Colbert's lancers
Sometime after writing the order to Ney around 8.00, Soult sent news to him about the position at Quatre-Bras:[33]

> Charleroi 16 June 1815
> M. marshal,
>
> An officer of the lancers had reported to the emperor that the enemy are assembling their troops nearby Trois-Bras; reunite the corps of Comte Reille and d'Erlon and also that of Comte de Valmy who at this very moment is moving to be with you. You must push back and destroy the enemy troops that you find there.
>
> Blücher was yesterday in Namur and it is not likely that he will take troops to Quatre-Bras, so you only need to be concerned about those from Brussels.
>
> Marshal Grouchy will make a movement to Sombreffe that I have informed you about, and the emperor is going to Fleurus. This is where you should send your reports to His Majesty.

We can confidently assume that Napoléon was not reporting back to Ney the reconnaissance report from Edouard de Colbert with the lancers of the Imperial Guard. These lancers must, therefore, be a different body of troops.

Grouchy had been ordered to establish a line of communication with Ney—an ideal role for light cavalry.[34] From the report, it is clear the line of vedettes between Ney and Grouchy were lancers.

Clearly, French headquarters knew that Quatre-Bras was going to be a focal point for the Allies. Soult urged Ney to attack. As we noted earlier, Ney was still at Frasné at 11.00 when he issued his orders to advance, a time that is recorded by Generals Foy and Bachelu. However, Ney must have had scouts at Quatre-Bras much earlier in the day. Gobrecht, with the 3rd and 4th Lancers, was with Jacquinot, and Wathiez, with the 5th and 6th, was with Ney, so the lancers mentioned must be the 1st and 2nd under the orders of Alphonse de Colbert. In support of the argument that Colbert's lancers were at Quatre-Bras, Jean Baptiste Berton, commanding the 14th and 17th Dragoons under the orders of General Chastel, which formed part of Excelmans's reserve cavalry, writes:[35]

> We said above that the 4th and the 2nd Divisions of the corps were placed on the evening of the 15th at Heppignies, the general ordered them to be united with the 3rd Infantry Corps to attack St-Amand. He sent a division of the Young Guard in reserve to the left of this village, with the light cavalry of General Domon. A brigade of lancers, commanded by Marshal-de-Camp Colbert, was placed beyond these troops, to maintain communication with the left wing.

This suggests that the brigade was with Ney on 16 June, or at least was deployed on Ney's flank. It is not impossible that the brigade fought at Quatre-Bras. Both the 1st and 2nd Lancers took a leading part in the combat at Genappe on 17 June, and thus are likely to have been with Ney at Quatre-Bras. Killed on 16 June was Mat. No. 637 Simon Bathziaux, of the 8th Company, and wounded from the 1st Lancers was Mat No. 872 Sergeant Julien Chaboudy in 9th Company.[36] The brigaded 11th Chasseurs à Cheval lost one man killed, two wounded and two missing, and further lost one man killed and one missing at Genappe.[37]

Given the brigade sustained losses on 16 June, and took a major part in the events of 17 June (seemingly brigaded with Jacquinot's 1st Cavalry Division), it does seem that Subervie's cavalry were placed between Grouchy and Ney. The fact that the division took losses on 16 June implies that a body of troops came into contact with the line of vedettes, or that the division was engaged in an action, possibly at Quatre-Bras. Did Ney have an additional cavalry force? Or were only portions of the regiments detached, leaving some squadrons with Vandamme? We cannot tell without further information. However, Durutte and d'Erlon never seem to have come across the line of vedettes in their journey to join the emperor, so they cannot have been strung along the roman road, and were perhaps further north.

With the receipt of this dispatch, Ney knew that the rearguard at Quatre-Bras was likely to be reinforced. Yet, once he had occupied Quatre-Bras and taken post at Genappe, what was he to do next? For all he knew, in all probability Wellington's entire command was marching south to confront him, and with the dispersed deployments asked of him, he no doubt reasoned that it was better to do nothing and see what happened at Quatre-Bras rather than facing the prospect of trying to defend Genappe against Wellington. Perhaps Ney felt the position he was in was better suited for operations than Genappe; and he was right.

Girard's report

Perhaps at the same time as receiving the emperor's news, at 10.15 Reille reported to Ney that an officer serving under Girard had submitted to him a report informing him that the enemy occupied Fleurus:[38]

> I have to inform Your Excellency of the report that was made to me verbally by one of General Girard's officers.
>
> The enemy continues to occupy Fleurus with light cavalry, with vedettes in front; two masses of enemy troops have been observed

on the Namur road, heading to the heights of Saint-Amand; they are forming bit-by-bit, and reached some ground where they can concentrate; their strength cannot be judged because of the distance. However, the general thinks that [each mass] was about six battalions strong in columns by battalions. There was also movement to the rear.

General Flahaut has informed me of the content of the orders he is taking to Your Excellency; I have warned Comte d'Erlon so that he can follow my movements. I would have started my move on Frasné as soon as the divisions were under arms, but after the report of General Girard, I will hold the troops ready to march, but will wait for Your Excellency's orders, and as you can warn me very quickly, little time will be lost. I have sent an officer to the emperor with General Girard's report.

Who had ordered Girard so far over to the right? Had Ney or Reille been level-headed enough to find out what troops were to their right flank? Certainly d'Erlon was to ordered to send pickets on the road to Mons. Girard's news had clearly unnerved Reille. But why did Reille not tell Ney where Girard was? Rather than heading directly off to Quatre-Bras, Reille was over-cautious and waited for clear instructions from Ney.
So, with Wellington bearing down on him along the Brussels road, and with two major Prussian forces on his right flank, where Girard and Donzelot were deployed, Ney perhaps reasoned that it was better to bide his time and see what happened. As it was, with every hour of delay Wellington was getting closer and Ney had issued no orders to concentrate his forces. The odds were stacking up against Ney.
Reille later sent word to Ney that Girard had been ordered to Saint-Amand.[39] With Girard detached, and d'Erlon and Kellermann still hours away, Ney had a very meagre force with which to oppose Wellington and the Prince of Orange. Reille was reluctant to advance—hardly surprising given the large number of troops assembling to his right—but why did it take Reille from daybreak to 10.00 to get ready to move forward? Was he waiting for 1st Corps to move up? The 1st Corps was strung out over a distance of twenty miles or so, it's leading division (that of Durutte) could not move off until 2nd Corps had left Gosselies. It seems Ney only issued orders, and seemingly reluctantly, at 11.00.

Reille's men seemed more concerned with food than fighting. Théobald Puvis, of the 93rd Regiment of Line Infantry, narrates:[40]

On the 16th, while the food distributions were made to the division. Whilst we were preparing for our movement, the artillery of the army corps and the cavalry marched past us to go take a stand in front of us on the road to Brussels. At noon, we put ourselves in motion.

The cavalry was seemingly Piré's command moving up. However, the enforced wait also allowed 3rd Division to move up.

Frasné
The scene now shifts to Frasné, a small village north of Gosselies. Little remains of the village from 1815, but of the buildings that do the most notable is the farm of Les Bons Villers, standing on the eastern side of the Brussels road at the junction with the rue de l'Encloître. The farm is clearly shown on the 1777 map, and was the southern limit of the village. Since the time of the battle, all the buildings shown on the 1777 map have been demolished. The farm, though, is a very evocative reminder of the fateful day of 16 June 1815.

It was in the fields around the village that Bachelu and Colbert had been engaged in a small-scale skirmish for some time, as Dutch-Belgian sources make clear, before Ney and Reille arrived. General Flahaut again:[41]

> I remained with him [General Lefèbvre-Desnoëttes] while awaiting the arrival of the troops under Marshal Ney and we saw, quite some distance in front of us, the English staff officers, who appeared to be examining our position. General Lefèbvre-Desnoëttes had some cannon shots fired at his cavalry, even though they were out of range. Finally, Marshal Ney appeared and the affair started, but there was no coherence in the dispositions. We took, as it is said, the bull by the horns, and launched the troops successively in the order they arrived.

A golden opportunity had been lost by Ney to achieve the mission objective set by Napoléon. Why Ney acted with timidity we cannot say. Marshal Ney's aide-de-camp, Heymès, writes:[42]

> It has been shown that on the 16th, at eight in the morning, there was at Frasné only the light cavalry division commanded by General Piré, together with the infantry of General Bachelu, and the two regiments of chasseurs and lancers of the Imperial Guard, which

were held in reserve behind the village; General Reille, with the two divisions commanded by Foy and Guilleminot [Jérôme], was en route to this point. The division under General Girard had been directed upon Ligny the preceding evening by the emperor, where that general was killed on the 16th. This division never re-joined the 2nd Corps, of which it formed a part.

Thus, when the whole of the 2nd Corps was brought together there were only four regiments of light cavalry, and three divisions of infantry and artillery available; in all between 17,000 and 18,000 men, not 40,000 as has been so often repeated. The light cavalry of the Imperial Guard should not be included in the number, for the emperor forbade their being engaged in any action.

The enemy, who occupied Quatre-Bras, at this time showed a force of 25,000 men with numerous artillery; his right covered the Bossu Wood; his centre was in front of Quatre-Bras; his left was lost in the direction of Namur, occupying the road to that place, and approaching our right flank.

In lieu of staff officers, in whom the marshal was deficient, officers of chasseurs and lancers of the Imperial Guard were sent in the direction of Marchiennes-au-Pont to meet the 1st Corps, with orders to press the march upon Frasné. The morning of the 16th was passed in reconnoitring the enemy and the ground upon which we were about to be engaged, and in awaiting the arrival of the 1st Corps and the reserves of the cavalry under General Kellermann [Comte de Valmy]. About eleven o'clock, General Flahaut brought orders to carry the position of Quatre-Bras and to march upon Brussels. The marshal made his dispositions immediately. Time passed. It was one o'clock and still the 1st Corps had not arrived; we had not even any tidings of it, but it could not be far off. The marshal did not hesitate to bring the enemy to action. The English were visibly receiving reinforcements, but their numerical superiority did not disquiet him. He thought that the sound of our cannon would cause the 1st Corps to hasten their arrival, and so he attacked the enemy. The division commanded by Guilleminot threw itself into the Bossu Wood, where it encountered strong resistance; however, at three o'clock, it was master of the wood, and threatened the rear of Quatre-Bras. The division under Bachelu met the enemy in front, upon the highroad, and the division led by Foy attacked the extreme left of the English. The enemy resisted at all points, but our attacks were impetuous. The cavalry division of Piré, although protected by our artillery, charged, but without success.

Colonel Baron Pieter Hendrik van Zuijlen van Nyevelt, the chief-of-staff of the 2nd Netherlands Infantry Division, narrates that:[43]

> At seven o'clock the enemy tested our position and carried out a few cavalry attacks which were driven back with small losses. Everything had been quiet in the position for more than an hour; the Prince of Orange gave the order for the troops to cook. Until this moment the enemy had shown only a small force; the troops we had to deal with included detachments of infantry of the line, as well as chasseurs, lancers and horse artillery of the Imperial Guard attached to the army corps of Comte Reille.

The time he gives was local to the writer, as there was no standard time before the advent of the railways, and the French and Allied armies would have had different times. We must also note that this letter is what the author thought he observed and deemed of sufficient importance to write down.

General Foy, commanding the 9th Infantry Brigade of General Reille's 2nd Corps, concurs about the activities of the Guard cavalry, noting in a letter of 17 June that:[44]

> The morning of 16 June passed quietly, but towards midday we set out for Quatre-Bras, an extremely important position where two highroads crossed. A reconnaissance by the chasseurs of the Imperial Guard had been driven back the day before by an enemy force which the men under General Lefèbvre-Desnoëttes identified as Nassau soldiers.

Early on the morning of the 16th, the 1st Hussars were spotted towards Nivelles. Zuijlen van Nyevelt reports about the initial troop positions against the oncoming French:[45]

> At five o'clock . . . the 2nd Nassau Battalion sent patrols forward which were shortly there, followed by the whole battalion. These patrols encountered the enemy patrols and small outposts of enemy cavalry which were pushed back with a few musket shots.

The 1st Hussars were between Quatre-Bras and Nivelles, acting as a flank-guard and checking on the movements of the Allied force from that area. A couple of other Dutch accounts mention French hussars appearing on the high ground to the west of Braine-le-Comte, heading towards Nivelles. Zuijlen van Nyevelt reports that the 1st Hussars were still in the area later in the day:[46]

> Around three o'clock in the afternoon ... The light cavalry brigade commanded by General van Merle [sic] (less a detachment on the road between Houtain-le-Val and Nivelles, as enemy hussars had appeared at this point earlier in the day) was positioned to the left of the highroad mentioned, as I recall, and the enemy doubled his attacks on the aforementioned farm, covered by the 5th Militia Battalion commanded then by Lieutenant-Colonel van Westenberg.

Following the initial advance to contact, the main attack began very slowly and very cautiously. Reille, like Foy, had served in Spain and had faced Wellington on the field of battle, and knew very well that Wellington had a habit of concealing the bulk of his forces. Reille's fear of running into strong, concealed Allied forces delayed that attack, as General Foy explains:[47]

> Reille thought that the battle might be similar to those in Spain, where the English troops would show when the time was right, and believed that we should wait until the troops were united before beginning the attack. But the marshal was impatient and reckless, and thought that our companies of voltigeurs were all that were required to capture the position.

For once Ney was correct, given that the crossroads were lightly defended, but no attack occurred for several hours. Picton's men were still about half an hour away from joining the line of battle. The position had to be held to give Wellington's troops a chance to deploy and redress the balance. But rather than attacking, Ney dithered and, uncharacteristically, heeded Reille's advice and made no major offensive movement until the divisions of Foy and Bachelu arrived.

Hindsight tells us the battalion of the 2nd Regiment of Light Infantry, with the Guard light cavalry, could have taken the position, but it was not to be. Every moment of delay brought more Allied troops closer to Quatre-Bras. Just as Blücher's men were on the march, so were Wellington's, who were coming to the aid of their Dutch allies, as a British officer writes:[48]

> On 15 June, everything appeared so perfectly quiet that the Duchess of Richmond gave a ball and supper, to which all the world was invited; and it was not till near ten o'clock at night that rumours of an action having taken place between the French and Prussians were circulated through the room in whispers: no credit was given to them, however, for some time; but when the general officers whose

corps were in advance began to move, and when orders were given for persons to repair to their regiments, matters then began to be considered in a different light. At eleven o'clock the drums beat to arms, and the 5th Division, which garrisoned Brussels, after having bivouacked in the park until daylight, set forward towards the frontiers.

On the road, we met baggage and sick coming to the rear; but could only learn that the French and Prussians had been fighting the day before, and that another battle was expected when they left the advanced posts. At two o'clock we arrived at Genappe, from whence we heard firing very distinctly; half an hour afterwards we saw the French columns advancing and we had scarcely taken our position when they attacked us. Our front consisted of the 3rd and 5th Divisions, with some Nassau people, and a brigade of cavalry, in all about thirteen thousand men; while the French forces, according to Ney's account, must have been immense, as his reserve alone consisted of 30,000, which, however, he says, Buonaparte disposed of without having advertised him. The business was begun by the 1st Battalion of the 95th, which was sent to drive the enemy out of some cornfields, and a thick wood, of which they had possession: after sustaining some loss, we succeeded completely; and three companies of Brunswickers were left to keep it while we acted on another part of the line: they, however, were driven out immediately; and the French also got possession of a village which turned our flanks.

Since the early hours, Ney had slowly pushed back the Allied troops to his front. Having only the Guard cavalry and the 2nd Regiment of Light Infantry, he had no troops to hand to initiate a more serious action. That he did nothing between the hours of 6.00 and 11.00 in ordering his troops to assemble at Gosselies was a major error on his part.

NOTES:
[1] Heymès, pp. 7-8.
[2] SHDDT: C15 5, *dossier 16 Juin 1815*. d'Erlon to Soult timed at 16.30.
[3] SHDDT: C15 5, *dossier 16 Juin 1815*. d'Erlon to Soult.
[4] SHDDT: C15 5, *dossier 16 Juin 1815*. Soult to d'Erlon. Copy of the now lost original order made by Marshal Ney's son.
[5] SHDDT: C15 5, *dossier 16 Juin 1815*. Durosnel to Nogues timed at 3.00, copied to general commanding 1st Division.
[6] AN: AFIV 1939 *Registre d'Ordres du Major-General 13 Juin au 26 Juin 1815*, p 31.
[7] AN: AFIV 1939, p. 32.
[8] AN: AFIV 1939, p. 32.
[9] SHDDT: C 15 5, *dossier 16 Juin 1815*. Lobau to Napoléon.

[10] Théo Fleischmen, *L'Armée impériale racontée par la Grande Armée*, Librairie Académique Perrin, Paris, 1964.
[11] SHDDT: C15 35 *Situation rapports Armée du Nord. Dossier 15 Juin 3e Corps de Cavalerie.*
[12] SHDDT: C15 5, *dossier 15 Juin 1815*. Grouchy to Kellermann. Copy made by Comte de Cases in 1865.
[13] Ian Smith, perssonal communication 1 December 2016.
[14] SHDDT: C15 3. *Rapport 26 Mai 1815.*
[15] SHDDT: C15 5, *dossier 15 Juin 1815*. Grouchy to Soult 16 June timed at 5.00.
[16] SHDDT: C15 5, *dossier 15 Juin 1815*. Grouchy to Soult 16 June timed at 5.00.
[17] *Le Moniteur Universel*, 18 June 1815, p. 3.
[18] SHDDT: Xc 206 *11e Chasseurs à Cheval. Dossier 1815.*
[19] Fleischmen.
[20] Chapuis, 'Waterloo' in *La Sentinelle de l'Armée*, 24 February 1838.
[21] AN: LH/1091/33.
[22] AN: LH/1168/88.
[23] AN: AFIV 1939 *Registre d'Ordres du Major-General 13 Juin au 26 Juin 1815*, pp. 35-7.
[24] SHDDT: C15 5, *dossier du 16 Juin 1815*. Copy of the now lost order made by Comte de Cases in 1865.
[25] AN: AFIV 1939 *Registre d'Ordres du Major-General 13 Juin au 26 Juin 1815*, pp. 37-40. See also: Emmanuel Grouchy, *Relation succincte de la campagne de 1815 en Belgique*, Delanchy, Paris, 1843, pp. 13-14. Grouchy states this is a verbal order, but it is written into Soult's order book, so clearly Grouchy is mistaken on this point, unless Soult recorded verbal orders.
[26] Emmanuel Grouchy, *Relation succincte de la campagne de 1815 en Belgique*, pp. 15-16. This order is not in Soult's order book, so we cannot be certain of its authenticity.
[27] SHDDT: C15 5, *dossier du 16 Juin*. Copy of the now lost original order made by Ney's son in 1837. See also: Emmanuel Grouchy, *Relation succincte de la campagne de 1815 en Belgique*.
[28] Emmanuel Grouchy, *Relation succincte de la campagne de 1815 en Belgique*, p. 15.
[29] SHDDT: C15 5, *dossier du 16 Juin*.
[30] Heymès.
[31] John Franklin, personal communication 7 October 2013.
[32] SHDDT: C15 5, *dossier 16 Juin*. Ney to Soult at 11:00. Copy of the original document made on 20 February 1890. We do not have the original order to compare this with, so we cannot tell if is a word-for-word copy of the original, or indeed whether it is an authentic document from 16 June that was copied at a later date.
[33] AN: AFIV 1939 *Registre d'Ordres du Major-General 13 Juin au 26 Juin 1815*, p. 40.
[34] AN: AFIV 1939 *Registre d'Ordres du Major-General 13 Juin au 26 Juin 1815*, p. 37.
[35] Jean Baptiste Berton, *Précis historique, militaire et critique des batailles de Fleurus et de Waterloo, dans la campagne de Flandres, en juin 1815*, J. S. Wallez, La Haye, 1818, p. 15.
[36] SHDDT: GR 24 YC 96.
[37] SHDDT: GR 24 YC 309
[38] SHDDT: C15 5, *dossier 16 Jun 1815*. Reille to Ney timed at 10.15. Copy of the now lost original document made by Ney's son in 1829.
[39] SHDDT: C15 5, *dossier 16 Jun 1815*. Reille to Duc d'Elchingen. Copy of the now lost original made in 1829.
[40] 'Souvenirs historiques de Theobald Puvis' in *Revue historique des Armées*, 1997 [no.3], pp. 101-29.
[41] John Franklin, perssonal communication 7 October 2013.
[42] Heymès, pp. 7-8.
[43] John Franklin, *Waterloo Netherlands Correspondence* [vol. 1], 1815 Limited, 2010, p. 45.
[44] Lemonnier-Delafosse, p. 270.
[45] Erwin Muilwijk, perssonal communication 1 December 2012.
[46] Erwin Muilwijk, perssonal communication 1 December 2012.
[47] Maurice Girod de l'Ain, *Vie militaire du Géneral Foy*, E. Plon, Nourrit et cie, Paris, 1900, pp. 271-2.
[48] John Booth, *The Battle of Waterloo*, Booth, Egerton, London, 1816, p. xlvix.

Chapter 3

Bachelu's Attack

At 11.00, Ney issued orders to Reille and d'Erlon to concentrate his command, and to begin the advance to Quatre-Bras from Frasné:[1]

> Conforming to the instructions of the emperor, the 2nd Corps will begin its movement and will occupy the following positions.
>
> The 5th Division will be in the rear of Genappes on the heights that dominate the town, the left flank lying against the main road. A battalion of two [illegible] will debouch in front along the Brussels road. The park and reserve will be deployed in the 2nd Line.
>
> The 9th Division will follow the movement of the 5th, and will take up a position in line on the heights, deployed to the right and left of the village of Banterlet.
>
> The 6th and 7th Divisions will debouch at Trois-Bras where I shall establish my headquarters. The first three divisions of the Comte d'Erlon will take up position at Frasné, the right-hand division will be established at Marbais with the 2nd Division of light cavalry of General Piré; the first is to cover your march and you are to send out reconnaissance patrols towards Brussels and on both flanks. My headquarters will be at Frasné.
>
> For Marshal Prince of the Moskowa
> Colonel aide-de-camp, Heymès
>
> The two divisions of the Comte de Valmy are to establish themselves at Frasné and Liberchies. General Lefèbvre-Desnoëttes and Colbert's division of the Guard are to remain at Frasné.

However, the order made a number of major assumptions:
1) d'Erlon and 1st Corps were at Gosselies;
2) Girard was not yet detached; and
3) Kellermann was close at hand.

Ney's order in no way reflected the troop dispositions as they were at 11.00: Girard was at Wagnelée and never headed back to join the rest of 2nd Corps; Kellermann was forty miles to the south; and 1st Corps was yet to arrive, being scatted between the River Sambre and Gosselies. For fact, Jacquinot's 1st Cavalry Division did not cover Reille's operations (that was done by Piré), no doubt because Jacquinot had not yet arrived. So, from word go, Ney's plan of operations fell to bits. Furthermore, Durutte's division from 1st Corps was always destined to attack at Ligny. This means that as soon as Durutte received orders, he was to head north from Gosselies on the Brussels road and then swing right onto the roman road and head off to join the emperor. It does mean that Ney planned on having the remaining three divisions at Frasné. In keeping three divisions he was being selective in understanding the emperor's orders. Napoléon spoke rather confusingly of sending a division with cavalry to Marbais and a complete corps in the same order. Ney clearly sent the minimal number of troops to support Napoléon—one division of infantry and one of cavalry.

Quatre-Bras in 1815 was known as 'Trois-Bras' or 'Three-Arms', the name Quatre-Bras being added after the battle. It was so called as it was the intersection of the Brussels and Namur roads. When supposed authentic documents, written by the French eyewitnesses, from the period call the place 'Quatre-Bras' we can quickly tell that they cannot be from 1815, as the term was not in common use. However, the label of 'Waterloo' was applied to 'Mont-Saint-Jean' as early as July 1815, so the reference to Waterloo in documents said to be from 1815 does not immediately call their authenticity into question. The modern-day village here did not exist 200 years ago, when all that existed on that hot June day was the 'Cabaret des Trois-Bras' standing at the crossroads, according to the 1777 Map. Where the cabaret stood is now a grassy field to the immediate north west of the junction. A print made soon after the battle in 1816 by Robert Bowyer shows a row of three houses on the west side of the Brussels road, before reaching the crossroads. At the crossroads, which occupy the middle ground of the engraving, we catch a glimpse of the southern gable of the cabaret, and the south face of the 'Ferme des Quatre-Bras', which was demolished not long after the 200th anniversary of the battle, after a long, but ultimately fruitless, campaign to save this noble and historically important building complex from destruction. Nothing remains of the farm, the cabaret or houses from Bowyer's engraving, and the location is now a soulless mass of modern tarmac and a neo-brutalist car showroom and small restaurant. North of the crossroads was another row of houses and the 'Cabaret la Baraque', standing at what was once the intersection of the Brussels and Namur roads before the new paved chaussee was built. It was from here that the rue de Banterlez branched west to Banterlez. This small village still retains the same street layout in 2017 as it did in 1777. The French only seem to have reached Banterlez on afternoon of the following day. Liberchies, now in 2017 is almost as it was in 1815—a small village standing to the west of the Brussels road. Many of the farms and houses clustered around the church, rebuilt after 1815, were clearly standing in 1815 and in many places, especially the outlying farms, the atmosphere of the place is little-changed since June 1815.

Laying the wanton destruction of the farm of Quatre-Bras aside, about the operation of his division, General Bachelu writes as follows:[2]

> The 5th Division of the 2nd Corps, commanded by M. Comte Reille took position at dusk on the 15th in the village of Mellet.
>
> This division was ordered on the 16th sometime between eleven o'clock and midday to start moving and head to the village of Frasné, where the lancers and chasseurs of the Guard had been busy the day before. He was followed at a distance of a quarter-hour by the 9th Division of the same corps, commanded by M. Comte Foy.
>
> When General Bachelu, at the head of the 5th Division, was in front of Frasné he found Marshal Ney and Comte Reille. Comte Piré's light cavalry division had already arrived and formed up into line of battle.
>
> The marshal ordered the 5th Division to form in close column and advance to the position of Quatre-Bras, which was occupied by the English. We had known that since the previous evening the position was occupied; and it was assumed that reinforcements had arrived in the night and early morning, but we could not establish the strength of the troops here.
>
> General Bachelu assembled his division and advanced in close columns by battalion on the point that was shown to him by the marshal himself. General Foy, who preceded the division by a few minutes, also received at the same time its direction of attack, being to the left of the one that was shown to the 5th Division.
>
> There were two marshy creeks to cross before ascending onto the plateau of Quatre-Bras, which slowed down the advance; the columns were only halfway to the position when they were charged by masses of British infantry, which appeared suddenly and so

strongly that the 5th Division and a brigade of the 9th were forced to retire, re-passing the ravine and returned to occupy a position in front of the village of Frasné where three brigades were maintained and fought until night.

Mellet is just over five miles from Quatre-Bras; around two hours march at most for the division. An eyewitness to the day writes in 1815:[3]

> The advance of our left wing commenced about two o'clock in the afternoon. The high standing corn, and the numerous copses and ravines which occurred between Frasné and Quatre-Bras, prevented our troops from ascertaining either the number or real position of the English. No precaution had been taken to clear away the under wood, and thus facilitate the march and the deploying of the infantry, and the division of Foy, which formed the advanced-guard, experienced much difficulty in advancing through the execrable roads.

Adjutant-Commandant Toussaint-Jean Trefcon, chief-of-staff to General Bachelu, adds some more detail, but contradicts his commanding officer in the time that orders were issued:[4]

> On the 16th, at five in the morning, we were already assembled and under arms, ready to fight. We remained three hours in this position. At eight o'clock we received orders to advance on Quatre-Bras. We made our way to this point, but due to some incorrect manoeuvres we did not arrive in our position until around noon. Our division was a little behind Genappe on the hills near this city. Enemy troops that were opposed to us consisted of a large division of Dutch troops, of about eight thousand men, commanded by the Prince of Orange in person.
>
> At three o'clock in the afternoon, Marshal Ney ordered us to attack. The division advanced to attack the Dutch who were at Piraumont. The force and impetuosity of our attack made them give ground. They retreated and were attacked by a vigorous charge of the 5th and 6th Regiments of Lancers who soon transformed this movement into a rout. The Prince of Orange was almost caught by our lancers, who brought us several pieces of cannon.
>
> Then we continued our march in the direction of Gémioncourt. The speed of our advance, attached to the extreme heat of the day, made this move quite painful. When we were turning into a small

valley situated near the Namur road, we were received by a violent discharge of musketry. It was the English hidden in the very tall corn who fired at us. At first, we could not see where the firing came from; our column hesitated for a moment. The English took advantage of this shouting loudly as they vigorously attacked us. The suddenness and violence of this attack forced us to retreat. We reformed in front of Piraumont, and it was now our turn to open a violent fire on them, supported by our artillery, which had remained in position at Piraumont. At that moment, the cavalry of General Piré arrived to charge the English, who in turn had to withdraw to their original position. This movement evoked the greatest admiration. Their squares were formed so remarkably that our chasseurs and lanciers were unable to attack them; it was an honourable combat which honoured all of those involved.

I ordered the retreat to Piraumont, which was nearly fatal for me. As I stayed back a little to rally the troops and hold my horse, who was angry, he became entangled in the corn or whatever and he began to kick, refusing to move. I felt the English on my heels and, unconcerned about being caught, I was going to throw down my arms, when suddenly, my horse decided to gallop off. I got away in fear, because the English were already close to me. Then it was our turn to continue against the English by resuming our march forward. Unfortunately, we had to stop soon because our cavalry had not been able to attack the squares, and they had received numerous reinforcements. We were then forced to abandon Piraumont and resume the position we had occupied at the beginning of the action.

About the attack of General Campi's brigade, Hippolyte de Mauduit reports:[5]

The 108th Line, commanded by Colonel Higonet, took a glorious part in this first attack. The regiment was three battalions strong and comprised some 1,340 bayonets, and found itself deployed to the rear-left of Bachelu's division. The enemy, after a murderous fire, retreated in the direction of Quatre-Bras, crossing a meadow which formed a shallow valley, and took position in corn fields on higher ground, having in front of them, forming a natural defence, a large thorn hedge.

The first three regiments of the division were able to cross this hedge, although with difficulty, as it had been cut down to two or three feet from the ground. However, the hedge in front of the 108th had not been cut down, and presented a formidable and impenetrable barrier a metre thick and from two to three metres high. Colonel Higonet, in the midst of enemy musketry, ordered a platoon of his grenadiers and sappers to make a large opening in the hedge, so that this barrier could be crossed by his three battalions. When the opening was practicable, the first battalion passed through and formed in line of battle to conform with the 72nd, which was formed to the right. But before this movement could be completed, a volcano of fire erupted along the line, almost at the feet of our soldiers. This most unexpected point-blank fire came from several English regiments which had hidden in the high corn fields. The fire made cruel ravages in our ranks and resulted in a retrograde movement in the other three regiments, who, upon returning to the hedge line were unable to cross it without much confusion.

In order to profit from this disorder, the English launched a charge. The 108th witnessed this confusion, and Colonel Higonet hastened to order his first battalion to about face so that it could re-cross the hedge and form up behind the other two that he formed up at the same time by turning them right into line. When he done so, he commanded them to level their muskets and give a defensive fire. With the 72nd being energetically pursued by the English up to the bayonets of the 108th, having cleared its front, began a terrible fire bringing death into the already confused ranks of the enemy. Colonel Higonet immediately ordered a bayonet charge. The English, who had survived the musketry, and wanting to retreat through the hedge, were closely pursued; the carnage was terrible. Captain Arnaud, son of a member of the Institute, whose sword was broken in a melee, seized a musket with a bayonet and put nine Englishmen out of action. Witnessing the success of the 108th, the other three regiments of the division, which had rallied, re-took the offensive and threw the enemy back to their first position. During this struggle the 108th had 400 men, including twenty-one officers, out of combat.

Despite the negativity of de Mauduit, the 72nd Regiment of Line Infantry at Quatre-Bras captured an Allied artillery piece; the officer who assisted in the capture of the artillery was Jean Denis Chapuzot. Chapuzot had been admitted to the regiment on 4 August 1811, was promoted to corporal on 6 June 1813 and promoted to sergeant a day later, before promotion to adjutant-sub-officer on 1 September 1813. He received his epaulettes of sub-lieutenant on 10 November 1813. He writes as follows about his military service:[6]

> I was wounded with a gunshot to the left knee at Wilna on 10 December 1812. I was wounded on 16 June 1815 at the affair of Fleurus with two gunshots, one which pierced my left shoulder, and the second gave me a strong contusion, causing a hernia of the stomach.
>
> I captured from the enemy, at the head of my three soldiers from the regiment at the affair of Fleurus on 16 June 1815 at the farm of Quatre-Bras, an ammunition caisson with its two draught horses which were taken to the artillery park of our division.

The action is confirmed by Allied eyewitnesses, including Zuijlen van Nyevelt who reported that:[7]

> The well-led attacks against the farm and against the wood resulted in the re-taking of many wounded and prisoners of war, and the enemy managed only to take away one howitzer and two 6-pounders which were, besides, taken back two days later.

Initially, the division of Bachelu ran into the 5th and 7th National Militia Battalions of the Dutch-Belgian army, and were supported by Piré's light cavalry. Zuijlen van Nyevelt reports about the initial troop positions against the oncoming French:[8]

> Around two o'clock, the 7th Line Battalion was deployed in closed column on the plain, but it soon received the order to move, first to the rear of the wood and then to the right. The 7th Militia Battalion followed this movement and crossed the wood, which was already under heavy attack from the enemy. At the same time the 5th Militia Battalion was placed more towards the left on the highroad to Charleroi and ordered to defend a farm situated on that highroad. The 1st Battalion of the 28th Orange-Nassau Regiment and the 8th Militia Battalion occupied the extreme right wing, and deployed in battle formation, but shortly afterwards received the order to retreat and to take position against and behind the Bossu Wood.
>
> The 1st Nassau Battalion was formed in line in front of the wood; the companies of Captain Werneck and Frittler were deployed as sharp-shooters. These troops were the object of repeated attacks by the lancers of the Imperial Guard.

Zuijlen van Nyevelt continues:[9]

> The enemy advanced in force under the most violent artillery fire, and pushed our troops placed in the woods back and took over part of the wood. The retreating troops placed themselves partly on the northern edge of the wood, while another part crossed the roads and deployed themselves on favourable heights situated to the left of the wood. The enemy emerging diagonally from the wood of Villers-Perwin and marching to the attack of our left wing, the general of our division pushed the 27th Jäger Battalion a few hundred paces ahead in order to cover the left of the 5th Militia Battalion. The detached companies were pushed back before having been able to form and rallied behind the aforementioned battalion. The enemy took advantage of this success, and placed a battery just ahead of the line of battle, which forced the latter to retire; this movement was executed in columns by divisions at the distance of the platoon so as to form square instantly.
>
> Meanwhile, the enemy pushing the 7th Line Battalion back was gaining a great deal of ground in the wood, and the 8th Militia Battalion had been forced to evacuate the area due to the fierce cannonade to which it was subjected. The 1st Battalion of the 28th Orange-Nassau Regiment and the 7th Militia Battalion stayed during the same time in reserve to the right of the wood while the two retreating battalions reformed on the height behind.

General Foy narrates Bachelu's assault against Picton's division as follows:[10]

> Bachelu's division, together with my own, reached the farm close to Frasné where Marshal Ney was in the adjacent field with the chasseurs and lancers of the Imperial Guard, and the light cavalry division under General Piré ... Bachelu marched in the direction of the small stream situated below Gémioncourt, and I followed in support on the left with my 1st Brigade, while allowing my 2nd to reform and wait by the farm at Frasné, before being relieved by troops from the next division. Having received our orders, Bachelu and I, at the head of the column, moved to the left in the direction the northern tip of the Bossu Wood. The enemy showed a great many troops outside of the wood and around the houses at Quatre-Bras, as well as on the road to Namur.
>
> Four cannon began firing at us and our heavy and light artillery responded. Four English and Scottish battalions formed in line of

battle, by battalion, on the heights above Gémioncourt, which was crossed by the road from Namur. They attacked our 5th Division, which at that moment was surmounting the plateau. The 2nd Light Infantry formed the head of the column of Bachelu's division. They did not anticipate the enemy attack and retired. The remainder of the division became disordered and abandoned their positions, not even stopping on the plateau behind Gémioncourt. I passed the stream near the house with my 1st Brigade and I ordered General Jamin, a dedicated, brave and excellent officer, to continue the advance with the 4th Light Infantry. I retired and subsequently formed the 100th Line on the height in the rear of Gémioncourt.

The 100th Line, by its good countenance, held the enemy column which pursued the 5th Division. The rest of my division formed on the height in front of Lerat [Lairalle], while the 5th Division rallied between Lerat and the hamlet of Piermont [sic]. The first prisoners that we captured announced that Wellington, with eight English brigades, had just arrived from Brussels and that other troops, including artillery, would arrive shortly. They also confirmed that there was already a considerable body of Belgian, Dutch and German troops at the crossroads.

Battalion Commander Claude François Marie Répécaud,[11] chief-of-staff of the engineers of 2nd Corps, writes:[12]

At noon, the Scottish troops had not yet arrived, and the English were still far off, but at the time of the attack, at one o'clock, we were the first there, and the others arrived later. They had arrived in large numbers when the division of Bachelu advanced along the road in order to attack in the flank the enemy position, which had established itself firmly in front of the Namur road. He forced one of the regiments to withdraw in the greatest of disorder.

Répécaud further notes that in this attack a regiment was routed, perhaps the 2nd Regiment of Light Infantry:[13]

I accompanied the division of Bachelu, but I had to stop or my company of sappers attached to this division would have been shot to pieces. There were some ridges on the terrain which disrupted the movements of the artillery, with General Bachelu needing this company to assist the artillery, I had to send the company forward and replace it with another, when I saw a mass of confused soldiers rushing towards me. Perceiving a battalion commander that followed them, I ran to him and induced him to put these scattered men back into some order, and he told me that this was as a result of his colonel, and that he did not know what had become of the colonel. So, I took it upon myself to order, on behalf of the commander, to reform these soldiers and put them into line at the left of a company of sappers that I had formed into line of battle a short distance away. The officer obeyed the order that I had improvised, but not without hesitation that I had given in my name. At the same time, there arrived a captain and the company of sappers that had remained with the division of Bachelu, who had hastily retraced their steps according to the order of the general himself.

A few moments later, having seen General Reille advancing, alone and on foot, stopped to see why this division, which was not supported by that of General Foy. I related what I had done in his name and he nodded his head in agreement.

Piraumont Farm was now in French hands, and the Dutch-Belgian defenders had withdrawn to the crossroads.

2nd Regiment of Light Infantry

The 2nd Regiment of Light Infantry was part of 2nd Corps. It formed, along with the 61st Regiment of Line Infantry, the 1st Brigade of General Bachelu's 5th Division. At Quatre-Bras, the 2nd Regiment of Light Infantry was, it seems, used as a skirmish screen. Bachelu, it would appear, advanced with the 2nd Regiment of Light Infantry thrown out in front as skirmishers, and then had the remaining three regiments advance on column by regiment, with the 72nd Regiment of Line Infantry forming the left of the line by the farm of Quatre-Bras, the 108th in the centre and the 61st towards Thyle.

Total losses for the 2nd Regiment of Light Infantry at Quatre-Bras are in the table below:[14]

2nd Regiment of Light Infantry

	Wounded	Wounded and Prisoner	Prisoner of War	Killed	Missing
1st Battalion	2	0	16	2	2
2nd Battalion	0	0	0	1	0
3rd Battalion	0	0	1	0	0
4th Battalion	0	0	6	0	1
Total	2	0	23	3	3

On 27 May 1815, the regiment mustered four battalions, comprising of ninety-eight officers and 2,468 men.[15] The regiment's paperwork admits to the loss of thirty-one men, 1.3 per cent of effective strength.

61st Regiment of Line Infantry

Brigaded with the 2nd Regiment of Light Infantry was the 61st Regiment of Line Infantry. The regiment's muster list, preserved in the French Army Archives, shows the following losses:[16]

61st Regiment of Line Infantry

	Wounded	Wounded and Prisoner	Prisoner of War	Killed	Missing (presumed prisoner)
1st Battalion	33	0	5	5	0
2nd Battalion	47	0	5	1	0
3rd Battalion	26	0	11	2	0
Total	106	0	21	8	0

The regiment had 1,196 effective rank and file at the start of the campaign. In total, 135 men were lost on 16 June, leaving 1,061 men in the ranks—a loss of some 11.3 per cent of the regiment. In addition, one officer was killed on 16 June and one other wounded. On 17 June, three men were lost. Thus, on the 18th, the regiment had 1,058 men in the ranks.

72nd Regiment of Line Infantry

Total regimental losses at Quatre-Bras are in the table below:[17]

72nd Regiment of Line Infantry

	Evacuated Wounded	Wounded and Prisoner	Prisoner of War	Killed	Missing
1st Battalion	89	0	16	7	5
2nd Battalion	73	0	9	6	11
Total	162	0	25	13	16

On 10 June, the regiment mustered forty-two officers and 953 other ranks. At Quatre-Bras, 216 men were lost, representing 22.7 per cent of effective strength. The heaviest losses were in the voltigeur company of 1st Battalion, which suffered over double the number of men wounded compared to the other companies. These losses impacted upon battlefield performance on 18 June.

108th Regiment of Line Infantry

The 108th Regiment of Line Infantry, commanded by Colonel Higonet, sustained heavy losses in the action at Quatre-Bras. These losses are detailed below:[18]

108th Regiment of Line Infantry

	Evacuated Wounded	Wounded and Prisoner	Prisoner of War	Killed	Missing
1st Battalion	0	0	3	11	0
2nd Battalion	0	0	1	7	0
3rd Battalion	0	0	1	5	0
Total	0	0	5	23	0

On 10 June, the regiment mustered sixty-one officers and 1,046 other ranks in three battalions. We only know the fate of twenty-eight men on 16 June. Therefore, we cannot give any further comment on the losses.

NOTES:
[1] SHDDT: C15 5, *dossier 16 Juin. Ordre Maréchal Ney 16 Juin 1815 à 11.00*. The document cited is a copy of the now lost original sent to the son of Marshal Ney by General Reille in 1829. This order is not found in the pages of General Reille's correspondence book preserved at the French Army Archives at Vincennes.
[2] Erwin Muilwijck, perssonal communication 6 June 2016.
[3] Pierre Giraud, *Précis des Journées de 15, 16, 17 et 18 Juin 1815*, Alexis Eymery, Paris, 1815, p. 65.
[4] Trefcon.
[5] Hippolyte de Mauduit, *Les derniers jours de la Grande Armée* (vol. 2), Paris, 1848, pp. 148-9.
[6] AN: LH/486/75.
[7] Erwin Muilwijk, perssonal communication 1 December 2012.
[8] Erwin Muilwijk, perssonal communication 1 December 2012.
[9] Erwin Muilwijk, perssonal communication 1 December 2012.
[10] de l'Ain, pp. 271-2.
[11] Répécaud was born at Besancon on 14 November 1782. He was the son of Jean François Répécaud, a merchant, and Marguerite Badez. He became a cadet at the Ecole Polytechnique on 22 November 1799 and graduated to the Engineering School at Metz on 22 December 1801. He graduated as a second lieutenant on 22 December 1802, and was promoted to captain on 1 January 1807 and to battalion commander on 16 October 1812. He served in the Peninsular War and in the Russian Campaign.
[12] Colonel du Génie Répécaud, *Napoléon à Ligny et le Maréchal Ney à Quatre-Bras*, Degeorge, Arras, 1847.
[13] Répécaud, 'Napoléon à Ligny, et le Maréchal Ney à Quatre-Bras' in *Memoires d'Academie de Arras*, 1832, pp. 191-2.
[14] SHDDT: GR 22 YC 19 *2er régiment d'infanterie Legere 1814 à 1815*.
[15] SHDDT: C15 34, *Situation Rapport 1e Corps 27 Mai 1815*.
[16] SHDDT: GR 21 YC 516 *57e régiment d'infanterie de ligne (ex 61e régiment d'infanterie de ligne), 1 août 1814-14 juin 1815 (matricules 1 à 1,800)*.
[17] SHDDT: GR 21 YC 599 *66e régiment d'infanterie de ligne (ex 72e régiment d'infanterie de ligne), 11 août 1814-27 février 1815 (matricules 1 à 1,800)*.
[18] SHDDT: GR 21 YC 790 *89e régiment d'infanterie de ligne (ex 108e régiment d'infanterie de ligne), 9 septembre 1814-7 juin 1815 (matricules 1 à 1,800)*.

Chapter 4

Foy's Attack

Maximillian Sebastien Foy was an artilleryman. He graduated from the artillery school at La Fere and saw his first action at Jemappes in 1792. General Foy, commanding the 9th Infantry Brigade of General Reille's 2nd Corps, concurs about the activities of the Guard cavalry, noting in a letter of 17 June that:[1]

> Upon our arrival at Frasné, we saw that the Bossu Wood and the hamlet of Quatre-Bras were occupied in force. We observed the British officers making a detailed reconnaissance. It was now that the emperor delivered battle with the Prussians in front of Fleurus, and we could hear his guns. I followed the division commanded by Bachelu; the division led by Girard was seconded to the emperor, while the division commanded by Prince Jérôme followed mine. The 1st Corps brought up the rear. The cavalry division commanded by General Lhéritier was behind us. Bachelu's division, together with my own, reached the farm close to Frasné where Marshal Ney was in the adjacent field with the chasseurs and lancers of the Imperial Guard, and the light cavalry division under General Piré. The marshal said that there was hardly anyone in the Bossu Wood and that it was to be captured immediately.

Marie Jean Baptiste Lemonnier-Delafosse's aide-de-camp to General Foy notes the following, but seems a little confused as to the French dispositions:[2]

> General Foy, by his movement, took possession of Gémioncourt farm and overwhelmed the enemy's left. For five hours we fought without a marked advantage on either side.

In this first advance, the 92nd and 93rd Regiments of Line Infantry moved off, and the 100th Regiment of Line Infantry and 4th Regiment of Light Infantry remained in reserve, until called upon to force back Picton's troops around 16.30. Major Pierre François Tissot, officer commanding the 92nd Regiment of Line Infantry, part of General Foy's 9th Infantry Brigade in 2nd Corps, notes:[3]

> On the 16th in the morning, Napoléon ordered General Kellermann to stand, with his body of cuirassiers, at Quatre-Bras, to strengthen the left. He ordered at the same time Marshal Ney to march forward with his troops, and take a good position beyond that of Quatre-Bras, since he had not taken it the day before, and, if the Prussian army stood to fight at Fleurus or near Gembloux, to send a detachment on the right flank of the Prussians.

Sergeant-Major Silvain Larreguy, of the 93rd Regiment of Line Infantry adds:[4]

> On 16 June there occurred the Battle of Ligny, which was taken and retaken seven times by our troops and the enemy. My corps was thrown into the Bossu Wood that hid the 90,000 men of Wellington; the fight was bloody, and the ground valiantly defended by the Scots, who were skilful marksmen, and fought to the sound of bagpipes, with their national dress, the short jacket leaving naked the thigh and leg. One moment our cavalry was overthrown, but our division, with Foy at the helm, remained steadfast and supported the fight with perseverance and fearlessness.

For the 93rd Regiment of Line Infantry, we are fortunate that several members of the regiment recorded their observations of the campaign, which are presented below. Théobald Puvis, of the 93rd Regiment of Line Infantry, narrates:[5]

> At noon, we put ourselves in motion. We had marched for an hour when to our right we heard a cannonade, which began quite close to us. We were ordered to leave the road to take a position on our right. No sooner was the movement begun than the enemy started the bombardment of our line which became more intense and some balls fell onto our column, but without worrying us very much. We could see perfectly well the enemy batteries firing on us, and was protected by a mass of infantry.

About three o'clock, we were deploying our masses and our whole line was in movement, supported by sharpshooters. We walked in the middle of the rye, which by its height obscured the enemy before us, but the balls did not come, which, like ours, also seldom reached their lines. This tension lasted until nightfall.

It seemed to us that with the enthusiasm which our army showed, without much resistance to fear, we could take the position occupied by the enemy. Why had we not done so? We had before us a small portion of the English army, who was surprised in his encampment by our rapid entry into the campaign.

But the same day, the emperor, with the Imperial Guard and the army corps commanded by Marshal Grouchy, had attacked the Prussian army on the side of Namur at Fleurus and had beat her, to go on to the English army which we had just met the vanguard of in the position of Quatre-Bras. The old soldiers blamed the reluctance that Marshal Ney had shown before the position of Quatre-Bras. Indeed, if it had been captured the same day, it would have been gained by a march on the enemy and he would not have been able the next day to rally his corps, surprised in their cantonments. On the evening of the 16th, we established our bivouac near a large village, which served as our ambulance.

About this action, General Reille writes as follows regarding the opening moves of the battle:[6]

> Your Excellency, at two o'clock ordered, as soon as the 9th Infantry Division was within range to support them, I gave the order for them to quit the wood and conquer the position of Trois-Bras. This movement was supported by artillery, the two divisions of infantry and a division of cavalry and was executed in good order despite the difficult terrain.
>
> The 5th Division of infantry was formed in column by battalion and marched against Gémioncourt with the 1st Brigade of the 9th Division and captured the farm. The 5th Division then crossed the ravine and marched to the position of Trois-Bras, with great unity and they came under the fire of a line of sharpshooters supported by artillery. They gained the plateau, but could not resist the fire from a line of enemy infantry.
>
> The English and Scottish infantry forced them to retreat back to the ravine. General Foy deployed the 100th Regiment of Line in the rear of the advanced post of Gémioncourt, and the good conduct of

the corps protected the retrograde movement and inflicted heavy losses.

General Jamin deployed the 4th Light Infantry to secure the great road in front of Gémioncourt. General Bachelu, with Generals Campi and Husson, marched to the plateau where the 108th Regiment of Line remained for a long time in the best order.

About the actions of the 100th Regiment of Line Infantry, Adjutant Romand[7] writes:[8]

> The regiment to which I belonged, having been established in the defence of our pieces of cannon, we remained with supported arms under the murderous fire of the enemy. The position was critical. Unable to see our comrades fall without being able to defend ourselves, I left my place of battle without orders, and I promptly came through to the front of the battalion, asking for good volunteers to follow me. I brought together about forty men with a drummer, which was necessary.
>
> With my sword in hand I went to charge the enemy. As I came to about half musket-range from the enemy line, I deployed my little party at intervals along a line. We commenced our vigorous volley fire, which was very effective, and lasted about five minutes. All of a sudden, a regiment of *sans-culottes* who were the Scottish, and had been masked by a hedge which dominated a gully which we had captured, appeared before us.
>
> Their discharge of musketry which he greeted us with killed two men and wounded several others, among whom I noticed was our drummer who was shot through the shoulder by a bullet. This small setback shook the courage of my soldiers. I felt myself that it was no longer possible to remain anymore in this dangerous position. I received a bullet to the head that forced me to fall back on my regiment and the rest of the men took their respective places besides me.

Another eyewitness to the events described by Reille was Jolyet, of the 1st Regiment of Light Infantry (part of 6th Division commanded by Prince Jérôme), who narrates that:[9]

> An aide to General Guilleminot brought me the order to gain the road and to march over the English. As we left the wood, we came under the fire of their artillery, to join the closed column of the 4th Light Infantry Regiment, who was attacking the withdrawing

English. I had my horse killed under me, and I lost a number of people in a very short time. The skirmishers of the 4th Light Infantry moved to the right and I was alone with my battalion in the middle of a fairly large plain, having before us the English in considerable masses.

Meanwhile, General Foy's French 9th Infantry Division advanced to Gémioncourt Farm. It seems that at first Foy's men encountered little resistance, as the Allied frontline was concentrated to the west of the Charleroi road. It was here that the Dutch jägers, who had established a skirmish line in front of the farm, had no choice but to fall back when faced with the advance of an overwhelming force. Some of the jägers fell back to Gémioncourt Farm, while others headed east towards Materne Pond. The 5th Militia Battalion, which had been ordered forward to support the jägers at Gémioncourt Farm, had for a time been able to hold onto some of the buildings and orchard before having to fall back also. In the action at Gémioncourt, the 5th Militia Battalion lost nearly 62 per cent of its original strength.[10]

Sometime between 15.00 and 15.30, the first of much needed reinforcements (Picton's division and van Merlen's Dutch-Belgian cavalry) arrived to aid Perponcher's hard-pressed troops. Wellington arrived at about the same time and, it seems, immediately took command. One of his first orders was to deploy Picton and Merlen on the Allied left flank. An eyewitness comments that:[11]

> At length, we arrived at Quatre-Bras, and attacked the position with the bayonet; but it was received with a fire so incessant and murderous that it was evident we had fallen into an ambuscade. Our troops, however, rushed with courage and impetuosity on an enemy whose force they disdained to calculate. The first brigade of the division of Bachelu, which led the right of the attack, imprudently advanced, without waiting until the columns that should have supported it were formed, and being suddenly charged by three Scotch regiments, which a wood on the right had concealed from our view, was driven back in disorder. These regiments, however, paid dearly for their first success, for eagerly pursuing the fugitives, they unexpectedly found themselves exposed to the fire of the second brigade, and part of the division of Foy, and were almost annihilated. In the meantime, our troops being engaged in a difficult and unfavourable country were unable to advance. The fire of the English was terrible, and it was necessary to have recourse to other dispositions.

Gauthier's brigade

The 92nd Regiment of Line Infantry was brigaded with the 93rd Regiment of Line Infantry, and formed the 1st Brigade of the 9th Infantry Division. The brigade was commanded by General Gauthier, who was wounded at Quatre-Bras and replaced by Colonel Jean Marie Tissot, officer commanding the 92nd Regiment of Line Infantry.

For the 92nd Regiment of Line Infantry, total regimental losses at Quatre-Bras are as below:[12]

92nd Regiment of Line Infantry

	Evacuated Wounded	Wounded and Prisoner	Prisoner of War	Killed	Missing
1st Battalion	33	0	2	7	3
2nd Battalion	37	0	0	9	14
3rd Battalion	30	0	4	8	1
Total	100	0	6	24	18

On 10 June, the regiment mustered forty officers and 998 other ranks. At Quatre-Bras, 148 men were lost, representing 14.8 per cent of effective strength.

The muster list for the 93rd Regiment of Line Infantry, preserved in the French Army Archives, shows the following losses:[13]

93rd Regiment of Line Infantry

	Wounded	Wounded and Prisoner	Prisoner of War	Killed	Missing (presumed prisoner)
1st Battalion	17	0	1	1	9
2nd Battalion	15	0	9	5	9
3rd Battalion	26	0	0	1	24
4th Battalion	0	0	0	0	0
Total	58	0	10	7	42

The regiment had 1,864 effective rank and file at the start of the campaign, of which 117 men were lost at Quatre-Bras—some 6.3 per cent of the regiment. One officer was killed on 16 June, and one wounded. On 17 June, three men were lost. Thus, on 18 June, the regiment had 1,744 men in its ranks.

Jamin's brigade

The 4th Regiment of Light Infantry was brigaded with the 100th

Regiment of Line Infantry. It was engaged in the action at Quatre-Bras in efforts to capture Gémioncourt.

Total regimental losses at Quatre-Bras for the 100th Regiment of Line Infantry are in the table below:[14]

100th Regiment of Line Infantry

	Evacuated Wounded	Wounded and Prisoner	Prisoner of War	Killed	Missing
1st Battalion	108	0	0	5	1
2nd Battalion	46	0	0	5	3
3rd Battalion	55	0	0	5	5
Total	209	0	0	15	9

On 10 June, the regiment mustered fifty-one officers and 1,070 other ranks. At Quatre-Bras, 233 men were lost, representing 21.8 per cent of effective strength. The heaviest losses were in the grenadier and voltigeur companies of 1st Battalion, and 4th Company of 3rd Battalion. These losses impacted upon battlefield performance on 18 June.

The regimental muster list for the 4th Regiment of Light Infantry preserves the total regimental losses at Quatre-Bras, which are detailed below:[15]

4th Regiment of Light Infantry

	Wounded	Wounded and Prisoner	Prisoner of War	Killed	Missing
1st Battalion	9	0	1	0	0
2nd Battalion	23	0	3	0	0
3rd Battalion	36	0	2	1	0
4th Battalion	75	0	19	7	12
Suite	14	0	5	0	2
Total	157	0	30	8	14

On 10 June 1815, the regiment mustered four battalions, comprising of ninety-four officers and 1,848 men. The regiment's paperwork admits to the loss of 209 men, a loss of 11.3 per cent of effective strength. The officers of the regiment killed in action were:[16]

Lieutenant Grand, 2nd Fusilier Company, 2nd Battalion
Lieutenant Mesnard, 4th Fusilier Company, 2nd Battalion
Lieutenant François Vidal, Carabinier Company, 1st Battalion
Lieutenant Jean-François Theron, Carabinier Company, 2nd Battalion
Sub-Lieutenant Nicolas Bouchard, 3rd Fusilier Company, 2nd Battalion

NOTES:
1. Lemonnier-Delafosse, p. 270.
2. Lemonnier-Delafosse, p. 361.
3. Pierre François Tissot, *Histoire de Napoléon, rédigée d'après les papiers d'État, les documents officiels, les mémoires et les notes secrètes de ses contemporains, suivie d'un précis sur la famille Bonaparte* (vol. 2), Delange-Taffin, Paris, 1833, pp. 277-8.
4. Silvain Larreguy de Civrieux, *Souvenirs d'un cadet, 1813-1823*, Hachette, Paris, 1912.
5. 'Souvenirs historiques de Theobald Puvis' in *Revue historique des Armées*, 1997 [no.3], pp. 101-29.
6. SHDDT: C15 22 *Registre Correspondence 2nd Corps Observation Armée du Nord*, p. 278. After-action report of 17 June 1815, Reille to Soult.
7. Louis Jacques Romand was born on 12 October 1780 and joined the 100th Regiment of Line Infantry on 21 May 1812. He had been promoted to sergeant-major on 1 November 1812 and to adjutant-sub-officer on 26 May 1813. He was admitted into the successor formation of the 100th Regiment of Line Infantry, the 81st Regiment of Line Infantry, on 23 April 1814 with the Matricule number 477. He was admitted to the military hospital at Charleroi on 17 June 1815.
8. Louis-Jacques Romand, *Mémoires de ma vie militaire, 1809-1815*, F. Barthelet, Besançon, 1981, p. 71.
9. Commandant Jolyet, '*Souvenirs du 1815*' in *Revue de Paris*, October 1903, pp. 545-55.
10. Andre Dellevoet, 'Cowards at Waterloo?' in *Napoleon*, Summer 2000 [No. 16], p. 31.
11. Giraud, p 66.
12. SHDDT: GR 21 YC 690 *76e regiment d'infanterie de ligne (ex 92e regiment d'infanterie de ligne), 4 septembre 1814-28 mars 1815 (matricules 1 à 1,512)*. See also: SHDDT: GR 21 YC 691 *76e régiment d'infanterie de ligne (ex 92e régiment d'infanterie de ligne), 25 avril 1815-27 juin 1815 (matricules 1,513 à 1,728)*.
13. SHDDT: GR 21 YC 701 *77e regiment d'infanterie de ligne (ex 93e regiment d'infanterie de ligne), 13 août 1814-22 décembre 1814 (matricules 1 à 1,800)*. See also: SHDDT: GR 21 YC 702 *77e régiment d'infanterie de ligne (ex 93e régiment d'infanterie de ligne), 22 décembre 1814-8 août 1815 (matricules 1,801 à 3,108)*.
14. SHDDT: GR 21 YC 734 *81e régiment d'infanterie de ligne (ex 100e régiment d'infanterie de ligne), 24 septembre 1814-1er mai 1815 (matricules 1 à 1,800)*. See also: SHDDT: GR 21 YC 735 *100e régiment d'infanterie de ligne, 1 mai 1815-16 août 1815 (matricules 1,801 à 2,248)*.
15. SHDDT: GR 21 YC 40 *4er régiment d'infanterie Legere, 1814 à 1815*.
16. SHDDT: Xb 572 *4e Legere, Dossier 1815*.

Chapter 5

Hurber's Charge

The Dutch-Belgian forces had slowly fallen back over the course of an hour as the divisions of Foy and Bachelu had advanced; the Dutch-Belgian line was about to break. The position had to be held at all costs to give Wellington's troops time to march to the Prince of Orange's aid. Despite his slow and cautious start, Ney had almost succeeded in his objective. However, with the timely arrival of van Merlen's cavalry, it gave the Prince of Orange an opportunity to buy the Allies some much needed time. van Merlen was outnumbered and many of his men had never seen action before. The outcome of the contest was sadly all too predictable, as Major von Balvern notes:[1]

> We barely had begun with the horses when the order to mount was sounded, while the [fodder] bags which had just been taken off needed to be re-attached quickly. This wasn't even completed, we had to march forward in columns by platoons, and from that column we were supposed to form line with our front to the enemy, but we were ordered to charge the enemy immediately, including the Red Lancers of the Imperial Guard. The haste which accompanied this manoeuvre caused the regiment not to fully adopt the battle order when it charged, which had the consequence that the attack turned out to be confusing and not beneficial. We were soon pushed back by the enemy cavalry, with the sabre in their hands, to the vicinity of a corps of Highland Scotsmen which was positioned in a row and received the enemy with deadly fire.

The failed charge is also recalled by Lieutenant Deebetz, who writes:[2]

> The said regiment [6th Hussars] had placed itself in battle order in front of the road from Quatre-Bras to Namur when it received the

order to take up a new position to the right, and come behind the road from Quatre-Bras to Nivelles. The movement with platoons to the right had already begun, so that a part of the regiment was already near to Quatre-Bras, when a staff officer rode along the side of the regiment, shouting 'Hussars charge!' If this order had been brought to the commander, or had been executed in an orderly fashion, it might have ended well, but instead the platoons wheeled away from the left wing and consecutively formed in line to the left and advanced for the charge, seemingly *'en fourageur'*. The outcome was a general retreat until behind the road of Quatre-Bras to Namur, where the regiment re-assembled

Lieutenant Henckens, of the 6th Chasseurs à Cheval, writes about the charge as he saw it:[3]

On 16 June 1815, at about two o'clock in the afternoon, we were half a league from Quatre-Bras when I received from Colonel Faudoas an order to reconnoitre the enemy with my platoon to the right of the Charleroi road in Brussels, and in front of Quatre-Bras. After the event at Berlaimont, Colonel Faudoas, worked upon by officers jealous of the favour I had enjoyed from Colonel Talhouet, held a grudge against the elite company and especially to my person, and was proved by addressing me as little as possible, so I was perfectly indifferent, convinced that I had done my duty and nothing more.

It was the first time I saw the colonel under fire. Since we had already been exposed to the cannon of the enemy, so it was under fire I gave my orders to my platoon, the first rank was composed entirely of legionaries, that Colonel Talhouet had chosen himself to join the Chasseurs de Berry, and further having taken the best for the elite company, these chasseurs immediately understood my intentions, it seems that the calmness with which I act on this occasion made such an impression on the colonel, he approached me and shook my hand galloping in front of the regiment, which was for me a mark of esteem that I have not forgotten for the rest of my life.

The reconnaissance made, with the support of the whole company, who received orders to follow me, my impression was that the forces we had before us were minimal, and that the enemy was not imposing. With daring, a great success was possible; to complete the reconnaissance, the regiment forced a battalion near the farm to retreat. We afterwards learned later that the farm of Gémioncourt, for lack of support, we confined ourselves only to this success.

Later that day reinforcements came successively to the enemy, but when I thought my gratitude to the total absence of cavalry, soon came hussars and dragoons with light artillery, the division of Piré, with all the 6th Regiment of Chasseurs à Cheval at the head, fell upon the enemy's cavalry, which was routed and driven back, while the servants of the artillery pieces in position were partly killed and the caissons harnessed and servants who could reach their horses followed the cavalry rout, the artillery pieces that remained there and were not spiked, probably because the means of doing so were lacking.

It was after this attack that Captain Esteve and I saw on a hill a meeting of officers without troops that our instincts told us to be the general staff enemy, we endeavoured to approach this group of officers, who departed at full speed and left us a horse officer that we took with us at the same time, being too exposed to fire of the infantry in square, in position behind a hedge, the rally was sounded for the division.

More detail on the events of the charge can be found from Dutch-Belgian eyewitness reports. Constant Rebecque, chief-of-staff to the Dutch-Belgian army, relates what happened next:[4]

Our battalions in the vicinity of Gémioncourt suffered greatly; they lost some ground but the prince rallied them with his very presence and example; our two cavalry regiments made several charges and checked those of the enemy. Colonel Boreel's hussars made an attack and were beaten back by the superior enemy force, and the prince was almost taken; his aide-de-camp, Count Stirum, was wounded by a sabre blow to the head. Our foot and horse artillery were overrun and sabred, and the enemy infantry entered into the Bossu Wood.

As the hussars made a hasty retreat towards the comparative safety offered by the Allied infantry and artillery at the crossroads, they overran the 5th Netherlands Militia Battalion on the Brussels road as it retreated from Gémioncourt Farm, as Dirk Toll, from the 5th Militia Battalion, explains:[5]

It is well-known that during the morning nothing of significance occurred, but between one and two o'clock the French attacked vigorously. The 5th Militia Battalion moved forward in column at double pace and deployed to the right of the farm of Gémioncourt, under a heavy canister and musket fire, but in the best possible order.

The farm was defended by two flanker companies belonging to our battalion, and two companies from the 27th Jäger Battalion; the first in front of the complex, and the others inside the farm buildings. Our troops suffered from the strong enemy attacks, by the tirailleurs in particular, who were supported by formidable columns. It was here that Lieutenant Wynoldie was killed while being surrounded by the enemy, despite attempting to cut his way free.

The corn was very high and while it remained so the enemy limited himself to attacks in columns and with skirmishers, supported by artillery fire, which was answered in the same manner. These attacks were followed by heavy enemy cavalry attacks, which we resisted, after having withdrawn our skirmishers, and by forming the battalion on the highroad in a formed body (*colonne en masse*), with front to all sides.

In the midst of the chaos, as the French chasseurs overran two artillery batteries, Captain Bijleveld, who commanded a half-battery of horse artillery, later recalled:[6]

The battery remained the entire day of the 16th in first line and played a big role in the battle; the battery of Captain Stevenaar, which had advanced that morning under the orders of Major van Opstall, was almost entirely destroyed by a charge of cavalry, the captain was killed, the major and two lieutenants wounded and of our equipment only one section remained, under the order of Lieutenant Wintsinger.

As Henckens noted earlier, the chasseurs had attacked a number of artillery batteries. One was the battery of Captain Geij van Pittius, as Lieutenant Wassenaar van St Pancras relates:[7]

The cavalry of General van Merlen rushed to our aid, but soon we saw these braves return in the direction of our position, my captain threw himself off his horse, the gunners crawled underneath the pieces, not perceiving the danger as grave, I remained for a moment in doubt, until I found myself in the middle of the melee and threw myself to the ground where we were packed together like herring. How I got out is still a dream and I was fortunate enough that no chasseur of the Guard has tried the sharpness of his blade on me.

About this chaos, Second Lieutenant Carel Emilius van der Wall, of the foot artillery battery commanded by Stevenaar, writes as follows:[8]

When the writer of this, on 16th June, in a forced march arrived at the battlefield of Quatre-Bras in a trot with the light cavalry brigade of General van Merlen, composed of the 6th Regiment of hussars; Colonel Boreel, the Belgian 5th Light Dragoons; Colonel Mercx and a half-battery of horse artillery; Captain Geij, our artillery, there had the following disposition: one Dutch battery of field artillery, of Captain Steevenaar, who was in position and in action forward to the right of the crossroads; another battery of horse artillery, Captain Bijleveld, occupied three points there on the road, and the one of Captain Geij, upon its arrival, took a position in front and left of Quatre-Bras, with the right flank against the highroad to Charleroi, while the light cavalry brigade then placed itself behind this horse artillery, which immediately started firing. To the left and forward of this gun line were English infantry regiments in columns of attack or squares, and to the right the Netherlands and Nassau units in similar order of battle, when the corps of Marshal Ney advanced, preceded by a numerous swarm of tirailleurs, who by their overwhelming numbers had ours yield.

Meanwhile, behind our left flank, a French cavalry regiment had taken position, which had encircled us through the high corn in the field. This regiment was indicated by Captain Geij to Colonel Boreel, whose hussars covered the horse artillery, where upon the aforementioned colonel sent First Lieutenant van Bronkhorst there with a platoon for reconnaissance, and whose éclaireurs got into action with those of the hostile regiment. The confusion of the next heavy fighting prevented the author to observe this French regiment any longer, but as he later learned it was driven off by the advancing English and Brunswick cavalry, and chased away around our left flank.

Now the light cavalry brigade received order to drive away the strongly advancing enemy tirailleurs, which they did with a charge *en fourageur*, but then met the heavy cavalry of Kellerman [sic], which had already charged the battery of Captain Steevenaar, sabreing the captain and one of his lieutenants, as well as many gunners, and now fought with our light cavalry.

The enemy cuirassiers, who were strengthened with a regiment of chasseurs à cheval, cut into our light horsemen and rode along with them while fighting and across and along the highroad, towards the farm of Quatre-Bras and straight towards the guns of Captain Geij, who diverged this cavalry stream with murderous fire from his battery, after which, nevertheless, a few enemy cuirassiers and chasseurs à cheval managed to come in from behind the right flank in-between the guns and exchange swords with our gunners. Meanwhile, the enemy cavalry was received with a formidable musketry fire from a regiment of Scots under General Picton, who were in and behind a dry ditch along the highroad to cover the aforementioned artillery positioned in line of battle, and partially beat them back, after which the canister of Captain Geij saluted them and many more fell down. A great number of enemy horsemen were still in a fight with ours and at last got out of each other behind our position, when part of the brave French cavalry mob retreated around our right flank and returned with the corps of Ney in order, even though still many of these brave ones were killed in and around our ranks.

The effect of both cavalry charges, the thundering gun and musketry fire, the rattling melee and the wild warrior cries, caused by the amazing intermixing of many thousands of soldiers, among which our undaunted Prince of Orange got in great danger, and his adjutant, Major Count van Limburg Stirum, received a sabre cut and others in ours and the enemy's ranks died or were wounded, now caused a lull in the main manoeuvres on both sides. The French tirailleurs wanted to benefit from this and took five of our limbered guns, of which three belonged to the battery of Captain Stevenaar (only moments before cut down with many of his gunners) and the other two to the battery of Captain Bijleveld. But when Captain Geij saw this he slashed into the French at the head of his horse gunners, retook the five guns from them, which belonged to his brothers-in-arms, and brought them back to his battery, formed them in line, and kept on firing with these united guns until in the night, after which he sent the recaptured guns back the next morning to their respective commanders.

Captain Henry Royen, of the 6th Hussars, notes the movement of his regiment before the battle commenced:[9]

> On the 16th during the morning at four o'clock, the regiment left its cantonments and elements of it were on field pickets. The entire 7th Company was put on field picket duty by General van Merlen on the height to the right of Cap de Bonne Esperance, above Binche, from where the mentioned company followed the regiment forming the rearguard. Moving up to Nivelles, where, at that time, the 1st, 2nd, 3rd, 4th and 8th Cavalry Regiments under the command of Lieutenant-General Collaert were in bivouac. The 5th Regiment left

its cantonments during the same morning and went with the 6th to Quatre-Bras.

Having arrived there, the 6th deployed *en bataille* near the so-called crossroads to the left of the highroad from Brussels to Charleroi; the road leading from Nivelles in its rear.

Standing in this position, and having received some enemy cannon balls, the regiment moved a little to the rear, and more specifically behind a farm, after which the enemy cavalry advanced and the regiment once again took its previous position, and from which position a charge was undertaken against two chasseurs regiments. When pushed back, the 5th Regiment advanced forward for as much as was possible, and the position allowed. When the 1st Squadron was formed, it charged immediately, which charge was followed by the other squadrons.

About the movements of the Dutch-Belgian cavalry against the French chasseurs à cheval, Brevet Subaltern-Officer J. B. J. van Doren, of the 5th Light Dragoons, writes:[10]

> At half-past three came General Baron van Merlen (of the Batavians-Belgians division under the command of Lieutenant-General Baron Collaert) with his light cavalry brigade of 1,100 horses-strong and a section of artillery, while the Picton division, 7,700 men-strong and divided into twelve battalions, as well as two batteries with twelve pieces, arrived at the same time from Brussels and debouched near Quatre-Bras.
>
> General van Merlen went in-between the Bossu Wood and the highroad of Brussels. Picton formed his division in two lines, each of six battalions; the first on the highroad to Namur, its right towards Quatre-Bras and its left towards a road that leads from that road to Sart-Dame-Avelines.
>
> While van Merlen executed his manoeuvre, Picton hadn't completed his when the Prince of Orange, ever more pressed by Foy and Bachelu, made use of the reinforcement he had received to sweep the slope of Quatre-Bras. He ordered General van Merlen, who was close to him with his brigade, composed of the 6th Regiment of Hussars (Dutch) and the Belgian 5th Regiment of Chevau-Légers, to charge with the first mentioned regiment upon two French battalions, which stood near the highway in square and supported by their skirmishers kept moving forward, while the chevau-légers, in case of failure, were kept in reserve.

Yet, the attempt wasn't fortunate. Colonel de Faudoas with the 6th Regiment of Chasseurs à Cheval, followed by the 5th Regiment of Lancers, attacked the 6th Regiment of Dutch Hussars vigorously, threw it in disorder and then fell upon the infantry that supported it, dispersed these and sabred the gunners on their pieces.

The prince noticed this and ordered Colonel Edouard de Mercx to resume the charge against the French cavalry with his regiment (the 5th Regiment of Chevau-Légers). The colonel then ordered Major Count de Looz van Corswarem to relieve the retreating infantry with part of the regiment, while he, in person, on the highroad to Charleroi with the other part charged the 6th Regiment of Chasseurs à Cheval, which was double his strength. Three times he rode through it in full trot and again made two subsequent charges, and after having fought for more than three quarters of an hour with the sabre, he made the chasseurs run. When next the chevau-léger wanted to move behind Quatre-Bras, to restore order among the intermingled men, an English infantry battalion fired heavily on them. They were under the assumption it was chasseurs of the aforementioned 6th Regiment, because the uniform of both regiments, green with yellow facings, except for the white epaulets of the chasseurs, gave reason for this mistake.

Colonel de Mercx, possessed with a never-ending courage, received in that fight four wounds, his horse was shot from under him and he was carried unconscious from the battlefield due to the heavy fall. Captain van Remoorter, after having made various charges at the head of his company, received a sabre stab in the confusion from a sergeant who before, in French service, had been in his company, and then his horse was shot from under him. The officers (at least the captains, all former officers in the former French Imperial army, who had been in several campaigns) distinguished themselves excellently, while the non-commissioned officers and chevau-légers, of which half of the regiment had shared the joys and sorrows of the French army, were possessed with a good spirit and also excelled in special bravery this day, were greeted at the end of the battle by their young field commander, Prince William of Orange.

With the first distribution of the Military William Order, Colonel de Mercx received the Order 3rd Class, while the regiment received twenty-seven of them, of which the author of this also got one. Later, several others were rewarded with it as well.

Lieutenant-Colonel Edouard de Mercx de Corbais, of the 5th Light Dragoons, writes:[11]

I arrived at Quatre-Bras on the 16th about three o'clock in the afternoon. I found Lieutenant Vandenzande with the 7th Battalion infantry companies and some Belgian 2nd Regiment of Nassau, plus two artillery batteries. We had before us 40,000 French, commanded by Marshal Ney and Jérôme Bonaparte.

The battle began soon; 6th Hussars was charged by two French regiments and brought back, but I charged them in my turn and repulsed them. I was long engaged in various charges, in which my regiment was covered with glory, and it never came to the idea of any of the brave, under my command, to flee.

Late in the afternoon, the British troops arrived and the Brunswickers and the Prince of Orange and the Duke of Wellington.

On 10 June, the 1st Chasseurs à Cheval mustered 445 other ranks. The regiment, it seems, took no part in the charges at Quatre-Bras, as no men are recorded dead or wounded. It is very likely that the regiment's horses sustained losses at Quatre-Bras and Waterloo, which no doubt would have vastly reduced the effective strength of the regiment, but no paperwork can be found that gives equine losses for the campaign for the regiment.[12]

Total casualties recorded for the 6th Chasseurs à cheval at Quatre-Bras were:[13]

Squadron	Company	Killed	Died of Wounds	Wounded	Prisoner of War	Missing Missing
1st	1st	6	0	3	0	0
	5th	0	0	0	0	0
2nd	2nd	3	0	0	0	0
	6th	0	0	2	0	0
3rd	3rd	0	0	0	0	0
	7th	0	0	1	0	0
4th	4th	0	0	0	0	0
	8th	0	0	0	0	0
Total		9	0	6	0	0

On 10 June 1815, the regiment mustered thirty-four officers and 526 other ranks. At Quatre-Bras, fifteen men were killed or wounded. Henckens states that the elite company was reduced to twenty-five men, which would represent a loss of over fifty men in the company, rather than then nine known losses. Even equating one man to three horses would make twenty-seven, still leaving over fifty men in the company. Therefore, Henckens's memoir seems very suspect in terms of the

casualties the regiment sustained. It seems that he elaborated the truth somewhat to make his part in the campaign more important than it really was.

Wellington arrives

Picton's divisions arrived at Quatre-Bras sometime around 16.00. An officer of the 92nd Regiment of Foot, writing on 21 June 1815, notes:[14]

> The 9th Brigade consisted of the 1st, or Royal Scots, 42nd, 44th and 92nd Regiments. The 8th Brigade, the 32nd, 28th, 79th and 95th. We marched thirty miles that night, and came up with the enemy about two or three o'clock next day, viz. the 16th. We were immediately marched into the field, as there was only one British division and some Brunswickers there before we came up. The 92nd took the position in a ditch to cover the guns and the cavalry, being the junior regiment—while the rest of the division went a little to the left to check the French infantry that were passing on there. We lay in a most disagreeable situation for upwards of an hour, having an excellent view, however, of the light, but exposed to a most tremendous fire, from their great guns, of shot, shells, grape, etc. which we found great difficulty in keeping clear of. I say keeping clear of, because you can very often see the round shot coming. This heavy fire was maintained against us in consequence of the duke and his staff being only two or three yards in front of the 92nd, perfectly seen by the French, and because all the reinforcements which were coming up passed along the road in which we were. Here I had a remarkable opportunity of witnessing the sangfroid of the duke, who, unconcerned at the showers of shot falling on every side of him, and killing and wounding a number of his staff, stood watching the enemy and giving orders with as much composed calmness as if he were at a review.

James Hope, a soldier serving in the 92nd Regiment of Foot, adds:[15]

> The Duke of Wellington, on perceiving that the enemy deployed fresh battalions towards our left, gave orders for the 3rd Battalion Royals, 42nd Regiment and 2nd Battalion 44th to proceed to the assistance of the 8th Brigade. The 92nd Highlanders were ordered to line a bank on the right of the road leading from Quatre-Bras to Ligny, on which the duke and his staff had taken post—the right of the regiment to rest on the farm of Quatre-Bras. The Hanoverian brigade was formed on the left of the 92nd, and the Brunswick

cavalry in rear of it. The Brunswick infantry were stationed, partly in rear of the left of the Highlanders, and partly in the wood on the right of the village. The few pieces of artillery we had with us were posted on the highway in front of Quatre-Bras. The only cavalry we had were those of the Duke of Brunswick.

Standing nearby was the 3rd Battalion of the Royal Scots, as an officer of that battalion writes:[16]

> I have great pleasure in detailing the conduct of the gallant 3rd Battalion of the Royal Scots; and though I have been present with the regiment at the battles of Busaco, Salamanca, Vittoria, Fuentes d'Onoro [sic], both stormings of San Sebastian, the passage of the Bidassoa, etc. (in all of which they bore a most conspicuous part, and suffered most severely), I can assure you they never evinced more steadiness and determined bravery than at the late battle. About half-past one o'clock on the 16th, the battalion was taken from its place in the centre of the 5th Division, by a movement to its own left, by order of Sir Thomas Picton, and instantly by command of that lamented officer brought into action by a charge upon a column of the enemy: it succeeded beyond our most sanguine expectations in routing this column, who afterwards formed under the protection of their cavalry, and then commenced a most galling fire upon us, which we returned with the utmost steadiness and precision.
>
> The battalion was brought into action under the most trying circumstances imaginable, and continued so for a long time; but they never for one moment lost sight of that character which upon former trials they had so well earned and maintained. The ground through which they moved was planted with corn that took the tallest men up to the shoulders; and the enemy by this, and the advantage of the rising ground, threw in volley after volley of grape and musketry, which did astonishing execution.

Brevet-Major Leach, of the 95th Regiment of Foot, writes about his operations against the 61st Regiment of Line Infantry and, presumably, the 2nd Regiment of Light Infantry:[17]

> Long before we reached this point, which consists of a few houses at the junction of four roads, we were aware that something not of an amicable nature was in progress between the Belgian troops under the Prince of Orange and the French under Marshal Ney, as a number of wounded Belgians were proceeding towards Brussels,

and an occasional cannonade was, moreover, heard in our front. The troops under the Prince of Orange had been driven back on Quatre-Bras, after some resistance.

We found the prince in possession of Quatre-Bras, occupying also a wood on his right, and a farmhouse in his front, as his advanced posts. The French were moving on in great force towards Quatre-Bras, and to a wood on the left of the road, at the moment of the arrival of our division. The Duke of Wellington instantly directed our battalion to occupy and to defend this wood; and we kept possession of it throughout the day, in spite of the many attempts made by the enemy to dispossess us of it, who kept us constantly engaged until night.

The remainder of our division, during this period, were engaged on our right in a fierce and desperate struggle against some heavy bodies of infantry and cavalry. The approach of the latter force obliged the different regiments to form squares, which resisted, with the greatest steadiness and gallantry, the repeated attempts to charge and break them, and strewed the field with cuirassiers and horses. Neither the charges of their numerous and daring cavalry, nor the incessant fire of musketry, supported by a powerful artillery, enabled the French to gain one foot of ground, although, at the most moderate calculation, they outnumbered the British in the proportion of two-to-one. The Duke of Brunswick fell early in the action, whilst setting a glorious example to his troops, which were chiefly new levies.

At around 16.30, trying to anticipate the next moves of Generals Foy and Bachelu, the Duke of Brunswick deployed his newly arrived troops, some being deployed to the Bossu Wood, and four battalions of infantry and four squadrons of cavalry were deployed in the same positions as occupied earlier by the Dutch-Belgians prior to Piré's first charge at Gémioncourt. Alten's 3rd British Division arrived at Quatre-Bras probably a little before 17.00; Cooke, with the 1st British Division, was not very far behind and Wellington still hoped that the Allied cavalry would appear before the long summer evening was over. Alten brought only two brigades, having left Ompteda's K. G. L. Brigade to cover Nivelles. Kielmansegge's unusually strong Hanoverian brigade (six battalions, over 3,300 men) was sent to reinforce Kempt and the 95th Regiment of Foot on the left. Halkett's men were sent to replace the Brunswickers, between the Bossu Wood and the Charleroi road south of Quatre-Bras. Piré's cavalry had disappeared before he arrived and he endeavoured to provide cover for the Brunswick troops to rally and to relieve the pressure on the 42nd and 44th Regiments of Foot, who were running short of ammunition and feeling the effects of the fire of the French artillery and skirmishers. According to Lieutenant William Thain, of the 33rd Regiment of Foot, 'the British Brigade advanced into line in column of companies at quarter distance'.

It seems while the French infantry were slowly moving forward, the cuirassiers now advanced along the highroad and threatened the Brunswick infantry battalions, supported, it seems, by horse artillery. It was now that the Duke of Brunswick was mortally wounded by a musket ball which passed through his left wrist and into his abdomen. James Hope, of the 92nd Regiment of Foot, relates that:[18]

> About four o'clock, the Duke of Brunswick, with his cavalry, advanced from Quatre-Bras to charge a French column of cavalry considerably in advance. Led by their undaunted prince, the troops charged in gallant style; but the duke, having received a mortal wound in the breast, his troops were seized with a panic, and began to retire from before their numerous foes towards the ground on which they had originally formed. This unfortunate affair gave the enemy a temporary advantage, and inspired his followers with fresh courage.
>
> The rear and flanks of the Brunswickers were assailed by their proud enemy, till they arrived almost at the farm of Quatre-Bras. The 92nd having been ordered to keep themselves hid from the enemy, the French troops no doubt fancied that the day was their own. As the enemy advanced in the direction of the 92nd, that regiment was ordered to be in readiness to fire. With their usual coolness and characteristic bravery, they prepared to repel their foes. When the fugitives had nearly all passed to the rear of the Highlanders, the French cavalry, who were advancing by the highway, received a volley from the 92nd, which stretched a number of both men and horses lifeless on the ground. A panic seized those who escaped the oblique fire of the 92nd. They fled in great confusion, confounded at meeting with such a reception, and at a point where they imagined resistance had ceased.

The two Brunswick infantry battalions retreated to the relative safety of the crossroads. The dragoons sensing that they now had the advantage, charged. In doing so they were met by a volley from the 92nd Regiment of Foot. An officer of the 92nd, writing on 21 June 1815, notes what happened next:[19]

The French cavalry was now beginning to advance in front of the 92nd, to take the village, and the Brunswick cavalry that were also in our front went on to meet them; but the French put spurs to their horses to charge, the Brunswickers then wheeled about and galloped upon the 92nd in the greatest confusion. The French were soon up with their rear men, cutting them down most horribly. The enemy also dismounted the two guns I have marked. We did not allow the flying Brunswickers to break through our regiment, but they passed around our right flank, close to the men's bayonets, having the French mingled with them cutting away. We of course could not fire to help them till they had cleared us. At the same instant, the road from the French lines towards the village was covered with cavalry charging at full speed. When the Brunswickers cleared our right, we wheeled our grenadiers back on the road, the ditch of which we lined, that they might fire when the first of the French should pass [house] no. two, the rest were to fire obliquely on the road and on the remains of those that followed the Brunswickers.

The volley was decisive. The front of the French charge was completely separated from the rear by the gap which we made, and nothing was seen but men and horses tumbling on each other. Their rear retreated, and the front dashed through the village, cutting down all stragglers. Our assistant-surgeon dressing a man behind a house no. four, who had had his bonnet cut in two, and a lance run into his side. Three of them came down the road through the grenadiers at full speed, brandishing their swords, and our rear rank firing at them all the way. Two were brought down, but the third (his horse gushing blood from all parts) had just cleared the regiment, when Col Mitchell made a cut at him with his sabre, which he dexterously parried, but an officer of the staff cut, with his sword, the hamstrings of the fellow's horse, and he was taken. The rest were likewise taken, and they tell me that eight pursued the duke a good way. I wonder how he got off, for I saw him in front not five minutes before the charge. The enemy's charge being repelled; it was now our turn to have our share of charging.

The French formed their cavalry again to charge, supported by infantry, and advanced past house no. two, when Adjutant-General Barnes, our old brigadier in Spain and France, who is undoubtedly fond of the regiment, came down to the front, and calling out 'Come on, my old 92nd', the men jumped from the ditch and charged in the finest style, up to the house no. two. He was then obliged to leave us, as it was not his duty to charge, although he could not resist the impulse. We were then moved forward from behind the house, with our brave Colonel Cameron at our head. When we jumped from the ditch, the officer with the regimental colour was shot through the heart. The staff of the colour was shattered in six pieces with three balls, and the staff of the king's colour with one. I got the remains of the regimental colours. When we moved from behind the house, and had passed the corner of the garden parallel to the road … we received a volley from a column on the right, which was retreating towards the wood. This fire killed Colonel Cameron and Mr Becher, and wounded a great many.

This column of the enemy kept us five minutes before we could clear the garden in advance to the wood. The fire here was dreadful. There was an immense slaughter among us at this time, but the French began at last to give way, and retreated up the side of the wood, keeping up, however, a tremendous fire, and killing a great many of our regiment. We had advanced so far that we were now completely separated from the rest of the line, and scarcely fifty men of those of us who went into action were remaining. A regiment of Guards was afterwards sent up to relieve us, but not before thirty of that fifty were hit.

Towards Piraumont, the duke deployed the 2nd Brunswick Light Battalion. Attached to the Brunswick staff was Karl Theodor Fischer, who writes as follows about the day:[20]

16 June, from Laeken passing through Brussels, after two hours, we crossed through a large forest (Bois de Soignes), through Waterloo, at about four o'clock in the afternoon, the regiment stood at Genappe, a small town in Brabant, beside many English, Hanoverian, Nassau and Dutch units. The French artillery could be heard already, holding a strongpoint behind a wood. Many injured and baggage trains being on the retreat came our way. Between the hours of four and eight o'clock, the regiment was under constant artillery fire of the enemy.

Our jäger occupied a hill, we stood behind them. Heavy grapeshot firing forced us to move backwards. At about five o'clock in the afternoon, Major Cramm[21] was mortally wounded, so too was the duke at six o'clock in the evening, and was a severe loss. One could well imagine the horror of the corps, especially because now Major v. Strombeck, Major Rauschenplatt, L. T. C. v. Heinemann[22], Maj. Bülow, Cpt. v. Pawel and some others either were killed on the spot or lethally or heavily injured, however the regiment stood its ground.

At six o'clock in the evening, supported by our artillery, the English units arrived, and after a terrible fire, the French retreated.

The army bivouacked on the battlefield, at ten o'clock at night. When the firing had ceased, I was at the head of some hussars escorting a horse cart filled with injured soldiers to Genappe, however we were unsuccessful, because nobody knew the collecting point for the wounded. Sergeant Pessler,[23] Volunteer Heinemann[24] and many hundred cried constantly for help, some cursed, some screamed, some prayed in pain, dreadful to listen to and watch. Roads and farms were filled with dying, dead or still-living wounded. Some of the doctors of our corps did not fulfil their duties,[25] ... several others, instead of staying, went back to Brussels. Here, too, I saw the cart transporting our dead duke, when I saw him, this went right through me. Maj. v. Cramm and Captn v. Pawel have been buried in a hole on the battlefield. Col Olfermann lost three horses being shot under him. The name of the place is 'Aux Quatre-Bras'. Corporal Woltereck had been divided by a ball, Sergeant Graumann[26] lost his entire right side, Pebler lost his right loin, the trumpeter's[27] head had been ripped off by a cannon ball.

Another officer in the Brunswick contingent writes on 29 June 1815:[28]

On the 15th, in the evening, about ten o'clock, a letter was brought from the Duke of Wellington's office, which contained an order that all the troops might be concentrated at the Allee Verte, near Brussels, on the following morning at daybreak. Orders were accordingly given and sent off as fast as possible: but, the dislocations being rather at a great distance, the troops could not arrive before five o'clock; when the duke, on the instant, marched through Brussels, and so on to the road to Waterloo. Directly afterwards, the Duke of Wellington followed, and, after showing a letter to the duke, changed his horse; they then set off together, and were as fast as possible followed by their suites. About ten o'clock, we arrived at Quatre-Bras, where we found part of the Nassau troops engaged, and heard that the French advanced very fast, and were exceedingly strong.

We then went on a hill to observe their approach; but hardly had they perceived the number of officers, but the rascals fired at us with grenades: so, we were obliged to leave the spot, and one narrowly escaped being killed. About twelve o'clock we returned; and the duke strongly expressed his wish of having an opportunity of meeting the French in equal force with his troops. To his great satisfaction, the Royal Scotch, the Hanoverians, and his own corps, arrived betwixt one and two o'clock. Tired and hungry as they were, they sang as they passed the duke, abusing and swearing against Buonaparte, wishing that they might soon meet him, and have an opportunity of setting the soldiers of the *Grande Nation* to rights. Hardly had we marched half an hour, when we saw the French expecting us on a hill. The Duke of Wellington then ordered to collect the troops as quick as possible, and to prepare for battle. At two o'clock all was ready, and the attack began.

The battle was very bloody, but we compelled the enemy to retreat. About half-past four, the French advanced again, and appeared double the number of the Allied army; but no fear was shown. The cannonade began most horribly, which in some respects put the train and baggage in confusion: however, the troops stood, and fought like lions; so, the French were again obliged to retreat, and were driven back to their position. Here they had a great advantage, being covered by a little wood, where they had placed all their artillery and riflemen. The Duke of Wellington most likely knew this, and ordered a fresh attack, to get the French out of the wood. The troops advanced the Brunswick division on the left wing. When they came near the wood, the French commenced a horrible fire with artillery and case-shot, which occasioned a great loss to our corps, in this attack, which was about seven o'clock in the evening; the duke was unfortunately killed on the spot by a case-shot. At this moment, I was not far from His Highness, and ordered our small carriage, thinking that he was only wounded—when, alas! to my inexpressible sorrow, I found he was dead. My feelings I cannot describe, but you will be able to form to yourself an idea.

Adjutant Heinrich Köhler, of the Brunswick general staff, recalls that:[29]

The brigade of Colonel Prince Bernhard von Sachsen-Weimar held the Bossu Wood, while the brigade of Major-General Count Bylandt [*sic*] was positioned behind the dairy farm of Gémioncourt. The skirmishing began early in the morning and continued with alternating success and failure until the afternoon. Marshal Ney had the 2nd Infantry Corps and the cavalry take a position in front of Frasné. At two o'clock the attack commenced from this position. The French division commanded by Baron Bachelu, with the support of the cavalry, advanced towards Gémioncourt. After a short and violent encounter, the Netherlands brigade of Major-General Bylandt was forced from its position and had to withdraw to Quatre-

Bras. The French division commanded by Comte Foy now moved into the line on the right and occupied Piermont [Piraumont], the light cavalry division commanded by General Piré, and his brigade of cuirassiers, advanced between the two aforementioned divisions. At this moment, the situation was perilous for the Prince of Orange, but towards three o'clock the English general, Picton, arrived with his division and immediately brought it into the line by taking a position on the left of Quatre-Bras along the road to Namur.

Shortly thereafter, the Duke of Brunswick arrived with his corps, and the 2nd Light Battalion under Major von Brandenstein was immediately detached in the direction of Piermont to cover the left wing and to occupy the wood nearby. The enemy troops in the wood were expelled and the position taken. Meanwhile, the two companies of Grey Jägers of the avantgarde were detached to the right to the Bossu Wood as well as small detachments of cavalry, the latter were ordered to occupy a position close to the wood and to observe the movements of the enemy from that position. The Line Brigade and the Leib Battalion formed the second line behind the division under General Picton, on the left of Quatre-Bras. However, the artillery and the 1st and 2nd Light Battalions had not arrived at this time.

The deployment of the English troops and the Brunswick corps into the line took place under a most violent cannonade from the enemy, who as stated previously, were deployed on the left and right of Gémioncourt in order to advance upon Quatre-Bras. This was the situation when a hussar regiment belonging to the Belgian cavalry arrived and made an immediate attack on the enemy, only to be beaten back and to flee in disorder. For this reason, our infantry formed squares and the Brunswick hussars, who had themselves only just arrived, moved to engage the enemy cavalry, which remained firm with the French infantry without attacking. Now the English division commanded by Count von Alten arrived in the field and formed on the right flank of General Picton's division.

Immediately thereafter, the Duke of Wellington personally ordered the Duke of Brunswick to advance without delay with four battalions and two companies from his corps on the road to Charleroi. The Leib Battalion, along with the 1st Light Battalion and the two light companies of the avantgarde advanced on the road and took a position between Schafferie [La Bergerie] and the stream; a skirmish line was extended to the front and right in order to make contact with the Allied troops in the Bossu Wood; the Brunswick hussars and the uhlans formed in rear of these troops. The 2nd and

3rd Line Battalions were positioned in, and close to, Quatre-Bras, as a reserve and to cover the possible withdrawal of the troops in the front line.

The enemy now deployed an artillery battery close to Gémioncourt and unleashed a relentless barrage against the Brunswick column. The losses sustained by the Brunswick battalions, who maintained their positions for a considerable time, in the face of this terrible onslaught were appalling. This continued until they received the support of two English batteries, which opened fire on the enemy and silenced their fire. It was now that Marshal Ney, from his advanced position, ordered Prince Jérôme Bonaparte to move with his division against the Bossu Wood; the enemy occupied Pierrepoint and immediately advanced along the edge of the wood. The Duke of Brunswick ordered the hussar regiment, which was hindered by the terrain and the close proximity of the wood, to retire onto the other side of the road towards Quatre-Bras, and collected the uhlans and attacked the enemy. However, the attack failed completely due to the strength and composure of the enemy infantry, and the uhlans were themselves compelled to retreat toward Quatre-Bras.

The division of cuirassiers threatened the two battalions positioned close to the road to Charleroi, and as the enemy was vastly superior in strength, the duke ordered the said battalions to retire. The 1st Line Battalion moved back towards the crossroads, but the Leib Battalion under Major von Pröstler, with whom the duke was stationed, positioned on the left of Schafferie, executed this movement as slowly and as well ordered as possible, under the most violent enemy cannonade. But the impact of the cannon balls into the column, the tremendous onslaught and the subsequent advance of the cuirassier regiment brought some confusion and disorder to the battalion. While the duke attempted to restore order, he was mortally wounded and died shortly thereafter.

Following this tragic event, the French cavalry attacked Quatre-Bras, but this was repelled by the Brunswick battalions positioned there. The English brigade under General Halkett, which was part of von Alten's division, was now ordered to expel the enemy from the Bossu Wood. The attack succeeded and the enemy was pushed back; only the 33rd Regiment of Foot, which advanced in square along the edge of the wood, was dispersed by the enemy cuirassiers.

The Brunswick infantry and cavalry were, it seems, no match for the French and had no option but to retreat, along with their British and

Hanoverian allies, faced with the onslaught of the French cavalry once more.

Wathiez's charge

In the charge, Wathiez's lancers took advantage of the flight of the Brunswick corps to fall upon the flank of Pack's brigade, which had just arrived on the field; most notably the 42nd and 44th Regiments of Foot which were formed in line well to the south of Quatre-Bras and the Namur road. The lancers seem to have circled behind the British infantry before they attacked, and certainly caught them by surprise. The 42nd Regiment of Foot scrambled to form square, but the cavalry were upon them before this was completed. An officer of the 42nd relates what happened:[30]

> The regiment was ordered to advance along with a Belgian corps to support the Prussians, who were under fire. In the march, owing either to their own superior quickness, or want of ardour in the Belgians, the latter were left behind; and in a field of standing corn, a column of French lancers advanced upon them—Colonel Macara ordered the regiment to form square, and in doing which two companies were left out, or were rather in the act of falling in when then they were pierced by the lancers, and in one moment overwhelmed and literally annihilated.
>
> The lancers then attacked the square and repeated the charge several times. One half of them were also mowed down, together with their brave colonel; upon which Colonel Dick took command, though wounded by a musket ball; he succeeded in rallying and forming them, into a diminishing square, and thus presented an undaunted resistance to the enemy. The lieutenant-colonel was at length from loss of blood carried from the field, but the gallant remnant of the men succeeded in putting the lancers to flight.

The *York Herald* newspaper reports that the 42nd Regiment of Foot lost thirteen officers and half of its effective strength in this attack.[31] A private in the 42nd writes, on 24 June 1815, about Quatre-Bras as follows:[32]

> About three o'clock in the afternoon of the 16th, we came up with them. Our whole force did not exceed 12,000 men, encumbered with knapsacks and other luggage. The day was uncommonly warm, and no water was to be had on the road; however, we were brought up, in order of battle.

> The French being strongly posted in a thick wood, to the number of 40,000 men, including cavalry and lancers, gave us very little time to look around us, here the fight commenced on both sides, in an awful and destructive manner, they having every advantage of us, both as to positions, and numbers particularly in cavalry, as the British dragoons had not yet come up. The French cavalry charged the British line of infantry three times, and did much execution, until we were obliged to form squares of battalions, in order to turn them, which was executed in a most gallant manner.

About the French lancers, Lieutenant Irwin, of the 28th Regiment of Foot, notes:[33]

> The lancers were in small bodies, concealed in the standing corn, which was extremely high, so that they could scarcely be seen on horseback. He received a wound in his leg; at the same moment, the cuirassiers advanced to charge the square of the 28th Regiment, and the lancers also advanced upon the other flank; another body of cavalry also advanced upon the third face of the square. The regiment remained perfectly firm and steady, the faces firing volleys as the cavalry approached. Only one of these bodies of cavalry came to the charge; the others faced about when within five or six yards of the square. Those that did charge were repulsed immediately: but the square remained steady, although not in a condition to pursue them, for they would not have known to which face to go, as the attack was on three sides. Col Sir C. Philip Belson exerted himself for his men to be steady, and not a man to stir until ordered: his horse was wounded in two places.
>
> The artillery was playing on the square for above an hour; and as it made openings by wounding or killing men, the regiment was very alert in closing in, for the lancers were very active and waiting in the standing corn to penetrate into these openings. Lieut Irwin, when wounded, was obliged to crawl into the square upon his hands and knees, to avoid being charged over by the lancers. One of the officers, (Capt. I.) was standing upon a sort of steep stony bank, when a party of French were rapidly advancing towards him: with a great presence of mind, he rolled a large loose piece of stone down upon them, which had the effect of diverting their attention from him. After standing the fire of artillery, and repeated attacks of cuirassiers and lancers, for above an hour and a half, the 28th Regiment was so much reduced, that Major-General Sir J. Kempt was obliged to send the Royals to join them, and their numbers were so much diminished.

Another general attack was now made upon the square, and Sir J. Kempt took refuge in the square. The enemy were repulsed as bravely as before; Third-Major-General Sir Thomas Picton came up and ordered Sir Philip Belson to advance the square, for the enemy were giving way. Three cheers were then given, and Gen. Picton and the square advanced in quick-time. The regiment deployed in double quick-time upon the march, as regularly as at a field-day, advanced to the charge, and drove the enemy over the hedgerow and adjoining road, and killed great numbers of them.

The 6th Lancers take the colours of the 44th Regiment of Foot

The charge of the 6th Lancers was sounded by Trumpet-Major Jean Joachim Baston. He was born at Cuers on 13 September 1782 and had joined the regiment on 21 August 1814, having served as trumpeter for the 13th Chasseurs from 1811 and 12th Hussars from 1813. He had been conscripted in 1803.[34] At the head of the 6th Lancers, Colonel Nicolas Marie Mathurin, Baron Galbois, was wounded. As his regiment charged forward, it was fired upon by Allied artillery at close range. A canister-shot hit Galbois in the chest, seriously wounding him.[35] Perhaps killed in the same deadly fire of artillery was Squadron Commander Rene Brard. About this, François Louis Malot, a captain in the regiment, writes:[36]

> During the campaign of 1815, I was wounded at Fleurus on 16 June where Commandant Brard and the Sub-Lieutenants Chassaigne and Morel of my regiment were killed.

Wounded while commanding the 2nd Company of the 2nd Squadron was Captain Jacques Philibert Rene Guillaume, having been appointed as such on 2 September 1812.[37] Captain Pigeau de la Belliere was also wounded.[38] Wounded in the same close-range artillery fire was Sergeant Jacques Aubert. He was born at Saint-Remy-de-Provence on 6 December 1787 and had been conscripted in 1807 to the 9th Hussars. He had passed to the 6th Lancers on 21 August 1814. He was unfortunate enough to be close by a howitzer shell when it exploded, the fragments lodging in his left hand.[39]

At the head of a squadron of the 6th Lancers was Lieutenant Armand Noel, an aide-de-camp to General Piré. He writes:[40]

> I was wounded on 16 June 1815 at Fleurus where a ball passed through my body during a charge led by General Piré at the head of a squadron of the 6th Lancers.

A French observer to Lieutenant Noel's injuries as described above comments:[41]

> Noel, lieutenant-adjutant to the staff of General Piré, who commanded a division of cavalry at Quatre-Bras, went in search of, along with many other officers from the staff, a flag that they observed floating in the middle of a group of enemy infantry with the view of capturing it. However, he was gravely wounded by a ball that passed through his torso. Left on the field of battle, his return to Paris was seen as nothing short of a miracle by his comrades who had considered him dead.

Turning to Allied accounts to confirm, or deny, this report, we find that a body of French lancers broke into the 44th Regiment of Foot and came very close to capturing their colours, and it seems took one, away albeit temporarily. It seems from the French sources that this was the 6th Lancers that had forced a passage into the square, with little initial resistance, as they had misidentified the lancers as Belgian cavalry, as Lieutenant Riddick notes:[42]

> We, from their appearance, supposed them to be Belgians, from their uniforms, and having been but a short time in the action, were still keeping the French army at bay with the bayonet, when the 2nd Battalion 44th Regiment were attacked in the rear by the lancers, who were slaughtering our supernumeraries and our rear-rank men.

Major G. O'Malley notes how the colours were partially snatched away by the French:[43]

> One very dashing fellow charged at the colours, wounding Ensign Christie, who carried one of them, with the lance . . . when Ensign Christie, in the most cool and praiseworthy manner, dropped the flag to save it, part of which the lancer actually tore off and possessed himself.

How much of the colour the lancer, seemingly Noel, endeavoured to take away with him is not known nor is its whereabouts. The lancer was killed soon after, and the fate of the part of the colour he carried is not recorded. Like with the colours of the 33rd Regiment of Foot, two colours where, it seems, temporarily in the hands of the French, making a tally of three colours captured, of which only that of the 69th Regiment of Foot was taken off the field of battle.

Napoléon's summons

The initial plan of operations for the day, as Napoléon had envisioned it, was for Ney to occupy Quatre-Bras and Marbais. Napoléon based his plan upon the notion that Wellington was not able to oppose Ney with any a major force. Furthermore, he supposed that Ney would have his forces concentrated around Gosselies and that he had sufficient troops to deal with Wellington. Contrary to Jeanin's early morning dispatch, the most recent update from Ney told Napoléon that rather than facing down 20,000-plus Allied troops, he told him that he was faced by a mere 3,000.

Therefore, for Napoléon, Ney had far more men than he actually needed, and assumed, therefore, that Ney had spare troops. These troops, he reasoned, were therefore available to be committed to action elsewhere. In the 11.00 dispatch, Napoléon knew that a division from 1st Corps was, in theory, heading off to Marbais, with two more in reserve at Frasné, and were therefore, in theory, free to be re-deployed. Plans were made accordingly at headquarters.

By 14.00, Napoléon realised that he faced a much larger Prussian force than he imagined. The presumption that Ney only faced a small element of Wellington's troops, which of course had been perfectly correct in the morning and afternoon of 16 June, led Napoléon to issue orders which would involve Ney in the much larger confrontation with Blücher. At 14.00, he sent the following order to Marshal Ney:[44]

> In front of Fleurus 16 June about 14.00 hours
> Sir marshal,
> The emperor charges me to let you know that the enemy has united a corps of troops between Sombreffe and Brye, and that at 14.30 hrs, Mr Marshal Grouchy will attack it with the 3rd and the 4th Corps; it is the intention of His Majesty that you will also attack what is in front of you, and that you, after having repulsed it vigorously, fall back on us in order to surround the corps I just mentioned to you. If this corps is pushed before, His Majesty will move in your direction in order to hasten your operations. Instruct at once the emperor of your arrangements and of what is happening on your front.
> Marshal of the empire, major-general,
> Duc de Dalmatie.

This order presumably arrived between 15.00 and 15.30, but we cannot be sure. The order outlined for Ney was for a *'manoeuvres sur les derrières'* by the left wing of the army against Blücher. However, the general concept of the situation wasn't explained to him. Rather than holding the Allies at bay, the order made Ney commit himself even more into the action at Quatre-Bras, as the order made it clear that the occupation of Quatre-Bras was to be completed before he was to manoeuvre towards Ligny. Ney didn't realise that the action at Quatre-Bras was of secondary importance, and that the decisive battle was raging at Ligny, but neither did Soult make this clear to Ney.

As the fighting developed at Ligny later in the day, between 16.00 and 16.30 Napoléon's order (timed at 15.30) arrived with Ney.[45]

Napoléon now made it clear that Ney was to manoeuvre to join the fighting at Ligny, along with Lobau and 6th Corps. This order was to have fateful consequences. By now of course, Napoléon had assumed, with only a single dispatch from Ney timed at 11.00, that he had pushed back the Allied troops at the crossroads, thus d'Erlon had three infantry divisions free to be able to march to Ligny down the Nivelles to Namur road, emerge on the Prussian right, and comprehensively defeat the Prussians. Napoléon knew when he got Ney's 11.00 dispatch that one infantry division and one cavalry division were already on the march to Marbais, yet he felt he needed more troops to deliver the *coup de grace* to Blücher. However, Napoléon made several assumptions:

1) That d'Erlon was at Quatre-Bras; and
2) The enemy presence at Quatre-Bras was still minimal and had been overcome.

In both cases, he was wrong—down to the lack of clear communication from Ney about what forces he faced. Ney had calculated the Allied troops at Quatre-Bras as 3,000, which it seemed did not factor in the reinforcements arriving on the field, which Adjutant-Commandant Jeanin (from 6th Corps) knew about all too well and stated that 20,000 troops were at Quatre-Bras. Napoléon could only make plans with the information he had (Ney had more than enough troops to push back 3,000 Allied troops, and had troops to spare to swing to the right and take part in the Battle of Ligny), yet this was based on the assumption that Ney's dispatch was accurate.

Napoléon had sent five dispatches to Ney, who had only sent a single one in return. Ney, by not reporting to headquarters and, either not being aware of the Allied troops moving to Quatre-Bras or only being concerned with the troops to his immediate front, had lulled Napoléon into a false sense of security about the left wing, with orders issued based on this. Ney's failure to communicate with headquarters resulted in orders being issued based on assumptions and outdated information. Had Ney told Napoléon at 11.00 that he faced 20,000-plus, it is very unlikely that the emperor would have issued the orders that he did and, we assume, based on no evidence at all beyond speculation, that 6th Corps could have taken a more active role in the battles of 16 June. Lobau could just as easily have been sent to Wagnelée, or have been sent to support Ney. This did not happen, I speculate, simply because Napoléon did not know what was happening on the left wing.

Ney's failure to communicate with headquarters and his gross underestimation of the number of troops he faced had catastrophic results—as a direct consequence, Ligny and Quatre-Bras were bloody and costly stalemates. Ney, in not keeping headquarters up-to-date with what was occurring, was a direct causation for the outcome of the day. Many historians blame Grouchy for not sending updates to Soult at headquarters on 17 and 18 June. When we look at the correspondence generated by Grouchy on those days, we see he sent reports to headquarters every couple of hours throughout the day. Ney, on 16 June, sent a single dispatch at 11.00, upon which Napoléon based the plan of action for the day. Grouchy has been damned by historians for his slowness to act on 17 and 18 June, which is totally incorrect, and yet Ney at Quatre-Bras did nothing between 4.00 and 14.00, other than engage in small-scale skirmishes. Ney is far more culpable for the outcome of the campaign than Grouchy ever was.

The other issue is that Napoléon assumed that d'Erlon, as ordered at 03.00 by Soult, had arrived at Gosselies by 7.00. Clearly this was not the case. Durutte's division does not seem to have arrived at the junction of the Brussels and Namur roads until around 15.30. This begs the question: why did it take d'Erlon nine hours to get from Gosselies to a point around four miles north? Allowing for a traffic jam and being delayed by Jérôme's division, which did not get to Quatre-Bras by 14.00, then surely Durutte was close behind, and thus would have been heading to Marbais by 14.30? Where was d'Erlon? We simply do not know. Kellermann's 3rd Cavalry Corps were riding as fast as they could to get to Ney at Gosselies. Roussel d'Hurbal, it seems, only arrived during the night, but had a march of forty miles across country, whereas the bulk of d'Erlon's troops had five miles at most to reach Quatre-Bras. The 16th was hot; horse and man needed regular water and time to rest. Tired and dehydrated men and horses were not effective cavalry. French cavalrymen were not issued water canteens for the simple reason that if a man had to find water for himself, he had to find it for his horse. Thus, the line of march would have been dominated by the need to use metalled roads, but also—and more importantly—to keep close to a source of water. When they arrived, Kellermann's troops were not fresh, well-fed, watered and rested, but travel-weary and in need of a rest before being flung headlong into action.

In reality, 1st Corps was spread out in a wide arc almost thirty miles deep from Quatre-Bras. The closest element of the force was Durutte, and he was at Gosselies—7 miles south of Quatre-Bras; around three hours away at most. Quiot was at Thuin, twenty-six miles away, or around seven hours at most by line of march, which would have taken him through Charleroi. Donzelot was at Jumet, some nine miles to the south and perhaps three hours away. Marcognet was at Marchienne-au-Pont, thirteen miles (four hours) away. Jacquinot's command was split with a brigade twenty-six miles to the south-west at Solre-sur-Sambre (a forced march of around six hours), and his other brigade at Bienne-sous-Thuin, some twenty-one miles from Quatre-Bras. d'Erlon's order was sent at 3.00, and had to cover twenty-six miles—perhaps an hour and a half at most for the courier—so, in theory, Quiot would have had his orders by 5.00 and been on the march an hour later, perhaps as late as 7.00. With twenty-six miles to cover, he could have reached Quatre-Bras in seven hours, assuming he did not get into a traffic jam crossing through Charleroi, where 6th Corps was. In spite of this, Quiot could have been at Quatre-Bras around 16.00, which seems realistic based on Durutte's time of arrival. Jacquinot's men clearly hit the route-march with speed to cover the twenty-six miles and to join with Durutte.

What we need to stress here is that the divisions of Quiot and Marcognet, and also Jacquinot, had to undertake a forced march before they went into action. The cavalry was expected to march no more than twenty-five to thirty miles a day, but not to fight a battle afterwards, yet this is what they had to endure. Quiot's men had to carry out a forced route march in full field service marching order for twenty-two miles and then fight a battle. During the Falklands War, the Royal Marine commandos undertook a 'yomp' of fifty-six miles in three days, carrying thirty-six kilograms of kit; marching eighteen miles a day. Quiot's men had to carry the same weight of equipment, march twenty-two miles, and then fight a battle. As with Kellermann's corps, Quiot's men were no doubt exhausted when they got to Gosselies around 16.30. Little wonder that Durutte's division was so far in front. In order to concentrate his forces at Gosselies, Ney asked Quiot's infantry and Kellermann's cavalry to undertake a 'yomp' and then fight a pitched battle, something not even the Royal Marine commandos in 2017 would consider, unless in extreme circumstances. Furthermore, a Napoléonic soldier did not have the same level of nutrition as a modern day Royal Marine.

What is considered difficult for modern-day commandos with modern-day nutrition was asking for an effort far greater: Ney was asking for superhuman efforts. Soult and Ney knew exactly where Kellermann and 1st Corps were; it was not concentrated. Yet Ney was still asked to fight a battle, with half his command being expected to 'yomp' to the rescue. Ney knew this. Did he delay the start of the battle to allow time for 1st Corps to assemble at Gosselies and for the men of Marcognet and Quiot to rest? We cannot know for sure, as we do not know when Marcognet got to Gosselies, and certainly Quiot did not arrive until well after the orders for concentration had been issued. The battlefield performance of Marcognet and Quiot's men and officers were undoubtedly affected by extreme fatigue and hunger.

1st Corps could not have been united around Gosselies until 16.00. d'Erlon himself says he got his orders for the day at 11.00—the same orders that Ney had sent to Reille at 11.00 cited before—noting that:[46]

> Towards eleven o'clock or midday, Marshal Ney sent me orders for my corps to take up arms and move towards Frasné and Quatre-Bras, where I would receive subsequent orders. My corps set off immediately, after giving the general commanding the head of the column orders to move quickly. I went ahead to Quatre-Bras to see where Reille's corps was engaged.

By 11.00, Durutte should have been at Gosselies, but Quiot and Marcognet had not yet arrived. The grave suspicion is that Ney had no idea where 1st Corps actually was. d'Erlon, on 15 June, had reported directly to Soult at Charleroi, from whence, on the following day, his marching orders (timed at 03.00) had come via Delcambre. I also suspect d'Erlon was totally ignorant of where his command was in reality. No doubt it would have come as a very nasty shock to Ney to realise that more than half his force was nowhere to be seen. In his 11.00 order, he seems to have been of the opinion that his command was close by and could be ordered up quickly as needed.

The sad fact was that he was totally wrong. When he issued his order at 11.00, he clearly did not realise where his command was. What can we make of this situation? Well, Ney cannot have issued his 11.00 order other than under the impression that his troops were all to hand, rather than being spread out behind him. If he had realised this, then the order to concentrate his forces would no doubt have occurred earlier—he may have known his true situation and issued orders in the manner he did for reasons of lethargy and indifference, if not over-confidence in easily sweeping aside Perponcher's men. Only when he realised that Perponcher was being reinforced in a major way did he realise, we suppose, that his plans had gone horribly wrong.

The grave suspicion is also that d'Erlon, in not sending his report to Ney on 15 June but to Soult, resulted in Ney having even less idea about where his forces were. Headquarters had no idea where Kellermann was, and d'Erlon, as we have just commented, had reported to Soult and not Ney; Ney had literally no idea where half his command was. The arrival of d'Erlon's dispatch saying his force was spread over an area of twenty miles must have come as nasty shock to Soult, and an even bigger one to Napoléon, as d'Erlon should, by the emperor's careful timetable and orders, have been at Gosselies in force and not spread out in a long line from Thuin to Gosselies. Furthermore, Napoléon's plan of action for the day was based on d'Erlon being where he was supposed to be (i.e. Gosselies) rather than being further south than Lobau's 6th Corps. Lobau and 6th Corps were in fact in front of d'Erlon, contrary to the wishes of the emperor. All Ney knew was that he was to be joined by d'Erlon at Gosselies on 15 June and by Kellermann on the 16th. Napoléon was issuing orders under a misapprehension.

In defence of Ney, he had been 'dropped in the deep end', as it were, by Napoléon. Ney had no staff, and no idea about what he was supposed to be doing. The first chance he got to meet and interview his senior officers was on the night of 15 June. He certainly met Reille, Jérôme, Bachelu and others, but Jacquinot, Quiot, Donzelot and Kellermann were all unknown quantities. With no staff he had to rely on second-hand information from Soult and from field officers, and assume troops where were Napoléon had meticulously planned for them to be. Sadly, despite all the planning in the world, Napoléon had not accounted for delays and the human factor. d'Erlon and Reille, and no doubt other commanders, were lacking in the fire and spirit of earlier years. Reille acted with, and urged, caution when facing Wellington. Yet this caution was the undoing of the emperor's plans. Defection of senior officers on 14, 15 and 16 June caused no end of problems; de Bourmont was just one notable example. Without an effective staff, and being generous to him, Ney, on the morning of 16 June, got a nasty shock when the true situation revealed itself to him. Not only was he facing half the Allied army, but his troops when he needed them were not to hand at Gosselies, and he had already been robbed of Girard's division from 2nd Corps.

Of course, Ney could have known the true sorry state of his command, and was either lethargic or so over-confident that he acted with no urgency on the morning of 16 June by issuing orders as late as he did for the concentration of the command, and that he was faced by a small rearguard. Either scenario is possible. In either, Ney was faced with a situation not of his making. To his credit, he held off Wellington with just three infantry divisions and three brigades of cavalry.

When Napoléon issued his 15.30 order to move to Ligny all his assumptions about what was taking place on the left wing were totally wrong: d'Erlon was nowhere in sight and could not quickly move to Brye; Kellermann was somewhere other than Quatre-Bras; and the rearguard at Quatre-Bras, as Napoléon had predicted, was now being majorly reinforced by Allied troops along the Brussels road. The dispersed nature of Ney's command made it impossible for orders to be executed in the manner and timescale Napoléon had anticipated. Poor marching discipline by d'Erlon wrecked any chance Napoléon had of concentrating his forces. d'Erlon would yet again prove to be a thorn in Napoléon's side, with as dramatic an effect. Ney could have easily pushed aside Perponcher at dawn on 16 June, but it seems Reille's caution put paid to any quick victory. Surely though, Reille knew where his corps was, and knew it would take an hour or so to get to Quatre-Bras, so why did Ney wait until 11.00 to issue orders? He seems to have lacked any urgency, and perhaps felt over-confident that what faced him was a small rearguard, which he estimated at 3,000. But, what would have happened if Ney had broken through at Quatre-Bras? Wellington's army was on the march south. If, as Napoléon planned, a single division was placed at Genappe to hold back all of Wellington's army, then he must have assumed that the forces coming from Brussels would be fewer in number than what happened in reality.

Either way, Ney was placed in a no-win situation; he had the troops to push Perponcher aside, but what then? In case the Allies were concentrating their forces, it was much better to attack with all his command unified. Yet why did he not issue orders to do so at daybreak? Why do nothing? If Reille counselled caution, it was better to let all 1st and 2nd Corps concentrate, and then attack—so the logical thing to have done would have been to issue orders at daybreak, not seven hours later. What we will never know is what Ney was actually thinking. But, at the same time, he knew Allied troops were heading from Brussels and from Mons, and it did not take more than a brief look at a map for Ney and/or Reille to realise that they would concentrate at Quatre-Bras.

The more time he spent doing nothing, the closer the Allied reinforcements were. Ney was caught between a rock and a hard place. He had to wait for 1st Corps to arrive, but every hour of delay brought the Allied troops closer. Yet he chose to wait and see what developed at Quatre-Bras, hoping 1st Corps and Kellermann would arrive quickly, despite being aware that he would have to face down an ever-increasing number of Allied troops.

Between 14.00 and 16.30, Ney, it seems, had devolved command to General Reille. From then on, the tactics of the battle changed. Bachelu and Foy reverted to reactionary skirmishing as opposed to co-ordinated, formal attacks. Any serious offensive operations were now restricted to Jérôme on the French left and Piré and Guiton's cavalry. No doubt Ney was waiting for the arrival of 1st Corps, who would then push through the Allies and enable Ney to move to Ligny. The arrival of much-needed reinforcements no doubt encouraged Wellington to attempt to regain the Gémioncourt Farm, and the Prince of Orange led forward the 7th Belgian Line to reinforce the jägers and 5th Militia, who were maintaining their position on the Materne Brook.

NOTES:
[1] Letter by van Balveren in *collectie van Loeben Sels*, box 1815, file II, no. 5, letter 2, dated 25 May 1841. Erwin Muilwijk, perssonal communication 1 December 2012.
[2] Notes from Lieutenant Deebetz on the basis of an oral account of a captain in the 6th Hussars, *collectie van Loeben-Sels*, box 1815. Erwin Muilwijk, perssonal communication 1 December 2012.
[3] J. L. Henckens, *Mémoires se rapportant à son service militaire au 6e régiment de chasseurs à cheval français de février 1803 à août 1816*, M. Nijhoff, La Haie, 1910.
[4] Erwin Muilwijk, personal communication 1 December 2012.
[5] W. J. Knoop, *Quatre-Bras en Waterloo*, Roelants, Schiedam, 1855.
[6] Letter of Captain Bijleveld, dated 3 June 1841, *collectie van Loeben-Sels*, box 1815. Erwin Muilwijk, personal communication 1 December 2012.
[7] Letter by Lieutenant Wassenaar van St Pancras, *collectie van Loeben-Sels*, box 1815. Erwin Muilwijk, personal communication 1 December 2012.
[8] *Bredasche Courant*, 5 July 1840. Erwin Muilwijk, perssonal communication 1 December 2012.
[9] Stadsarchief Zutphen: *collectie van Loeben-Sels*.
[10] J. B. J. van Doren, *Strategisch verhaal van de veldslagen tusschen het Fransche leger en dat der Geallieerden op 15, 16, 17 en 18 Junij 1815, Mont-Saint-Jean*, Amsterdam, 1865. Erwin Muilwijk, perssonal communication 1 December 2012.
[11] Roland-Marchot, *Notice biographique sur le général-major Édouard de Mercx de Corbais*, Namur, 1855, pp. 75-7.
[12] SHDDT: GR 24 YC 254.
[13] SHDDT: GR 24 YC 282.
[14] Booth, pp. 77-8.
[15] James Hope, *Letters from Portugal, Spain, and France, during the memorable campaigns of 1811, 1812 and 1813 and from Belgium and France in the year 1815*, Michael Anderson, Edinburgh, 1819, p. 225.
[16] Booth, p. 52.
[17] Jonathan Leach, *Rough Sketches of the Life of an Old Soldier*, Longmans, Rees, Orme, Brown and Green, London, 1831, pp. 366-8.
[18] Hope, p. 227.
[19] Booth, pp. 77-8.
[20] Karl Berthold Fischer, from Karl Theodor Fischer's campaign diary of 1815 in *Braunschweig Magazin*, January 1912 [Edition 1], translated by Hans Kolmsee and the author.
[21] Cramm, c/o the Hussar Rgt. His successor was Maj. v. Oeynhausen.

[22] Heinemann took over command after Col. Olfermann was injured. He was succeeded by Col. v. Herzberg.
[23] Sgt. Albrecht Pessler from Wedlenstedt, died 16 June.
[24] Hussar Friedrich Heinemann from Oker is listed as wounded.
[25] Statement probably incorrect. In Laeken, a hospital with three sections has been established. Here, the list of dead, wounded and missing has been produced.
[26] Heinrich Woltereck from Braunschweig. Friedrich Graumann from Goslar died that day.
[27] Name missing, may be the dead could not be recognised.
[28] Booth, pp. 92-3.
[29] John Franklin, personal communication.
[30] The *Morning Chronicle*, 24 June 1815.
[31] *York Herald*, 24 June 1815.
[32] National Library of Scotland: *Caledonian Mercury*, 3 July 1815.
[33] Booth, p. 79.
[34] AN: LH/134/23.
[35] Ian Smith, personal communication 12 February 2013.
[36] Ian Smith, personal communication 12 February 2013.
[37] Ian Smith, personal communication 12 February 2013.
[38] Ian Smith, personal communication 12 February 2013.
[39] AN: LH/64/22.
[40] Hilarion François marie de Forsanz, *Le 3e régiment de chasseurs d'Afrique*, Nancy, Berger-Levrault et Cie, Paris, 1898, p. 392.
[41] Lefol, *Souvenirs sur le prytanée de Saint-Cyr sur la campagne de 1814, le retour de l'empereur Napoléon de l'île d'Elbe, et la campagne de 1815, pendant les Cent-jours*, Montalant-Bougleux, Versailles, 1854, p. 71.
[42] William Siborne, *Waterloo Letters* ed. H. T. Siborne, Greenhill Books, 1993, No. 167.
[43] Siborne, *Waterloo Letters*, No. 166.
[44] AN: AFIV 1939 *Registre d'Ordres du Major-General 13 Juin au 26 Juin 1815*, pp. 41-2.
[45] AN: AFIV 1939 *Registre d'Ordres du Major-General 13 Juin au 26 Juin 1815*, pp. 42-3.
[46] SHDDT: C15 5, *dossier 16 Jun 1815*. Letter from d'Erlon to Duc d'Elchingen in 1829.

Chapter 6

Jérômes's Division

While Ney was digesting his orders from the emperor, Prince Jérôme ordered his 6th Infantry Division to attack Pierrepoint Farm. Outnumbered, the Dutch-Belgian garrison withdrew to the Bossu Wood, pursued by Jérôme's men. Bourdon de Vatry, aide-de-Camp to Prince Jérôme, narrates the day's events as follows:[1]

> On the 16th, we had before us Brunswick and Nassau troops. Soon we heard in the east a heavy cannonade. Marshal Ney, who marched at our head of column, made us attack the important position of Quatre-Bras, defended on our right by English and Scottish regiments, and on our left by German troops occupying the Bossu Wood, at the head of which had been built some fortifications.
>
> When Jérôme's division marched to attack the wood, an officer of high-rank, wearing a green uniform covered with medals and decorations, wanted to harangue his troops. Standing, hat in hand, he exclaimed in French: 'My friends, do not fight, let us be peaceful, I bring it to you as a brother … '.
>
> Before he could finish his sentence, Captain de Brea, arriving at the ruin with his carabinier company to assail the rampart, from the top of which the speaker harangued, gave the order to open fire. The unfortunate babbler fell dead, riddled with bullets. We thought at first that it was the Duke of Berry, but recognised him as the Duke of Brunswick.
>
> A furious battle, fought with the bayonet, began in the Bossu Wood. Prince Jérôme was shot in the hip. Fortunately for him, his sword in solid gold, which the projectile had first hit, resulted only in a severe bruise which soon paled. Overcoming his grief, the prince continued to remain on horseback, at the head of his division, giving

everyone an example of courage and selflessness. His composure produced the best effect.

The rampart was the ditch and bank surrounding the wood. However, contrary to the writer's explicit identification of Captain de Brea, we note he quit his regiment, the 1st Regiment of Light Infantry, on 1 June 1815, so cannot have been at Quatre-Bras.[2] Therefore we cannot be certain if this episode in the battle actually took place. As the French attacked, Prince Jérôme's staff became obvious targets. In the action, Captain Louis Alexandre Druez, the aide-de-camp to General Guilleminot had his horse shot from under him.[3]

At Quatre-bras, the 1st Battalion of the 1st Regiment of Light Infantry was commanded by Jean-Baptiste Jolyet. His account of the fighting at Quatre-Bras was written many years after the battle, but incorporates many fascinating details:[4]

> On the 16th, the regiment remained in its camp until midday, at which time most of our army corps set out on the road to Brussels; we heard the cannon on our right and saw smoke in front of Fleurus. Soon the cannonade was also heard in front of us, when we arrived near Frasné, for it was in front of this village that several of our divisions were engaged in battle with the English. Our regiment moved towards the left of the road near a wood, where we discovered masses of English infantry posted on the heights at the junction of roads to Brussels and Nivelles (the position of Quatre-Bras). Towards four o'clock in the evening our 2nd Battalion advanced into the wood, and after securing it, moved towards its northern edge and engaged the English regiments there. I remained at the back until almost six o'clock in the evening, waiting for instructions.
>
> Eventually, an aide-de-camp of General Guilleminot brought me the order to gain the road and march against the English. I found myself under cannon fire as soon as I left the wood in closed columns in order to support the tirailleurs of the 4th Light Infantry, who were engaged with the English. I had my horse killed under me and lost a lot of men in a very short time. The tirailleurs of the 4th Light Infantry moved to the right and I found myself alone with my battalion in the middle of a large plain, having considerable numbers of English troops in front of me.
>
> Two cavalry regiments, one of cuirassiers and one of lancers, then appeared and launched several attacks against the English squares, but as they were unsuccessful they retired. Seeing that I was alone,

and being unwilling to lose any more men, I moved towards a large farm which served as a rallying point and two companies of the 3rd Battalion joined me. We were pursued by a cloud of English skirmishers, who were supported by artillery and columns of infantry. Nevertheless, we were able to maintain ourselves in the surroundings of the farm until nightfall. I then began to retreat, and was soon joined by our colonel, who had been wounded at the beginning of the action, and who, despite the injury, came to look for us. He told me that the army corps was camping behind Frasné. After calling back for the 2nd Battalion, which had remained at the edge of the wood, we re-joined our corps.

De Jongh, of the 8th National Militia Battalion, writes about the initial troop positions and the action in the woods:[5]

> In the morning of the 16th, around two o'clock, I received orders through Aide-de-Camp Count van Hogendorp to report with His Excellency the lieutenant-general commanding the division, who ordered me to defile through Nivelles in the utmost silence with my battalion and join the 27th Jäger Battalion, which H. E. [His Excellency] already had marched off to take position near Quatre-Bras. H. E. the lieutenant-general gave me the command of both these battalions and ordered me to place myself under the command of His Highness the Prince Bernhard von Sachsen-Weimar, commanding the 2nd Brigade of the division. In the morning at four o'clock, I arrived with both battalions at the position of Quatre-Bras and received the order of the mentioned prince to have the 27th Jäger Battalion take a position forward-left of the highroad to Frasné, and the relief of a Nassau battalion, which had been there during the night facing the enemy.
>
> When this was done, the prince ordered me to place my battalion in reserve behind the houses of Quatre-Bras, in which position it remained until about two o'clock in the afternoon, when Major Amerongen, aide-de-camp, in consequence of orders of H. E. the divisional general moved my battalion forward of the highroad, in front of the Bossu Wood and placed it in a sort of hollow-way, my right wing leaning against the left wing of an Orange-Nassau battalion, which was already arranged in order of battle. Having been here with them for a while in battle, under fire from an enemy battery of three pieces, I saw the Orange-Nassau battalion move to the rear, as a terrible panic had spread among them. I was in front of the centre of my battalion and my right flanker company was

interpenetrated by the Nassau battalion. I spurred my horse and assisted by the brave Captain Sijbers, acting Adjutant-Major, I immediately brought the company back into the line of battle. I discovered the Nassau men had been frightened by His Royal Highness the Prince of Orange, who rode in front of our line of battle, accompanied by staff and ordnances, under the fire of the enemy battery.

An aide-de-camp of His Royal Highness brought me the order to position me towards the rear against the Bossu Wood. The cannon balls of the enemy artillery, from which the battalion had been covered by the hollow road, now started to fall in it, by which the sergeant-major standard-bearer and two NCOs from the Standard Platoon were heavily wounded, a corporal and several men were killed and heavily wounded. There arose some confusion among the battalion; I had it deploy with files to the right under the fire from the three enemy pieces, gave the officers and men a short and concise speech, addressed their duties for king and country, inspired their honour and there immediately reigned the most beautiful tranquillity. Major Count van Stirum, aide-de-camp of His Royal Highness the Prince of Orange, brought me the order to detach two companies left in front of the wood, for which I deployed the 5th and 6th Companies.

Next I remained with the four companies in this position, exposed to the enemy cannonade, which killed and wounded some men. The reported aide-de-camp once again joined me, to throw the battalion into the wood; I protested with all discretion against this, giving him in consideration that it was a waste for a battalion, composed of young men, to fight dispersed as skirmishers in a wood and that I had rather marched forward to take away the three guns that were firing upon me. When this report had been brought to His Royal Highness, I received further orders from Colonel Lord Somerset, to move into the wood without further ado, to traverse it and on the other side engage the enemy attacks. At this moment, the 5th and 6th Companies were engaged with the enemy *en tirailleurs*. I had the company commanders move through a thick hedge in the wood and then had the men follow in order and on the other side of the hedge assemble the companies again.

I remained with Captain Sijbers outside of the wood until the entire battalion had defiled it, traversing the point of the wood and found on the other side part of the 7th Line Battalion engaged with the enemy. I then started to engage with the four companies under my command and chased the French away, but as they were reinforced, they in turn attacked me and pushed me back into the wood, while fighting. At this moment, I was wounded by a piece from a howitzer grenade and crashed to the ground. I was lifted up again immediately, because this wound had only caused a heavy contusion. It was impossible to properly maintain the order among my troops inside the wood. The French, who were protected by artillery fire from the other side of the wood, entered into it. I retreated while fighting through the wood on to the highroad between Hautam-Leval [sic] and Quatre-Bras, closer to Quatre-Bras, and formed four companies there and had myself bandaged.

My adjutant-major took a cavalry horse from an officer of the jägers who led it and retreated in isolation and helped to mount me, and I marched to Quatre-Bras, where I found the divisional and brigade general, who had me placed with platoons in column on the left wing of the corps of Brunswick troops. Major-General van Marle [sic] had given me a saddle and, assisted by Surgeon Wilson, this was put on my horse. At that moment, Surgeon Wilson was wounded by a piece from a howitzer grenade against his left leg (heavy contusion); this was a great loss for me and my battalion. This brave officer had to leave the battlefield on the 15th [sic], but he reported back to me on the 18th, jumping on two sticks, when the first enemy attack began and fulfilled with the most beautiful inspiration his duty during that bloody and honourable day, by bandaging the wounded on the battlefield. In the evening of the 16th, the firing ended on both sides at ten o'clock. That night we bivouacked on the battlefield near Quatre-Bras.

With the 7th Line Battalion was Captain Henry Scheltens, a former officer of the grenadiers of the Imperial Guard of Napoléon:[6]

> In the morning of the 16th we took up our arms, we passed an inspection and were given the order to load our muskets. There could be heard the thunder of cannon on the line occupied by the Prussians.
>
> Here we are on the road to Quatre-Bras. We marched by platoons at full distance on the highway, up against the Bossu Wood where we were made to stop. Some bullets passed over the column. No sooner had we taken a moment to rest than an English officer of the staff of the Duke of Wellington brought us the order to march forward, head to the right column, to carry us through wood and the other side of the flank as skirmishers. The movement began with regularity. We kept the 12th Platoon in reserve. My battalion

commander ordered me to follow the movement of deployment. The line was well commanded, but a charge of cuirassiers made us retire to the woods, after that we were half an hour in this position. I could not reach the wood in time, but I escaped between the wheels of an abandoned ammunition caisson. The charge passed and I succeeded in my escape, and I ran to join my men in the wood. We sounded the recall, it was night.

It was in the charge of the French cuirassiers that the Prince of Orange was rescued by two companies of the 7th Belgian Battalion. Sergeant Winsinger (brother of the deceased general of artillery), was part of one of these companies.

We lost pretty much all of our men due to the musket balls, the cannon balls and the cavalry charge. Lieutenant Carondal was killed. Gérard was made a prisoner and several officers were wounded. I had received a bullet in the shako, she had shaved my head, one centimetre lower, I was burning!

I believed, and then I was convinced, that if the French had made the head of the column and marched resolutely forward on Quatre-Bras, the position would have been captured. The English were not online with sufficient strength to be able to withstand the shock. The battalion was reformed. It lacked many men. We returned on the 16th evening, bivouacking on the highway, near the farm of Quatre-Bras.

Prince Bernhard von Sachsen-Weimar, with the Nassau troops, noted that he led a bayonet charge against the French to regain some of the wood:[7]

> On the 15th, the French fell upon the Prussian army, and pressed it very much. My brigade continued on the left wing of the Dutch army, the headquarters of which were at Braine-le-Comte—my division lay in Nivelles. A battalion of Nassau were at Frasné, and also a battery of Dutch horse artillery. When the Prussians retreated towards Fleurus, the post at Frasné was attacked and driven back. The infantry threw itself into a wood on the right, and the artillery retired fighting to Quatre-Bras. At this important post I had drawn my brigade together, and was cannonaded by the enemy who I managed to keep at a distance.
>
> I maintained this post through the whole night. Towards morning, on the 16th, I was reinforced by a battalion of Dutch yagers [sic], and a battalion of militia. Soon after arrived my general-of-

division and the Prince of Orange. With the latter I went to the outposts, and by this order undertook a reconnaissance, with a battalion and two cannon. Towards noon, the enemy showed strong columns, and began to cannonade us. It is said he had three corps of his army engaged against us on this day. We had only five battalions to oppose to him, and the skirts of a wood to defend to the utmost. The Duke of Wellington himself was present at the beginning of the action: I kept my ground a long time against an enemy thrice my number, and had only two Belgian cannons to protect myself with.

The enemy took the point of a wood opposite me, and incommoded my left flank. I, without loss of time, took some volunteers, and two companies of Dutch militia, and recovered my wood at the point of the bayonet; I was at the head of the storming parties, and had the honour to be one of the first in the wood. In cutting away some branches, I wounded myself with my sabre very slightly in the right leg, but was not a moment out of battle—it is in fact not worthwhile to mention this wound; I write to you about it only that you and my good mother may not be alarmed by exaggerated and foolish reports. While I manfully defended my wood; the enemy drove back our left wing as far as Quatre-Bras.

It was on this occasion that the brave Duke of Brunswick was killed by a ball, which entered his breast. Strong columns of infantry turned my right flank; I asked for orders how to act, but received none. When I saw myself surrounded on all sides, and my people had expended all their ammunition, I retreated in good order through the wood to the neighbourhood of Hautain-le-Val. The Hanoverian Alten Division supported me, and recovered the wood, but lost it again; at last it was forced by the English with great loss, and maintained through the night. I bivouacked for the night in the wood.

Brigaded with the 1st Regiment of Light Infantry was the 3rd Regiment of Line Infantry. It was near Pierrepoint Farm that the regiment overran an artillery battery. Captain Charles-François Durousseau-Lagrange,[8] at the head of the grenadier company of the regiment's 2nd Battalion, charged an Allied artillery battery. He writes as follows about this event on 28 September 1815:[9]

> In the affair of Quatre-Bras against the English, supported by a part of his company, he repelled the enemy with sufficient success to make him abandon a howitzer which he captured. He was able to

have it driven back to the artillery park of 2nd Corps and was evidenced by a written statement of General-de-Brigade Pelletier, commander of the artillery.

Clearly, he and his men also overran the horse team and limber for it to have been driven back to the French artillery park. In this action he suffered a bruise to the right shoulder. He was wounded again at Waterloo with a gunshot, which passed through his torso.

With the first attack led by the 1st Brigade checked and pushed back, Prince Jérôme ordered his 2nd Brigade, commanded by Marshal-du-Camp Jean Louis, Baron Soye, to attack. The vanguard was formed by the 1st Regiment of Line Infantry, with the 2nd Regiment of Line Infantry moving up in support.

Major Jean Louis Beaux, the temporary commander of the regiment, writes as follows:[10]

> At Ligny the 2nd Corps suffered horribly from the English, whilst not engaged for various reasons, was the 1st Corps, which took no part in the affair. However, their presence was to be decisive in the affair at Mont-Saint-Jean.
>
> There was made an extraordinary effort by the troops of 2nd Corps to resist the enemy for many hours despite having no more ammunition. Those with malicious intent went to the artillery park and the baggage wagons and cried 'look, here is the enemy! Here is the enemy! Save yourselves!', and thus a great disorder was spread in the rear of the army, and the wagons were pillaged. The army was not informed of this event until they had captured the position.

In this attack, Sergeant-Major Paul Joseph Marie Viara led forward a group of sharpshooters and attacked the enemy artillery, which was firing on the regiment. They forced the enemy gunners to abandon a piece, which was captured by the group of sharpshooters. However, the Allied troops counter-attacked, and Viara suffered a gunshot to the head and another to the right knee. But, for his action, he was awarded the Legion of Honour.[11]

Captain Robinaux, of the 2nd Regiment of Line Infantry, narrates that:[12]

> On the 16th, we attacked the English at Quatre-Bras; the French left is in front of Frasné to Quatre-Bras, the centre is at Ligny, and the right to Sombreffe. The British and Prussians were attacked at the

same time, General Blücher, who was defeated, retired to Tilly, and marched all night to arrive at Wavre, where he concentrated his remaining troops.

In the action, the regiment lost one officer killed and five men wounded. Brigaded with the 2nd Regiment of Line Infantry was the 1st Regiment of Line Infantry. Mortally wounded leading the 1st Battalion was Pierre Deperonne. At the head of the 2nd Battalion, Commander Michel Jean Meulot was shot in the foot.[13] Similarly wounded was Captain-Adjutant-Major Louis Charles Joseph Beissac.[14]

As the regiment attacked, officers and men fell dead or wounded. Captains Pierre Cesar Bunel and Charles Marie Signault were shot dead, and so too were Lieutenants Louis Germain Alexandre Leroy, Jean Baptiste Alexandre Rey and Sub-Lieutenant Simon Charles Herlobig.[15] Captain Jean Jacques Lemonnier was wounded, as well as fellow captain, Augustin Joseph Hilarion Mouton, Lieutenants Charles Jacques Adolphe Henry, Blaise LeCorps and Meyer, Sub-Lieutenants Bechamiels, Genton, Leiris, Maigret, Martinieau, and Peronnet.[16] Lieutenant Honoré Bel, who served in the 2nd Fusilier Company of 2nd Battalion, was wounded with a musket ball lodged in the heel of his right foot.[17] Fellow lieutenant, but of the voltigeurs, Edme Cloix, suffered a gunshot wound to the right arm.[18] Lieutenant Simon Cottan had a musket ball pass through the right side of his torso. The wound, though severe, was not fatal, as he died in 1851.[19] Fellow lieutenant, Charles Thomas Henry, a native of Blois, was shot in the right elbow.[20]

About the start of the action, Colonel Pierre Heymès, aide-de-camp to Marshal Ney, writes:[21]

> The division of Guilleminot threw itself into the Bossu Wood, where it experienced a strong resistance; however, at three o'clock, it was master of the wood, and threatened the rear of Quatre-Bras.

About this movement, General Foy narrates the assault of Jérôme against the Dutch troops in the wood as follows:[22]

> The marshal directed the division to the Bossu Wood, by the main road of Brussels, as well the cavalry division of Lhéritier. The enemy marched on the left of the road to Namur. When he arrived, there began an exchange of artillery and musket fire. About four o'clock in the afternoon, the English, probably being eager to gain the road

to Namur, they marched incessantly to Piermont, despite our artillery fire which caused them considerable loss, seized the village and carried the nearby woods. This circumstance forced us to extend the right wing.

To the left, Prince Jérôme captured the Bossu Wood and was chased out by successive reinforcements which the enemy had received.

The observations about General Lhéritier's cavalry is interesting and, perhaps, is further proof, contrary to all histories of the battle, that the 2nd and 7th Dragoons were indeed involved in the battle. General Samuel François Lhéritier de Chezelles was born at Vienne on 6 August 1772. He commanded the 11th Cavalry Division, the senior division in Kellermann's 3rd Reserve Cavalry Corps. His command comprised the 2nd and 7th Dragoons under the command of General-de-Brigade Cyrille Simon Picquet, and the 8th and 11th cuirassiers under the orders of General-de-Brigade Guiton. Certainly, the two cuirassier regiments fought at Quatre-Bras, but did the two dragoon regiments?

The 7th Dragoons had two men wounded in 6th Company on 16 June.[23] The brigade seems to have been in action, we suppose, in the evening, along with Donop's cuirassiers, to replace the troops of Piré and Guiton.

In the action, the Dutch-Belgians had lost heavily. The 7th Line Regiment lost sixty-four men dead and wounded, the 27th Line Regiment 144 men, the 5th Dutch Militia some 199 men dead and wounded, and the 8th Dutch Militia just thirteen dead and wounded. A total of 420 men were killed or wounded, and a further 265 were listed as missing, making a total of 685 men lost.[24]

Bauduin's brigade
The casualty data for the brigade is incomplete, and where the data exists the losses are incredibly low. The reason for the low number of losses recorded is not known. Did the brigade suffer very few casualties? Or is the paperwork of both regiments incorrect in some manner? We simply cannot tell at this distance in time from when the muster lists were compiled in June 1815. On 27 May 1815, the 1st Regiment of Light Infantry mustered seventy officers and 1,858 other ranks in three battalions. The 4th Battalion comprised eighty officers and 105 men.[25] The regiment's paperwork declares seven men lost on 16 June and fifty-nine on 18 June.[26]

Brigaded with the 1st Regiment of Light Infantry was the 3rd Regiment of Line Infantry. Wounded in the regiment was Sub-Lieutenant Dominique Botto, who served in the Grenadier Company of the 1st Battalion. Wounded in the 2nd Fusilier Company of the same battalion was Sub-Lieutenant Jean Amboise Fleury, suffering a gunshot wound to each leg. Lieutenant Claude Glorget, of the 4th Fusilier Company 1st Battalion, was wounded. Commanding the Voltigeur Company of 2nd Battalion was Jean François Tourbier, who was also wounded.

The 3rd Regiment of Line Infantry at Quatre-Bras recorded the loss of just three men wounded, seven prisoners of war and two killed; a total of twelve men. At Genappe on the 17 June five men were wounded.[27]

Soye's brigade

The brigade comprised the 1st and 2nd Regiments of Line Infantry. Total regimental losses for the 1st Regiment of Line Infantry at Quatre-Bras are in the table below:[28]

1st Regiment of Line Infantry

	Wounded	Wounded and Prisoner	Prisoner of War	Killed	Missing
1st Battalion	67	0	0	12	28
2nd Battalion	46	1	1	9	28
3rd Battalion	35	0	0	4	17
4th Battalion	9	0	0	1	24
Total	157	1	1	26	97

Total losses were 282 other ranks dead, wounded, missing or prisoner of war. On 10 June, the regiment mustered fifty-nine officers and 1,736 other ranks. At Quatre-Bras, 16.2 per cent of effective strength was lost. In total, 1,454 were in ranks on the morning of 17 June.

Total losses sustained by the 2nd Regiment of Line Infantry at Quatre-Bras are as below:[29]

2nd Regiment of Line Infantry

	Wounded	Wounded and Prisoner	Prisoner of War	Killed	Missing
1st Battalion	48	4	2	3	9
2nd Battalion	6	0	1	2	0
3rd Battalion	30	9	1	11	0
4th Battalion	40	3	0	3	2
Total	124	16	4	19	11

In total, the regiment lost 174 men. On the June, the regiment had 1,730 other ranks, and so the casualties represent a 10.1 per cent loss of man power, giving the regiment some 1,556 men under arms on the morning of the 18th. It seems that the 2nd Battalion was held in reserve, as it lost far fewer men than the remaining three battalions. The regiment's archive lists that in the 1st Battalion, Captain Claude Joseph Giro was wounded.[30] Also wounded was Pierre Gobon.[31] Killed at the head of the voltigeur company was Honoré Fiacre Tamponet.[32] Wounded in the action were Lieutenant Antoine Amelot[33] and Gabriel François Pergaud.[34]

2nd Foot Artillery

Attached to Jérôme's division was the 2nd Company 2nd Foot Artillery. The 7th Company formed the 12-pounder reserve battery of the corps, but we do not know where the battery was deployed. The two companies sustained the following losses:[35]

2nd Regiment of Foot Artillery

Company	Wounded	Wounded and Prisoner	Prisoner of War	Killed	Missing
2nd	2	0	0	0	0
7th	1	1	0	2	1
Total	3	1	0	2	1

It is clear from the losses that the two batteries came under enemy musket or artillery fire. The reserve battery lost seven men, so it seems the battery was a target for the Allied troops. These six 12-pounders were the heaviest guns on the field in terms of calibre, and no doubt due to their range and hitting power were a major threat to the Allied lines.

NOTES:
[1] Emmanuel Grouchy, George Grouchy, *Mémoires du maréchal de Grouchy* (vol. 4), E. Dentu, 1873, pp. 99-102.
[2] SHDDT: Xb 565 *1e regiment d'infantere legere, dossier 1815*.
[3] France Ministère de la guerre, *Annuaire officiel des officiers de l'armée active*, 1822, p. 3.
[4] Commandant Jolyet, '*Souvenirs du 1815*' in *Revue de Paris*, October 1903, pp. 545-55.
[5] *Nieuwe Militaire Spectator*, Nr 1 [Vol. 20], 1866. Erwin Muilwijk, perssonal communication 1 December 2012.
[6] Erwin Muilwijck, personnal communication.
[7] Booth, p. lxxvi.
[8] Charles-François Durousseau-Lagrange was born at Montron on 25 June 1780, and died on 11 December 1857. He had joined the army in 1797 and, after being promoted through the ranks of the regiment's sub-officers, he was promoted to second lieutenant on 28 March

1807. He was wounded at the Battle of Heilsberg on 10 June 1807, and again at the Battle of Eckmuhl on 24 April 1809. Promotion to captain came on 17 November 1780, and command of the grenadier company came on 12 February 1813. In front of Hamburg on 16 September 1813, he was wounded when he was trapped under his horse, which was killed during an enemy cavalry charge. He was rescued by his regiment. He remained with the 3rd Regiment of Line Infantry during the Bourbon Restoration, and, as we have seen, served during the Hundred Days campaign. He was placed on half-pay due to his Waterloo wound on 28 September 1815, and pensioned-off on 3 May 1817.

[9] Author's collection.
[10] Letter dated 25 June 1815 published in the *Journal de Rouen*, 27 June 1815, pp. 3-4. The author of the letter is anonymous; however, we do know that he served in 2nd Corps. Given as he speaks of Jérôme's division, it seems likely that he served under Jérôme. The author speaks of his regiment and that he attended the briefing at Waterloo where the day's orders were issued. Presumably, therefore, he is a regimental colonel or a brigade commander. If a colonel, this narrows the author down to one of four men: Despans Cubières, of the 1st Regiment of Light Infantry, was wounded early on 18 June; Hubert Vautrin, of the 3rd Regiment of Line Infantry, had his left leg shattered by a cannon ball which was amputated in the field hospital; Colonel Tripe, of the 2nd Regiment of Line Infantry, was not wounded; and Major Lebeau, of the 3rd Regiment of Line Infantry, was wounded with a gunshot wound. The writer was wounded about 20.00, and clearly it seems he remained with the regiment. Vautrin, of the 3rd Regiment of Line Infantry, being in a field hospital would perhaps have been incapable of remaining with the regiment. It is not certain that the field hospital was in operation about 20.00, as the writer places the event after the defeat of the Old Guard and the rout was in process. Therefore, it seems likely on balance that the writer is Major Lebeau of the 1st Regiment of Line Infantry.
[11] AN: LH/2704/63.
[12] Pierre Robinaux, Gustave Léon Schlumberger, *Journal de route du Capitaine Robinaux 1803-1832*, Plon-Nourrit, Paris, 1908.
[13] AN: LH/1298/59.
[14] AN: LH/165/53.
[15] SHDDT: M59.
[16] SHDDT: M59.
[17] AN: LH/166/3.
[18] AN: LH/555/16.
[19] AN: LH/601/4.
[20] AN: LH/1285/74.
[21] Heymès, p. 16.
[22] de l'Ain, p. 272.
[23] SHDDT: GR 24 YC 158.
[24] Dellevoet, p. 31.
[25] SHDDT: C15 34, *Situation Rapport 2e Corps 27 Mai 1815*.
[26] SHDDT: GR 21 YC 8 *1er régiment d'infanterie de ligne dit régiment du Roi, 1 mai 1814-6 décembre 1814 (matricules 1 à 3,000)*.
[27] SHDDT: GR 21 YC 31 *3e régiment d'infanterie de ligne dit régiment du Dauphin, 16 juillet 1814-17 décembre 1814 (matricules 1 à 1,800)*. See also: SHDDT: GR 21 YC 32 *3e régiment d'infanterie de ligne dit régiment du Dauphin, 17 décembre 1814-1 juillet 1815 (matricules 1,801 à 2,135)*.
[28] SHDDT: GR 21 YC 8. See also: SHDDT: GR 21 YC 9 *1er régiment d'infanterie de ligne dit régiment du Roi, 6 décembre 1814-3 juillet 1815 (matricules 3,001 à 4,386)*.
[29] SHDDT: GR 21 YC 19 *2e regiment d'infanterie de ligne dit regiment de la Reine, 20 mai 1814-21 août 1814 (matricules 1 à 2,997)*. See also: SHDDT: GR 21 YC 20 *2e régiment d'infanterie de ligne dit régiment de la Reine, 9 septembre 1814-6 juin 1815 (matricules 3,000 à 4,723)*.
[30] Claude Joseph Girot was born on 23 April 1766 and admitted to the regiment on 23 June 1807 from the 16th Regiment of Line Infantry. He commanded the 4th Company of Fusiliers of 1st Battalion in 1815.
[31] Pierre Gobon was born 14 July 1784 and was admitted to the regiment on 6 July 1814 from

the 17th Regiment of Line Infantry, in which he had served since 12 July 1812. He was wounded at Quatre-Bras.

[32] Fiacre Tamponet was born on 28 August 1769 and was admitted to the regiment on 6 July 1814 from the 140th Regiment of Line Infantry.

[33] Antoine Amelot was born in Paris on 24 April 1793 and was admitted to the regiment on 6 November 1811, upon graduating from the military school of Saint-Cyr, and placed in the Voltigeur Company of 1st Battalion. He served in the Grenadier Company of 3rd Battalion in 1815.

[34] Gabriel François Pergaud was born on 16 March 1780 and was admitted to the regiment on 1 May 1813. He was wounded at Quatre-Bras while serving in the 5th Company of 3rd Battalion.

[35] SHDDT: GR 25 YC 21 *2e Artillerie à Pied*.

Chapter 7

Kellermann's Charge

By now, all of Ney's forces had been committed to action. He had yet to take Quatre-Bras, or more correctly 'Trois-Bras'. The arrival of Soult's order, timed at 15.30, had made it abundantly clear to Ney that he was to occupy Quatre-Bras with all haste and, upon doing so, to head to Ligny. With 1st Corps now marching to Ligny to face the fresh crisis of Wellington's men arriving in force, and to execute the emperor's orders, Ney had no troops to hand which had not seen action other than part of Kellermann's 3rd Cavalry Corps. It had not long arrived before it was sent into action. General-de-Brigade Jean Baptiste Berton writes:[1]

> The morning of 16 June, the corps of cavalry composed of two regiments of dragoons, four of cuirassiers and two of carabiniers, under General Kellermann, passed the river and at Charleroi and marched to Frasné, a division of lancers and chasseurs of General Jacquinot had been posted at Marchienne.

If Berton was correct writing just a few years after the events, then Kellermann was still not across the River Sambre on the morning of 16 June, and neither was Jacquinot. Given that Kellermann did not arrive at Quatre-Bras until after 18.00, I feel Berton's comments are correct. Given headquarters had no clue where Kellermann was, then the orders issued to him meant that Soult's couriers had to search a vast tract of land to find over 2,000 cavalry. Given the emperor openly criticised these men, we do wonder how long it took for Soult's men to find Kellermann.

This no doubt delayed Kellermann getting his orders to move out. To make matters worse, once he had received his orders, and before Kellermann could leave his positions, 6th Corps had to file through the narrow streets of Charleroi, followed by elements of 1st Corps, and only then could his cavalry cross the River Sambre. Once over the river, with 1st Corps marching on the Brussels road, the column would have been a mile long, if not longer, and then he would have had to travel cross country. With the Brussels road occupied by a slow-moving traffic jam, and cavalry been unsuited to march through Gosselies, Kellermann must have moved cross-country or taken another road. Due west of Gosselies was a vast tract of forest, so Kellermann moved east of the road through the corn and wheat fields flanking the Brussels road.

Sensibly, Kellermann, it seems, had left the carabinier brigade in reserve as he was dubious of its loyalties. Lhéritier's dragoons and Donop's cuirassiers did not move up until around 19.30 and were to take part in the action in the late evening. An eyewitness writes:[2]

> The left wing, which was at this moment engaged with the English army at Frasné, and which had succeeded in repelling the English from the heights of Frasné to the farm of Quatre-Bras, was greatly enfeebled; and what added still to the error of having moved away this important reserve of Marshal Ney was that Napoléon had not the consideration to inform the marshal of this subtraction of the greater part of his force.
>
> The 1st Corps had moved off in its new direction upon St-Amand, about an hour away, when the English army, being considerably reinforced by the Prince of Orange, resumed the offensive, and began to repel with much vigour our tirailleurs and advanced columns. On the flank of the highroad to Brussels was a wood; the English occupied the verge of it, and were separated from us by a hollow-way in the form of a ravine.
>
> But, between the wood and the ravine were numerous plateaux, which formed advantageous positions for cavalry. Some of them were either in advance of the ravine, or had an easy passage over it. These plateaux were suddenly covered with battalions of infantry supported by a formidable cavalry, which confident in their reinforcements, now boldly advanced; and threatened to charge and pierce our opposed line. Our troops, wearied by their previous advance, seemed to retreat from new efforts. The moment was critical, and it became necessary to call up the reserve. Marshal Ney, however, a little alarmed at these appearances, because he reckoned upon his 1st Corps in reserve, he now sent it the order to come up, and to charge the enemy. But how great was his astonishment and embarrassment when he learned that Buonaparte had already marched it off to another point.

> He immediately ordered the 8th and the 11th Cuirassiers, who happened to be at hand, to charge the first battalions. This charge was executed with the greatest bravery.

Kellermann had not long arrived at Quatre-Bras with Lhéritier's division (the division of Roussel d'Hurbal had yet to arrive) when he received the order to charge the Allied centre to 'overthrow the mass of the Allied infantry.'[3] The reality, however, seems that rather than a suicidal charge, what Ney needed was an offensive movement to rescue Bachelu's division, as an unknown French general notes as follows about why the cuirassiers charged:[4]

> The Prince of the Moskowa, who from the beginning of the action, had been ordered to seize Quatre-Bras, had made the mistake to postpone the attack on this position; the whole corps of Comte d'Erlon was wasting its time in marches and counter-marches. General Foy's division was the first to advance on this point, and was greeted by a fire so deadly he believed that they had fallen into a trap.
>
> We were ignorant of the fact that Lord Wellington had advanced his army. The French maintained their fire with firmness, and continued to approach the 1st Brigade of Bachelu's division, by a reckless audacity, rushed forward to wait for the support columns that were to be formed; and suddenly found themselves charged by three Scottish regiments in an ambush from a wood on their right, and was forced to retreat in disorder. But the Scots were soon punished by the Prince of the Moskowa, who lead forward the charge with his usual impetuosity, strongly supported by the cavalry. Pierre-Henri, of the 8th Cuirassier Regiment, captured the flag of the 69th Regiment of British infantry. Fired upon in turn by the French, the Scots are almost completely destroyed, and the position was captured. Lost to the English at the affair of Quatre-Bras was a considerable portion of the legion of Brunswick and three Scottish regiments, the Duke of Brunswick remained on the battlefield, and a large number of officers of distinction. On our side, Prince Jérôme was among the wounded.

So, Kellermann had been ordered up to attack the Allies and, when pushing back the Allied troops attacking Bachelu, over-extended their charge caught up in the ardour of pursuit and headed off north to do as much damage as they could to the Allied army. Kellermann galloped off, caught up in the moment (just as Ponsonby's men would do on 18 June), as did, it seems, General Lhéritier with Picquet's dragoon brigade. Far from being a mad 'death or glory' charge, Ney had acted rashly in sending forward his only fresh cavalry force (Guiton's brigade) and Kellermann either lost control or led the cuirassiers, as at Marengo, to win the victory, take the crossroads and literally bludgeon aside Wellington. This scenario is far more likely than Ney ordering a suicidal charge for no reason, according to accepted wisdom of the battle. About the charge, Colonel Pierre Heymès, aide-de-camp to Marshal Ney, writes:[5]

> A little before three o'clock [sic] General Kellermann, at the head of two regiments of cuirassiers, arrived to partake of our labours; he only waited long enough to let the horses recover their wind then executed a brilliant charge which had all the success desirable. He cut to pieces several squares of Scottish infantry, routed others, took a colour, and, notwithstanding the most vigorous resistance, managed to establish himself at Quatre-Bras. If the 1st Corps, or one of its divisions, had arrived at this moment the day would have been one of the most glorious to our army; but the conquest which our cavalry had just achieved could not be supported, and the marshal had no reinforcements at his disposal to call upon, for the three divisions of the 2nd Corps were already seriously engaged.

Kellermann himself, writing in the third-person, tells us what he thought about the seemingly suicidal order:[6]

> It was not a time to deliberate the orders: The general rushed as a devoted victim to death at the head of 600 cuirassiers, without giving them time to reconnoitre and calculate the number of enemy troops, he led them headlong into this pit of fire.
>
> The first enemy regiment he met was the 69th Regiment composed of Scots, who made a discharge at thirty paces, but without being stopped, the cuirassiers, lying against their horses, destroyed them completely, and overthrew all that stood in their way. Some even penetrated into the farm of Quatre-Bras and were killed. Lord Wellington had only just had time to jump on a horse and escape this terrible attack.
>
> The charge of the cuirassiers had succeeded against all odds: a large gap had been made, the enemy was shaken, and the British legions were drifting about in the uncertain expectation of what would happen next: the smallest support of the cavalry reserve and slightest movement of the infantry engaged on the right would complete success.

Without 1st Corps, Ney had no infantry reserve with which to support Kellermann. Despite the lack of infantry support, Kellermann's charge was initially spectacularly successful. The cuirassiers charged the square of the 30th Regiment of Foot, as Ensign Macready writes:[7]

> We soon reached Quatre-Bras, and on turning the end of the wood found ourselves bodily in the battle. The roaring of great guns and musketry, the bursting of shells, and shouts of the combatants raised an infernal din, while the squares and lines, the galloping of horses mounted and rider less, the mingled crowds of wounded and fugitives (foreigners), the volumes of smoke and flashing of fire, struck out a scene which accorded admirably with the music.
>
> As we passed a spot where the 44th, old chums of ours in Spain, had suffered considerably, the poor wounded fellows raised themselves up and welcomed us with faint shouts, 'Push on old three tens—pay 'em off for the 44th—you're much wanted, boys—success to you, my darlings.' Here we met our old colonel riding out of the field, shot through the leg; he pointed to it and cried 'They've tickled me again, my boys—now one leg can't laugh at the other.' I saw an officer of the 33rd pass near us. I did not know him personally, but he was a tall, young man and I think named Furlong; he bent forward and seemed hit about the body. Hamilton showed us where our regiment was, and we reached it just as a body of lancers and cuirassiers had enveloped two faces of its square. We formed up to the left and fired away ... On our repulse of the cavalry, a general outside the square (said to be Sir Thomas Picton) thanked us warmly, and some seconds after, in still louder terms, damned us all for making such a noise, and asked if we had no officers amongst us.
>
> We were half a minute in the square laughing and shaking hands with all about us, when we were ordered to pursue and, dashing out, were soon brought up by a line of skirmishers, with whom we kept up a briskish fire. Lockwood, one of our grenadiers, came out with us and dropped with a shot in his head; he was a noble fellow and as he was led by the regiment, he recognised his men and bade God bless them, as he knew they would do their duty. The cannonade and skirmishing was lively on both sides, while the heavy fire from the wood in our rear showed that the Guards and the enemy were hotly disputing it.
>
> On the left of our company were some Hanoverian jägers, one of whom had joined a soldier of ours named Tracy; a skirmisher dashed out from their line to a clump of cover and shot the

German, on which Tracy ran over to him and before he could carry him off, he shot him dead. This enraptured their officers, who loaded us with praises in the gibberish we talked together, such as 'English and Hanover *fielle* good for the *Franceusens—Franceusens a la monde capoote*, etc.' till the advance of the enemy's cavalry obliged us all to retire to our columns. They made a faint charge on our regiment and some others, but being uniformly repulsed retired, and we occupied our former ground. The regiment came down to us, and we descended the slope towards our right in the direction of a ravine, across which, with one of Picton's corps (the Royals, they said), we drove a heavy body of infantry after a severe fire. The enemy were retiring from the wood, and the Guards pressing them very closely. A retrograde movement was perceptible along their whole line, and it was performed in beautiful style. Their columns and skirmishers kept their alignment and distances as if on a parade; the dimness of the evening made the firing doubly vivid, and amid its rattle was occasionally heard the bugles sounding the 'advance and fire'. We had no cavalry to spoil this spectacle.

Standing nearby was the 3rd Battalion of the Royal Scots, as an officer of that battalion writes:[8]

> After being engaged for some time in a line, the battalion was formed into a square to resist the enemy's cavalry, who were then advancing in great force; and I have the pride of stating, that though charged six or seven times by an infinite superiority of numbers, the French cavalry never for an instant made the slightest impression upon the square of the Royal Scots.
>
> The high encomiums given to this battalion on the morning of the 17th, by the general officers both of brigade and division, for its conduct on the 16th, have made me very proud of being a Royal Scot. The cuirassiers never were able to make the smallest impression upon our squares, nor did we lose one single man by the cavalry. We were at the very commencement of the action sent with Sir James Kempt's brigade, by order of Sir T. Picton, and remained apart from our own brigade the whole day. The 42nd and 92nd were chiefly engaged near a village, in which the commander of the forces remained with the headquarters for a great part of the afternoon. Our battalion and the 28th formed one square, and it so happened that the cuirassiers charged that part of the square in which the Royals were posted.

Capture of the British colours
In the audacious attack, the French cuirassiers took two colours that day: one from the 69th Regiment of Foot by the 8th Cuirassiers, and one from the 33rd Regiment of Foot by the 11th Cuirassiers.

The 33rd's colours: lost and recaptured
John White, a historian who has studied the 33rd Regiment of Foot, comments:[9]

> After the 33rd had advanced through the fields west of the Brussels road, it took up a position about 300 metres east of the elbow of the Bossu Wood, on a small hill. In its right front were some Brunswick units (infantry and cavalry) and in its front was a line of French light infantry. Very soon after its arrival, French units of infantry moved in its right front towards the Brunswickers. The 33rd gave a volley and marched up to the French in the direction of the Bossu Wood. The result was that the enemy pulled back. By now, the 33rd had come into a position about 250 metres from the wood and under the heavy fire of some French guns. At the same time, Guiton's cuirassiers approached further to the east. The battalion suffered heavy casualties from the French gunfire and the attempt to form square was very much impaired; to make matters even worse, rumour spread that the cavalry was in the rear of the battalion and it got into disorder for fear of being cut off. As a result, the battalion fled towards the wood, but here it was more or less restored by Sir Colin Halket.

Thain, of the 33rd Regiment of Foot, notes:[10]

> The enemy were making an attempt to turn our right by a wood upon which it was approached. We gave them a most beautiful volley and charged, but they ran faster than our troops could do, we consequently did not touch them with the bayonet; soon after this they brought up five pieces of cannon to bear direct upon us, which did great execution and threw us into a little disorder, upon which a strong column of their cavalry came out from behind a farm where they had been in ambush and charged us. The 30th, 69th and 73rd threw themselves into squares and our regiment was ordered to take advantage of the hedge of the wood, in the rear of which we formed line and kept up an excellent fire, which together with that of our squares made them sheer off, not however before they broke the 69th and took one of their colours.

Lieutenant Pattison, however, is adamant that the 33rd Regiment of Foot stood against the initial charge and retreated into the woods to escape artillery fire:[11]

> I think it must have been between four and five o'clock in the evening that Sir Colin Halket's brigade advanced to that spot which is intersected by four roads, and from which fact the battle derives its name, being Quatre-Bras, or Four-Arms. At this period the Scotch division under Sir Thomas Picton was actively engaged a little in advance on the great road which leads to Charleroi. Immediately on getting there, orders were given for the brigade to move forward to the right, and support the right of Picton's division.
>
> A movement agreeably to this order took place, each regiment advancing in open column of companies, preserving their respective distances, so as to deploy into line when necessary. The ground through which we had to advance was much undulated, and in full crop of rye, which in that rich and luxuriant country grows excessively high, and on this account obstructed observation.
>
> As we advanced, the leading company of our regiment reached a prominent part of the field and observed the French cavalry advancing to the charge. Orders were then given to form square to receive the enemy. The enemy, perceiving we were prepared for them, instead of advancing made a movement to the left, broke in upon the open columns of the 69th Regiment, which being on a low part of the field, had not observed them. The havoc that then took place was very great, and one of their colours, I think the regimental colour, was carried off in triumph.
>
> All this took place with amazing rapidity and despatch, and the 33rd was not left long to contemplate objects with indifference. As I have already observed, we were made aware of the approach of the cavalry and that by the grenadier company, it having reached rising ground and having formed square, upon that company the whole regiment were placed as a beacon in presence of the enemy. Immediately a park of artillery was opened at point-blank distance upon our column. The destruction consequent upon this was fearful. At this time, Captain Hay, having moved from the head of his column to encourage the face of the square fronting the enemy, was cut in two by a cannon ball, and poor Arthur Gore's brains were scattered upon my shako and face.
>
> It was soon found necessary to deliver the regiment from this untoward situation, which was done by deploying into line in an

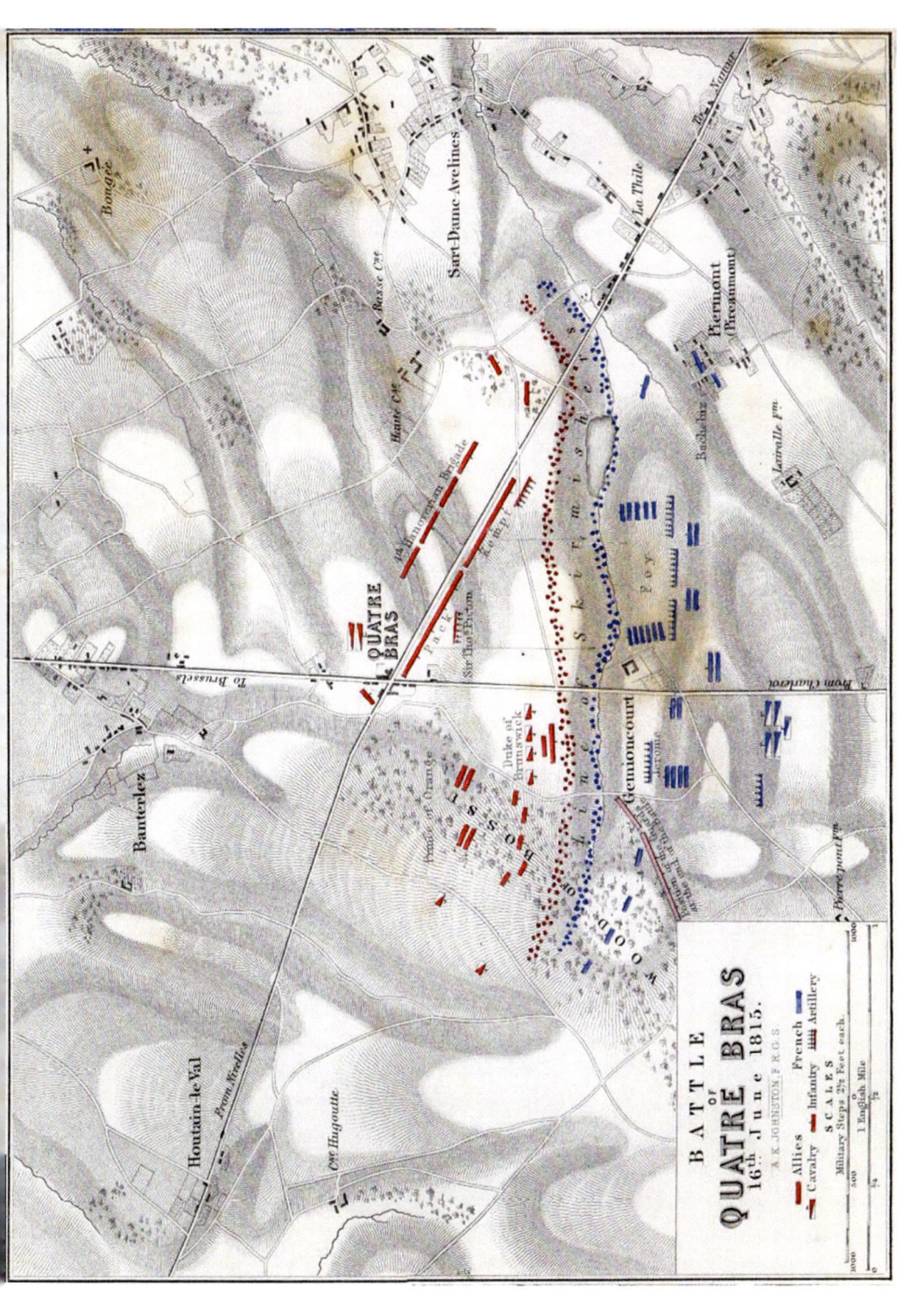

Map of the Battle of Quatre Bras by Siborne. The troop depositions are generally accurate for the start of the battle.

Above: The monument to Belgian soldiers at Quatre-Bras. (© D. Timmermans; napoleon-monuments.eu)

Below left: The monument at Quatre-Bras to the 5th Dutch-Belgian Light Dragoons which was involved in the cavalry action against the French 6th Chasseurs a Cheval and Pire's Lancers. (© D. Timmermans; napoleon-monuments.eu)

Below right: The monument to the fallen soldiers of the British army at Quatre-Bras. (© D. Timmermans; napoleon-monuments.eu)

Above: The monument to the Dutch cavalry that fought at Quatre-Bras. (© D. Timmermans; napoleon-monuments.eu)

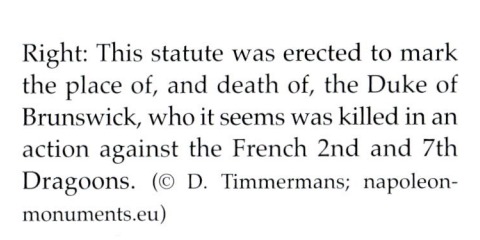

Right: This statute was erected to mark the place of, and death of, the Duke of Brunswick, who it seems was killed in an action against the French 2nd and 7th Dragoons. (© D. Timmermans; napoleon-monuments.eu)

Above: Chantelet farm which was the location of Marshal Ney's headquarters on the night of 17/18 June.

Below: Quatre-bras, the centre of the Allied positons on 16 June. (© D. Timmermans; napoleon-monuments.eu)

Above: The gateway to Gemioncourt Farm. The farm was contested by the Dutch-Belgians and the French under the command of General Bachelu. (© D. Timmermans; napoleon-monuments.eu) Below: The approach to Gemioncourt Farm, showing the unevenness of the terrain, which was to prove a disadvantage for the attacking French. (© D. Timmermans; napoleon-monuments.eu)

Southeast of the extreme southern part of the Bois de Bossu, at about 1,300 and 1,600 metres west of the high road of Brussels respectively, were the farms of Grand and Petit Pierrepont. Both of these farms are in the low ground of the stream of Odomont, which comes up near the farm of Grand Pierrepont and then flows towards Rêves. (© D. Timmermans; napoleon-monuments.eu)

Above: The farm at Quatre-Bras, the centre of the battlefield of 1815, and which is threatened with demolition. (© D. Timmermans; napoleon-monuments.eu)

Above: The Bergerie Farm stands just south of the crossroads and was contested on the 16th by the French and Dutch-Belgian forces. (© D. Timmermans; napoleon-monuments.eu)

Below: Looking north from the crossroads towards Genappe in a print published in 1816.

Above: The bridge and river at Genappe. This bridge was hotly contested on 17 and 19 June. It was a vital river crossing for the attacking and retreating French. (© D. Timmermans; napoleon-monuments.eu)

Left: Monument in the church at Genappe to Major Edward Hodge of the British 7th Hussars who was killed in the action on 17 June. (© D. Timmermans; napoleon-monuments.eu)

angular position. Upon getting into this new position, we were supported on the right by a regiment of Brunswick cavalry, which behaved with great intrepidity. In advance, near the corner of the wood, a regiment or brigade of Brunswick Infantry were fiercely engaged.

At this time the 33rd moved towards them, but upon getting near the wood, a report being spread that the cavalry were in the rear, the regiment entered it and dispersed.

Private William Hemmingway recollects that the men of the 33rd Regiment of Foot in the wood had opened fire against the cuirassiers.[12] The following statement was written about the capture of the colours of the 33rd Regiment of Foot:[13]

> That the French cavalry coming suddenly upon the 33rd at Quatre-Bras, there was no time to form square, and they were ordered to disperse and run into the wood. But they did not all effect this; some were made prisoners, and my informant, along with a young officer, was somehow cut off, and concealing themselves in the corn, they saw the French cavalry returning from the edge of the wood.
>
> The story proceeded as follows: when I looked up, I saw a cuirassier with one of the colours, which he was bringing off. Shouting, I said to Mr— 'We are disgraced forever, for there is our colour, but if you will allow me, I'll fire at that man.' He replied 'It is as much as our lives are worth if you do, but I won't say you will not.' On which I fired, when the Frenchman was very near us: he fell: and I stripped the colour (or cut it) from the staff, gave it to Mr—, and told him to get away with it into the wood, which he reached safely. I reloaded and fired again, but without effect, and was soon surrounded by the French, when I threw down my musket and cried prisoner. They seized my fob, in which I had two *francs*, and one of them cut it off, which I resisted, for which I got some blows with the flat of a sword and was marched off. Amongst other prisoners they got the sergeant-major of our regiment, and we were standing together when the Brunswickers charged.
>
> We took to our heels, ran in among the horses and escaped. When I re-joined without arms and belts, I was questioned, and Mr— having told the commanding officer that a corporal, whose name he did not know, had given him the colour, etc. but that he was killed or taken; the colonel told me that if we both survived he would try and do something for me, and I have now an extra four pence a day for saving the colour.

About the cuirassiers, Morris, of the 73rd Regiment of Foot, later wrote:[14]

> On reaching the town of Nivelles, we were informed of the advance of a large French army, commanded by Napoléon, and that they had been engaged with the Prussians the day before at Ligny; we passed through the town and halted on an extensive common, and could then distinctly hear the sound of artillery. Some commissariat wagons coming up, we received three days' allowance of provisions, consisting of salt beef and ship's biscuit, it being impossible to provide, on the moment, fresh provision for so many.
>
> We were now ordered to fall in and advance, and we soon heard the firing of musketry, as well as artillery. We were urged forward with the utmost celerity and, about three o'clock, entered the field of battle, at Quatre-Bras, notwithstanding our fatigue, having marched about twenty-seven miles exposed to a burning sun. Our brigade at this time consisted of the 30th, 33rd, 69th and 73rd, commanded by Major-General Sir Colin Halket. The ground, for a considerable distance, being covered with rye, and of an extraordinary height, some of it measuring seven feet, prevented us from seeing much of the enemy; but, though we could not see them, they were observing us. We continuing to advance, the glittering of the tops of our bayonets guided towards us a large body of the enemy's cuirassiers, who, coming so unexpectedly upon us, threw us in the utmost confusion. Having no time to form a square, we were compelled to retire, or rather to run, to the wood through which we had advanced; and when we rallied, the 69th unfortunately lost their king's colours.

Clearly, the high corn standing in the fields that day greatly obscured what the Allied infantry could see and had a major impact on the performance of some regiments, as we have seen.

The 69th lose their King's Colour
The capture of the colours of the 69th Regiment of Foot is one of the best-known episodes of the battle. An eyewitness to the events surrounding the capture of the colours was Trumpeter Jean-Baptiste François Charonnet. He was born in January 1797 at Dieppe, the son of Boniface Charonnet and Marie Azire. He was admitted to the regiment as *'enfant de troupe'* on 6 January 1802, upon the death of his father in a military hospital aged just thirty-one. Boniface Charonnet had served in the regiment and at his death his widow requested to Colonel Merlin, the regiment's commanding officer, that his eldest son, then aged eight,

be admitted as *'enfant de troupe'* along with Gille François Charonnet, then aged seven.

Charles Charonnet (aged four), and François Napoléon Charonnet (aged twenty-two months) were also to be admitted to the regiment. Jean-Baptiste Charonnet was made trumpeter on 1 April 1810. Despite his age, just eighteen at Waterloo, he had served in the campaigns of 1808, 1809, 1810, 1811 and 1813 in Germany, and 1814 in France. In 1815, he had the matricule number eleven and served in 2nd Company, 2nd Squadron. Following Waterloo, he passed to the Royal Guard on 29 November 1815.[15] He writes as follows, and adds more detail to Kellermann's own comments, about the cavalry charges:[16]

> The brigade was composed of the 8th and 11th Cuirassiers. General Kellermann prescribed that the 8th were to charge the English squares to open a passage and then move to the right and left to unmask the squadrons of the 11th, which marched in the second line, who charged and pushed back all those in their front.
>
> This provision did not allow the possibility for the cuirassiers to retreat. They charged the English dragoons which advanced upon their head of column, their *élan* was lost and the order was given for the 8th to retire.
>
> The troopers of the 11th who were now in the first line began a new effort, were the first to be turned about: the English dragoons [actually Dutch-Belgian] sabred them: the brigade withdrew in disorder. Kellermann, who was dismounted and without his hat, was in an instant in the middle of the cuirassiers who rescued him.
>
> The trumpeters who were placed close to the standard, and were placed at equal distance from each other, sounded the assembly amidst the dust that enveloped the men. The regiment rallied: the duty trumpeter to Colonel Garavaque was killed and was replaced by Charonnet.
>
> The horses were blown, the officers passed along the ranks, the cuirassiers were able to drink a drop of water and then recommenced the charge.
>
> The colonel and his trumpeter examined the terrain, who then gave the signal for the regiment to advance. Meanwhile he dismounted from his horse, and walked around his horse, checking his girth and curb chain, some gunshots were directed towards him, the balls whistled passed his ears. In a calm voice, he spoke to the little trumpeter, to ask what the English were doing. Charonnet replies 'these are not skirmishers who fire at us, these are *cantinieres*'.

The trumpeter being fifteen years old was not aware of the uniform of the Scottish troops.

The colonel remounted his horse, and remained in the same position to observe the enemy. The regiment approached, the cuirassiers did not let their chief out of their sight and made jokes in lowered voices: he is getting angry they say, look at what this will bring us.

Slowly he put his hand on the hilt of his sword and he quickly drew the bright shining blade. To the soldier this firm movement is a good preparation after a careful reconnaissance. A shiver ran down the ranks as the colonel spoke 'we will charge, we fight and not retreat. Make no cuts with the sabre, only points, aim at their bellies and turn your point for a quarter-round in order to pull the guts out of these buggers.'

They set off at the trot against the corner of a square whose three faces were formed by 4,000 Scottish troops, the fourth side was not yet formed. At the command 'Charge!' the cuirassiers fell on the Scots.

The colonel was eighty paces in front of the regiment; he made his black horse jump and so was the first to make entry into the square. The cuirassiers overthrew the Scots who fled or laid down on the field, and leaning against their horse's necks, the cuirassiers pinned down to the ground those who were trying to avoid their sabres. The horsemen were fighting the entire square, which cut down and completely dispersed the Scots.

In a moment, the enemy line was crossed, the rally was sounded; the 11th Cuirassiers contained the English cavalry [actually the Dutch-Belgians of van Merlen's brigade], the 8th sweep across the field again; the three sides of the square of the 69th were literally marked out by the dead. In the middle of the square, the lieutenant-colonel and the standard-bearer where lying flat to the ground, making no movements, the latter still held the colours in his hand, for which he was killed. Cuirassier Henry jumped to the ground and took up the colour. In order to mount his horse again as quickly as possible, he passed his precious trophy to Corporal Borgnes who was close to him. Borgnes left quickly at the gallop taking the colours with him, followed by the horse of Cuirassier Henry, who had not been able to re-mount his horse due to its irregular movements, being very nervous due to the noise of the battle. Borgnes arrived in front of the regiment, saluted by the cuirassiers with loud cheering.

Charonnet is perfectly correct in his observation that the standard-bearer of the 69th Regiment of Foot was lying on the ground. Mike

Robinson, in his book *The Battle of Quatre-Bras*, notes that the colour party of the 69th was in the centre of the battalion. Ensign Ainslie was carrying the regimental colour; the king's colour being carried by Ensign Keith. The colours were defended by the colour-sergeants and Major Lindsay, who fell wounded alongside Lieutenant Pigot. Ensign Ainslie fell to the ground and his body covered the regimental colour. The king's colour was taken by Cadet Christopher Clarke, who was wounded twenty-three times in endeavouring to save the colour, but he too fell to the ground, the colour being taken from his prone body.[17]

George Barlow, of the 69th Regiment of Foot, recalls the loss of the colours thusly:[18]

> The scene of the action lay upon ground diversified with little dales and gently rising slopes covered throughout with rye and wheat: in the course of manoeuvring, the 69th for a moment found itself at the bottom of one these little dips, and being formed in squares was perfectly secure; a certain personage who shall be nameless sent down the order that the 69th should deploy into line; it was obeyed, and scarcely done when a strong body of French cuirassiers showed themselves close in rear of our flank; we happened to be in a small hollow and the height of the surrounding corn precluded a view of everything beyond the above distances.
>
> The enemy approached close to the regiment unperceived; and rushed out as from an ambuscade on the flank of the line. An attempt was made to form square, but the proximity of the cuirassiers and the instantaneousness of their attack rendered it impossible—in a word they rode through and over our little battalion of 400 men; one colour was taken in the confusion which ensued, the other was preserved; many of our unfortunate men were sabred and wounded, but no prisoners made, as the neighbouring regiment, taking warning from our example, threw themselves into squares before the cuirassiers could reform, they kept up such a terrible fire that the greater part of our gallant enemy perished on the spot.

Lieutenant Pigot, also of the 69th Regiment of Foot, notes:[19]

> I was wounded at the same time as with Major Lindsay: he commanded no. 1 [Company], I commanded no. 2. Poor man, the loss sustained by the grenadiers, nos 1 and 2 Companies was greatly attributed to him, halting those companies, making them face to the right about, in open column and commence firing upon the

cuirassiers. But for that we should have got into square, as it was those companies who were really cut down.

It is hardly surprising that the 69th Regiment of Foot fared badly, as like many in the French, Hanoverian, Prussian and Dutch-Belgian armies, the men had little experience of fighting. Indeed, one historian comments that:[20]

> The 2nd Battalion 69th (South Lincolnshire) Foot was another inexperienced battalion having no Peninsula experience. In all British battalions, it was normal for there to be a small number of men, perhaps a dozen or so, who had joined the ranks underage—that is, under eighteen. However, in the 2nd Battalion 69th Foot the number was 159, nearly 30 per cent of the other ranks. Thus, even amongst those men who had served since 1811 there were many who had not yet reached their twentieth birthday. The average length of service amongst the privates was only three and a half years, less than any other British regiment at Waterloo. Only twenty men had served ten years or more and 44 per cent of all privates had joined in 1813 or later. The average age was twenty-one years old, with over a quarter of the men aged fifteen to nineteen. This cumulative inexperience probably proved fatal to a great number of these young men.

About the charge and the capture of the colour, General Picquet, commanding the 1st Brigade of the 11th Cavalry Division, writes:[21]

> I confirm that the following individuals named below were most distinguished on 16 June, during the charge of the regiment against the square of the English 69th whose colours we took away. The attack cost us the loss of 200 men.
> The Marshal-du-Camp Baron Picquet.
> Captain Bertrand, promoted squadron commander
> Lieutenant Rohas, promoted captain
> Lieutenant Lancesseur, promoted captain
> Sub-Lieutenant Pelle, promoted lieutenant
> Sub-Lieutenant Petit Fils, promoted lieutenant
> Sub-Lieutenant Rigaud, promoted lieutenant
> Sergeant Massiet, promoted sub-lieutenant
> Adjutant Parent, promoted sub-lieutenant
> Captain Bisson, made Officer of the Legion of Honour
> Captain La Fargue, made Officer of the Legion of Honour

Squadron Commander Guillaume, made Officer of the Legion of Honour
Paris, 5 July 1815
Colonel Garavaque

For General Picquet to write the document, and for it to be countersigned by Colonel Garavaque, the document clearly indicates Picquet and his brigade were on the field at this time and witnessed the charge. We do note, however, that the loss of 200 men is much higher than the regiment's muster list presents.[22] No doubt this latter figure includes men who had had their horses killed. Of the men listed, only two mention 16 June on their service papers.

Picquet, for some inexplicable reason, gives Adjutant Parent the rank of sub-lieutenant. Alexis Parent was born 19 November 1776 at Lyon, in the department of the Rhone. He enlisted in the 25th Chasseurs on 20 November 1793, and passed to the chasseurs à cheval of the Consular Guard on 9 November 1799. Allowed leave from 7 September 1802, he was recalled to the 8th Cuirassiers on 14 November 1803. He was promoted to corporal on 15 October 1806, to fourrier on 12 July 1807, sergeant on 21 February 1808 and sergeant-major on 9 August 1809. He was then promoted to sub-lieutenant on 1 June 1812 and following his return from Russia was promoted to lieutenant-adjutant-major on 8 July 1813. He was promoted to captain-adjutant-major on 8 January 1815. He was awarded the Legion of Honour on 28 September 1813, and was discharged from the regiment on 11 December 1815.[23] About Quatre-Bras, he writes:[24]

> I was wounded with a canister shot to my left side on 30 October 1813 at Hanau, and suffered a gunshot to the left leg on 31 March 1814. I suffered a gunshot wound, where a musket ball passed through my upper body, on 16 June 1815 at the Battle of Fleurus.

Louis Bernard Massiet was born on 10 May 1797. He was admitted to the 8th Cuirassiers on 30 September 1811, promoted to corporal on 26 December 1812, corporal-quartermaster on 26 January 1813, sergeant-major on 11 May 1813, and to adjutant-sub-officer on 3 July 1815. Regarding Quatre-Bras, he notes:[25]

> At the affair of 16 June 1815 at Fleurus, I had a horse killed under me charging the English battalion squares, and I took part in the final charge on my third horse.

Massiet retired from the army in 1857 as colonel of the 12th Regiment of Dragoons, and stated he took part in the capture of a colour at Quatre-Bras.[26]

It seems Garavaque had missed some names off the list of men nominated for promotion on the list prepared in 1815, since he writes to Colonel Tancarville, formerly chief-of-staff to the 3rd Cavalry Corps at Waterloo, on 28 October 1818 that:[27]

> My dear colonel,
> I wish to point an error has been made in the names given at the affair on 16th June 1815 at Quatre-Bras. That given by General Berton is Lamy, it should be Henry. This name was given to me during my last visit to Paris with no uncertainty by M. Alix, quartermaster of the 1st Mounted Regiment of the Royal Guard and ex-quartermaster of the 8th.

The M. Alix mentioned by Colonel Garavaque was without doubt Cesar Hector Alix. He was born at Marle on 22 July 1790, and was conscripted to the 8th Cuirassiers on 21 July 1808, promoted to corporal on 12 October 1808, corporal-quartermaster on 15 May 1810, second lieutenant on 12 August 1812 and to lieutenant-quartermaster on 14 April 1813. He was discharged from the regiment on 11 December 1815. As Garavaque states, he served in the Royal Guard, being admitted on 22 April 1818.[28]

Tancarville, writing to Soult on 16 June 1815, notes that the colour was captured by Troopers Henry and Albisson, confirming what Garavaque notes.[29] Pierre Henry was born at Chataillon-les-Sons, in Aisne;[30] Albisson has proven much harder to track down. Charonnet also presents another man as taking the colour—Corporal Borgnes.

Antoine Borgnes was born in 1789 at Mantes, Seine-et-Oise. He joined the regiment on 6 March 1812 and survived the horrors of the Russian campaign before being promoted to corporal in March 1813. Following Waterloo, he was discharged and enlisted in the Mounted Gendarmes of the Seine-et-Oise in 1816, and served until 1823.[31]

It seems, therefore, that the colour of the 69th Regiment of Foot was taken by Cuirassier Pierre Henry, Cuirassier Albisson and Corporal Borgnes, and that a separate colour, perhaps the regimental colour of the 69th, was taken for a short period by Sergeant-Major Massiet. Albisson, Valgayer and Mourassin have been more problematical to track down, and more research is needed on this subject.

End of the charge

Kellermann's attack had been devastating, two colours had been taken and three regiments virtually ridden down. A French eyewitness writes in 1816, perhaps exaggerating the charge, but nonetheless offers a view point from the French contrary to that of General Foy and Kellermann:[32]

> At ten o'clock, the battle began with an attempt by the enemy to take over the farm of Quatre-Bras, whose occupation seemed to be essential for the deployment of their forces. This partial engagement, which lasted nearly three hours, was soon followed by a general engagement. Charges of the French cavalry were crowned with the most brilliant success. The marshal was everywhere and the English were crushed. A body of cuirassiers, after opening a path through enemy squares, penetrated to the farm of Quatre-Bras, which Lord Wellington had established as his headquarters. This bold attempt was admired by both armies and pushed in the English lines so greatly that the cuirassiers returned to their positions without having experienced a loss proportionate to what they had done to the enemy.

The cuirassiers now tried to push through their effort straight on the crossroads of Quatre-Bras. It was now that Ney felt the lack of fresh infantry, as Bourdon de Vatry recalls:[33]

> The position at Quatre-Bras had just been taken by Kellermann's cavalry, Marshal Ney was impatiently awaiting the arrival of d'Erlon's corps, when he learnt that the emperor had altered the course of the direction of march of the corps, and had summoned it to join him at Saint-Amand . . . as the infantry of 1st Corps did not come, since it had been sent to the battlefield of Ligny, the enemy re-occupied the Quatre-Bras position and we were only too happy to prevent the English from going to the aid of the Prussians.

Ney had been expecting 1st Corps, but what arrived instead were two messengers from headquarters, telling him to send 1st Corps to Ligny with all haste. We can only begin to imagine the rage that would have filled Ney at this moment. Kellermann had almost succeeded in taking the crossroads; all that was needed was for the attack to be followed up immediately by infantry. Bachelu and Foy's forces were recovering, licking their wounds from Wellington's devastating attack that had cost them dearly. Without much-needed support, however, the stamina of the cuirassiers soon ran out, and out of desperation he hurled Piré's men forward once again.

Two days later, Ney would do exactly the same thing—hurl squadron after squadron of cavalry at the same target and hope and pray that the cavalry broke through, as with no immediate support Ney bargained that cavalry alone could break out and carry the position. It failed at Quatre-Bras, and Ney knew it, yet he did exactly the same at Waterloo. Lieutenant Henckens, of the 6th Chasseurs à Cheval writes:[34]

> As Ney endeavoured to take control of Quatre-Bras, and the infantry corps of d'Erlon failed him, Kellermann's cuirassiers were charged with this objective, with us in support. The charge of the cuirassiers began at seven o'clock and was admirable, but did not have the success that Ney expected from it: it was taken over by us, with the same courage.

General Delort, writing in 1820, notes (no doubt from tales he had been told of the charge, as he did not witness the charge in person) the following about this attack:[35]

> But soon the fire and deadly ambush of British troops in the Bossu Wood threw disorder into the ranks of the cuirassiers. Their flight, which turned to rout, also led other battalions to rout; the baggage was plundered, and it is not without difficulty that the officers were able to rally their troops shaken by the consequences of this reckless charge that cost the loss of several brave men due to the nature of the terrain, and especially the position the enemy were in.

General Foy caustically notes his thoughts about this charge as follows:[36]

> A Brigade of cuirassiers was ordered to make a feather-brained charge against the infantry, it was repulsed with losses and fled in disorder as far as Frasné, and more than half a league in our rear encountered the artillery reserve which it scattered, and the baggage wagons that were moving up from Gosselies were pillaged and spread terror everywhere.

An eyewitness writes that the fire of the Allied infantry threw back the cuirassiers:[37]

> But these battalions, being supported from behind with the infantry which filled the wood, were enabled to return such a terrible fire

upon us that our cuirassiers, being repelled in their attempt to pierce them, were compelled to make a wheel round; and as always happens in such cases, retired in much disorder. It was in this charge, which, however unfortunate, was executed with the greatest resolution, that a cuirassier of the 11th Regiment took a colour of the English 94th Regiment.

The retrograde movement which was now sensibly beginning, and the multitude of wounded soldiers who threw themselves into the rear, began to excite a manifest terror amongst their comrades. The wagoners, the servants, the attendants of the camp of all kinds, saved themselves with precipitation; and communicating their panic to all they met soon clogged up the road to Charleroi. The rout indeed in this point (Ney's command) was beginning to be complete; everyone was flying in confusion; and the cry of 'the enemy, the enemy' was general.

But the evil was not in fact as great as it appeared, and therefore was repaired. This marshal, the bravest amongst the brave, was not to be daunted or confounded by a slight disaster. General Roussard, with his division of cuirassiers, hastened in a long trot into the front of the English, and reassured the fugitives by his presence, and in good part re-established the battle. Our infantry, taking their position upon the heights of Frasné, were compelled to abandon all purpose of a more forward movement; they confined themselves, therefore, to maintaining this position, and they succeeded in it.

Such was the effect of Napoléon's withdrawing the 1st Corps from Marshal Ney. And the 1st Corps was as useless to the emperor as it would have been effectual to Marshal Ney. It was employed only in marching and in returning.

Without infantry support and facing virtually point-blank artillery, Kellermann's cuirassiers had no option other than to return to the French lines. During the retreat, Kellermann's horse was killed. According to myth, he barely escaped capture by hanging onto a cuirassier's horse. General Kellermann writes about his actions that day as follows:[38]

> Near Frasné, June 16, 1815 10 p.m.
> Sir marshal,
> I executed the charge that you have ordered me to do; I encountered the enemy infantry, posted in a small valley beneath their guns. On the spot, without giving the troops time to think, I rushed at the head of the 1st Squadron of the 8th with Gal Guiton,

against the Anglo-Hanoverian infantry, in spite of the extensive fire from the front and the flanks. Both lines of infantry were knocked over, the greatest disorder was in the enemy line, which we crossed two to three times, the most complete success was ensured [here was added a space line: 'With the results which you was waiting for'], if the lancers would have followed us, the cuirassiers, shot upon from all sides, could not exploit the advantage that they had obtained by this most resolute and fearless charge against an infantry which did not let itself be intimidated, and which they fired with the greatest coolness as if during an exercise.

We took a flag of the 69th which was taken by the Cuirassiers Valgayer and Mourassin. The brigade, having taken an enormous loss and seeing that they were not supported, withdrew in the usual disorder as in similar circumstances, my horse was knocked down by two shots, and I fell under it. I was barely able to escape. The Gal Guiton, the Colonel Gavaraque was unhorsed as well as numerous officers and cuirassiers. I was hurt in the knee and the leg, but nevertheless I shall be there tomorrow on horseback. Roussel's division is bivouacking in the plain close to Frasné, Lhéritier 's division has not joined up, I will try to address orders to him.

I am respectfully
Signed: the Comte de Valmy (Kellermann, the young)

Kellermann's official report to Ney seems to imply that Lhéritier's command was to yet arrive on the field, but Guiton's cuirassiers were under Lhéritier's order, and, as we have already noted, we know that Picquet's dragoon brigade had arrived by the time the charge commenced, along with Picquet himself. So, does Kellermann mean that Guiton's men had yet to re-join Lhéritier and Picquet? Perhaps so. In addition, Kellermann's report does confirm that Donop had arrived, perhaps also with the carabinier brigade. Guiton's losses appear to have been minimal when we consult the regimental muster lists. The 8th Cuirassiers lost the following men in the charge:[39]

	Killed	Died of Wounds	Wounded	Wounded and Prisoner	Prisoner of War	Missing
Total	7	0	0	1	5	2

The 11th Cuirassiers also sustained the following losses among the men during the charge:[40]

Squadron	Company	Killed	Died of Wounds	Wounded and Prisoner	Prisoner of War	Missing
1st	1st	1	0	3	0	4
	5th	0	0	1	0	5
2nd	2nd	2	0	0	0	2
	6th	1	0	0	0	1
3rd	3rd	0	0	0	0	2
	7th	2	0	1	0	3
4th	4th	0	0	0	0	2
	8th	0	0	0	0	4
Total		6	0	5	0	23

For the 3rd Company 2nd Regiment of Horse Artillery, which accompanied, the following casualties occurred:[41]

	Killed	Died of Wounds	Wounded	Wounded and Prisoner	Prisoner of War	Missing
Total	0	1	2	0	0	1

In total forty-nine men were lost at Quatre-Bras from the brigade. The 8th Cuirassiers had lost fifteen men.[42] It is likely the brigade lost a number of horses, but we do not have that data. Picquet gives 200 men lost for the 8th Cuirassiers, so losses to effective strength due to dead or wounded horses could be double or triple the loss of man power. Even so, the loss of forty-nine men does contradict the notion that the regiments were badly mauled.

Histories of the battle, based on the eyewitness testimonies of men who served at Quatre-Bras, state the cuirassiers routed and the two regiments were massacred.

This is clearly not the case, as the brigade sustained very few losses indeed.

The British Guards are scattered

With Kellermann and Piré's men pushed back, Wellington sent forward Maitland's command to clear the Bossu Wood. The British Guards debouched out of the wood, and threatened to overwhelm Ney's left flank. In response, Ney hurled forward the two brigades of Kellermann's corps that had just arrived on the field, and, it seems, the Red Lancers.

Charge of the Red Lancers

Towards evening, the ever-increasing tide of Allied troops had pushed Prince Jérôme's French 6th Infantry Division back to its original positions, south of the Bossu Wood, but not without cost to the Anglo-Dutch. As the 1st (Royal Scots) Regiment of Foot emerged from the wood, they were caught by the lancers of the Imperial Guard. Lieutenant l'Hotte[43] of the lancers recalls:[44]

> During the campaign of 1815, June 16, the day of the Battle of Ligny and Quatre-Bras, an infantry division commanded by King Jérôme, composed of young troops, was surprised at about three o'clock and was completely routed by enemy infantry suddenly bursting out from a wood. My father, whose regiment was placed in reserve between Quatre-Bras and Ligny, is then detached with his platoon to return the fugitives, and found the King Jérôme in the middle of the skirmishers, trying in vain to rally his division. He charges instantly, releasing the king, and with his small detachment, pushes the enemy infantry back in the woods where she was routed. Seven of his brave lancers remained on the field of battle.

The lancers fell on Nassau troops and the 27th Jägers. Another eyewitness was Colonel Baron Pieter Hendrik van Zuijlen van Nyevelt, the chief-of-staff of the 2nd Netherlands Infantry Division, who narrates that:[45]

> The 1st Nassau Battalion was formed in line in front of the wood, the companies of Captain Werneck and Frittler were deployed as tirailleurs. These troops were the object of repeated attacks by the lancers of the Imperial Guard, but led by His Serene Highness himself, they managed to repel these attacks with great composure.

Colonel van Nyevelt continues that:[46]

> The regiment of Red Lancers of the Imperial Guard and the 6th Chasseurs à Cheval engaged the 27th Jäger Battalion before they were formed entirely and broke them. In that action the battalion lost a lot of wounded and prisoners who, however, mostly managed to escape and return during the night. From then on the enemy were in possession of the largest part of the ground stretching in front of the position, directed all his efforts towards the centre and attempted to pierce it by marching on the farm of Quatre-Bras.

Wilhelm Grunsbosch, of the 27th Jäger Battalion, notes that the 1st, 2nd and 6th Companies were deployed in skirmish order to repel an attack by French infantry, leaving the 3rd Company to cover an artillery battery. The French were concealed by a line of hedges. The regiment of light horse lancers of the Imperial Guard caught the 5th and 6th Companies in the open.[47]

The 'Red Lancers' were counter-charged by the Dutch-Belgian 6th Hussars and 5th Light Dragoons. An eyewitness to the events was Count Renesse-Breidach d'Elderen, a former lieutenant with the 5th Belgian Light Dragoons, who recalls what he observed:[48]

> In the meantime, our Dutch hussars had joined the fray with the French cavalry, whom they initially pushed back until they were themselves driven off. Our 1st Squadron was sent to their aid, but this was not strong enough, so the colonel then gave my captain the order to charge with his company. However, when we rode down the slope, the 6th French Chasseurs attacked our left flank; we charged them and drove them off, despite the fact that they numbered 400 men, and our company merely 105 men, but unfortunately we were attacked from behind by the Red Lancers of the Guard, the 1st Chasseurs à Cheval and cuirassiers, and the fight became general. We fought with all our might. Our colonel was severely wounded, as was a captain. I received a blow in my face with the flat of a sabre and was stabbed by a lance through my cloak, which I had fortunately rolled around myself.

During the charge, the Red Lancers had twenty-three men killed or wounded, and fifty-seven horses were killed.[49]

Donop and Picquet

By 20.00, give or take, the cuirassier brigade of General Donop also appears to have arrived. Donop's men appear, along with Picquet's dragoons to have gone into action at the close of the day. In the action that commenced in the late evening, Sub-Lieutenant Victor Baudinet de Courcelles, of the 3rd Cuirassiers, was wounded. He was to make a name for himself at Waterloo, having two horses killed under him and, for his bravery in the battle, was recommended for the Cross of the Legion of Honour immediately after the Battle of Waterloo.[50] Donop's own son, Claude Frederic Donop, was also wounded at Quatre-Bras while acting as aide-de-camp to his father.[51] Late in the evening at Quatre-Bras, with Piré's and Guiton's brigades totally exhausted and licking their wounds, Donop's brigade appears to have been moved onto the field to provide a much needed cavalry screen to allow Ney's infantry divisions to retreat back to Frasné.[52] An officer in the 3rd Battalion 1st Foot Guards recalled Donop's cuirassiers as follows:[53]

> On the evening of the 15th, we heard that the French were passing the frontiers, and we received orders to hold ourselves in readiness to march; at two o'clock we received our orders to march, and were oft' at three. We passed through Braine-le-Comte, and proceeded to a bivouac near Nivelles. While we were setting ourselves down, an order came to move immediately to the left through Nivelles—having passed it, we heard the firing very close, and soon met many wounded Belgians coming in. At five o'clock, General Maitland galloped up, and ordered the grenadiers to drive the French out of a wood, and in about half an hour we perfectly cleared it. When we opened at the end of the wood, the enemy threw in a most tremendous fire of round and grapeshot, from which we found it necessary to retire.
>
> We got out of the wood in another part, and they immediately advanced columns to attack us, which deployed very regularly, and drove us a short way back. However, we advanced again; and they gave way, and retired to their guns. They then advanced upon us, and having driven us back a second time, their cavalry attempted to charge; but a square of Black Brunswickers brought them up, while we were simply slipped into the wood on our right, lined the ditches, and paid them handsomely. Our loss was very severe, and we found great difficulty in forming our line again.
>
> At last we effected it with the 3rd Battalion of our regiment, and then we drove everything before us. We kept possession of the wood all night. The Prussians and French had been engaged from two o'clock in the morning in the position of Fleurus; and the former had been driven back. The French then tried to get possession of the road to Brussels. They had a severe contest with the Dutch, and one of our divisions, and had succeeded in driving the Dutch out of a wood, (Bossu, I think it is called). We arrived at the very moment the French skirmishers were appearing. We dashed in and cut them up properly, though our loss was severe. Out of eighty-four, I had only forty-three left in my company. At night, the remains of the battalion bivouacked at the head of the road, and during the night we received a strong reinforcement. They call this the action of Quatre-Bras (where two highroads cross).

This body of cuirassiers, along with Picquet's dragoons, also seem to have run against the British 1st Regiment of Foot Guards:[54]

> The cuirassiers, scattered all over the field, were cutting at our men here and there; but there were a goodly number that got into the wood notwithstanding ... I have said that the cuirassiers had got in amongst us and as I had got pretty far from the wood before they made their appearance, how I was to get back again was the question. I made for the wood when I saw of batch of them coming to where I was, I threw myself on my face as if I had been shot, running the risk of being trampled by the horse's hooves rather than be cut down with the sword; and by such means I got to the edge of the wood, but the place I came to was a thick, high thorn hedge.
>
> There was no time to be lost as the dragoons were cutting at our men as they were getting through the hedge, and I saw it was either do or die in the proper sense of the word. Regardless of the thorns running into my hand, I put one hand on the top of my firelock and the other on top of the thorns, and gave myself a poise, and over I went, heels overhead. My military hat had kept the thorns from running into my head, but it stuck there and I have never seen it since. I soon got another as there were plenty lying about whose owners did not need them anymore. When we got into the wood we made the cuirassiers pay for their attack. We pelted them through the hedge, and although they were strongly reinforced, they never were able to take the wood again; so, we kept up a hot fire on them till it was dark when it ceased.

Behind the cavalry came French infantry, as an officer in the 1st Foot Guards notes:[55]

> We passed the wood, and found ourselves in the presence of an immense body of French cavalry ready to charge. From the difficulties of the ground, we could not manoeuvre, and retired into the wood; the cavalry charged in after us, did us no harm, and were all cut to pieces; but their light troops advanced in such numbers as to oblige us to evacuate the wood at ten o'clock, after four hours hard fighting, till night closed the business.

The British line of Guards had been broken and the men fled back to the wood. This had been the last major attack by the French forces and it had succeeded in halting the advancing Allied line of infantry.

However, the French cavalry had earned the admiration of at least one British senior officer. Augustus Frazer, a senior artillery officer in the British army, writes on 17 June 1815 as follows about the French cavalry:[56]

> The enemy's lancers and cuirassiers are the finest fellows I ever saw. They made several bold charges, and repeatedly advanced in the very teeth and in the rear of our infantry. They have severely paid for their spirit—most of them are now lying before me. Had we but had a couple of brigades of British cavalry, we should have gained a decided advantage.
>
> We had but one Belgian regiment of hussars and some Brunswick hussars, and both felt their inferiority, and made weak efforts against the enemy's cavalry, who, pursuing them amongst our very infantry, made a mingled mass of the whole. I have never seen a hotter fire than at some times of yesterday, nor seen more of what is called a melee of troops. Our wounded at the close of last night was said by the adjutant-general to be 5,000. Of the killed, I have heard no estimate, but it must be severe. Great part of the action having been fought in standing corn, the dead are not easily discernible, and many of the wounded may never be found. The Duke of Brunswick, I believe, is killed. I saw and spoke to him in the course of the day, but did not see him fall. Of the artillery, I hear of no officers killed.
>
> Rogers's and Lloyd's brigades have suffered much, especially Lloyd's, which was attacked by two brigades of French artillery, concealed in a wood. A French column came out of the wood on their right flank, and attempted to get in their rear, but soon retired from a sharp fire with great loss. The Duke of Wellington ordered some Belgian cavalry to their support. Our infantry behaved most admirably, setting good examples to our Belgian and German allies. Poor Cameron of the 92nd is dangerously, but I hope not mortally, wounded. Blücher fought obstinately, but lost ground; we in consequence retrograde a little. The ammunition carriages of the horse artillery are sent off to the front of Soignes, near Waterloo. Ross and Bean are known to be near Brussels and coming up. The British cavalry have made also very forced marches, and are at this moment in the field. Sir Henry Hardinge has lost his left hand by a cannon-shot. The brunt of the Prussian action was in the road from Namur to Nivelles. The action seems now recommencing—we shall retire to make our communication with Blücher.

Beyond two officers, Donop's brigade recorded no losses on 16 June. The muster list of the 2nd Dragoons for the period 1814 to disbandment in 1815 exists at the French Army Archives at Vincennes. However, the document was damaged in the 1940s, and is not available for researchers to consult until it has been conserved sometime close to 2020. Therefore, we are not able to obtain losses for the regiment at Quatre-Bras. However, one officer was wounded at Fleurus:[57] Joseph Muller, born 18 February 1767, was admitted to the regiment with the rank of corporal on 18 August 1797 from the 19th Cavalry Regiment, into which he was admitted as an *enfant de troupe* on 2 July 1772. Promoted to squadron commander on 9 March 1814, he was wounded at the Battle of Fleurus.

Squadron Commander Dieudonne Rigau, of the 2nd Dragoons, states, however, that the regiment attacked Fleurus.[58] The brigaded 7th Dragoons lost two men wounded in the action at Quatre-Bras,[59] thus it seems that all of Lhéritier's division was in action that day.

Summary
Around 21.00, 1st Corps arrived. By this time the fighting was largely over, bar sporadic clashes of vedettes and pickets. Heymès, aide-de-camp to Marshal Ney, writes:[60]

> General d'Erlon arrived in person around nine o'clock in the evening, having completed his journey and received orders from the marshal. The corps was to take up bivouacs in the rear of Frasné, and was to spend part of the night to march to this location and to establish a rally point.

Marshal Ney continues his narration of the battle as follows:[61]

> Frasné, 16 June, 22.00
>
> Monsieur, I attacked and moved against the English in the positions of Quatre-Bras with the greatest of vigour, but a wrong movement by Comte d'Erlon deprived me of a good victory, for at that moment the 5th and 9th Divisions of General Reille were totally cut up. The 1st Corps marched to Saint-Amand to join the left wing of Your Majesty, but at that critical moment the corps began to retreat to re-join myself, thus not a single man was of use.
>
> The division of Prince Jérôme acted with great valour. His Highness was slightly wounded, so I in reality only had three divisions of infantry, a brigade of cuirassiers and the cavalry of General Piré. The Comte de Valmy performed a very good charge.

> Everyone did their duty except the 1st Corps. The enemy lost a lot of men, for our part we took a cannon and a flag. We have lost perhaps 2,000 men killed and 4,000 wounded.
>
> I have asked the Generals Reille and d'Erlon to submit reports to Your Excellency.

Ten days later, on 26 June 1815, Marshal Ney provided more information:[62]

> On the 16th, I received orders to attack the English in their position at Quatre-Bras. We advanced towards the enemy with an enthusiasm difficult to be described. Nothing resisted our impetuosity. The battle became general, and victory was no longer doubtful, when, at the moment that I intended to order up the 1st Corps of infantry, which had been left by me in reserve at Frasné, I learned that the emperor had disposed of it without advising me of the circumstance, as well as of the division of Girard of the 2nd Corps, on purpose to direct them upon St-Amand, and to strengthen his left wing, which was vigorously engaged with the Prussians. The shock which this intelligence gave me confounded me.
>
> Having no longer under me more than three divisions, instead of the eight upon which I calculated, I was obliged to renounce the hopes of victory; and in spite of all my efforts, in spite of the intrepidity and devotion of my troops, my utmost efforts after that could only maintain me in my position till the close of the day. About nine o'clock, the 1st Corps was sent to me by the emperor, to whom it had been of no service. Thus 25,000 to 30,000 men were, I may say, paralysed, and were idly paraded during the whole of the battle from the right to the left, and the left to the right, without firing a shot.

Ney, in the second letter, quite correctly blames the outcome of a stalemate due to having less than half of his troop allocation with him. General Reille, commanding 2nd Corps, describes the battle as he witnessed it on 17 June 1815:[63]

> In accordance to Your Excellency's orders yesterday, I ordered my army corps to quit their camps and to move on the road to Gosselies, and to be in positions at Trois-Bras and at Genappe, the light cavalry divisions and the 5th Division of infantry which were stationed at Mellet arrived in front of Frasné, in front of the enemy which had occupied the Bossu Wood and Trois-Bras. Your Excellency at two

o'clock ordered, as soon as the 9th Infantry Division were within range to support them, I gave the order for them to quit the wood and conquer the position of Trois-Bras.

This movement was supported by artillery, the two divisions of infantry and a division of cavalry and was executed in good order despite the difficult terrain. The 5th Division of infantry was formed in column by battalion and marched against Gémioncourt with the 1st Brigade of the 9th Division and captured the farm. The 5th Division then crossed the ravine and marched to the position of Trois-Bras, with great unity, and they came under the fire of a line of sharpshooters supported by artillery. They gained the plateau but could not resist the fire from a line of enemy Infantry.

The English and Scottish infantry forced them to retreat back to the ravine. General Foy deployed the 100th Regiment of Line in the rear of the advanced post of Gémioncourt and the good conduct of the corps protected the retrograde movement and inflicted heavy losses. General Jamin deployed the 4th Light Infantry to secure the great road in front of Gémioncourt. General Bachelu with Generals Campi and Husson marched to the plateau where the 108th Regiment of Line remained for a long time in the best order. An English officer was made prisoner and told us that 15,000 troops had been ordered to quit Brussels at three o'clock in the morning, and had arrived at two o'clock in the evening to join the attack with Lord Wellington.

General Piré debouched on the right, where the terrain was very difficult for his horses, and he arrived at the left of the 6th Division. These two divisions acted under Your Excellency's immediate orders. He will send his report directly to the general commanding.

Our attack on the left flank of the enemy was pushed back, and we suffered from then until night from the fire of sharpshooters all along our front line. Our artillery caused considerable losses to the enemy who wanted to gain the Namur road. We remained in contact with the emperor via the farm of Pirémont.

This day cost the enemy a lot of men. His losses were certainly greater than ours. Ours number about [illegible] killed, of whom [illegible] were officers, [illegible] were wounded of whom [illegible] were officers. If the troops employed in attacking this position did not succeed, it was because the enemy's forces was three time stronger than ours. I only have praise for the manner in which Generals Bachelu, Foy and Lacroix, the chief-of-staff, as well as various marshals-du-camp, who commanded the troops, acted under my direct command. A cannon and howitzer were taken by the 72nd Regiment of Line and the 4th Light Infantry. A colour was also captured by that regiment, but the man who carried it off was killed and it was retaken.

Your Excellency, you observed the deeds of the 6th Division commanded by Prince Jérôme and the cavalry of General Piré. I will send a detailed list of all the officers and soldiers who have particularly distinguished themselves and have the right, therefore, to promotion or decoration.

After ten hours of fighting, Ney had held off a superior force. From the French perspective, after the first well co-ordinated attack, the French offensive broke down, with haphazard attacks to meet new situations as they arose. Indeed, Pierre de Witt notes 'the Anglo-Netherlands-German superiority as such cannot be disconnected from the way the French staff handled the action: both are inseparable'.[64]

Marshal Ney had fought to a bloody standstill, but he was faced with more than double the number of troops and it does both him and Reille credit that they had held back the Allies.

The main problem for Ney at Quatre-Bras must have been that he had no idea about was happening behind Bossu and Delhutte Woods. The heavily wooded terrain, as Jeanin had pointed out earlier in the day to the emperor, made assessing the number of Allied troops and their location virtually impossible. The field of Quatre-Bras also played its part in the outcome of the battle in another way: the high crops, standing well over six feet high according to some eyewitnesses, made it impossible for infantry and foot artillery to see what was going on around them with any degree of clarity. Furthermore, the high crops would have slowed the advance of infantry and cavalry which had to push their way through, and even mounted officers, just as Jeanin reported, would have found it difficult to judge the strength of enemy forces which might be facing them. The high crops resulted directly in the 69th Regiment of Foot losing a colour. If the terrain hindered the French assessing the forces at Quatre-Bras, it also hindered the Allies. It seems Wellington clearly was not aware that by late afternoon he greatly outnumbered Ney, as at no stage did he ever commit his forces en masse, press home his advantage and crush Ney.

Perponcher had chosen his terrain well. Ney, despite Tancarville's information about a column heading from Mons, and the emperor's concern about a column coming from Brussels, had no exact idea on where or when they would arrive. He perhaps guessed that the British had come from Brussels, but what of the column from Mons? This is why the 1st Hussars were detached towards Nivelles, and Colbert was somewhere on the Brussels road between Quatre-Bras and Ligny. Despite losing the initiative, and spending the period between 4.00 and 11.00 inactive, Ney had prevented the overwhelming Allied forces from crushing his own.

Total losses sustained by Reille's 2nd Corps in the battle are presented below:

2nd Corps

	Wounded	Wounded and Prisoner	Prisoner of War	Killed	Missing (Presumed Prisoner)	Total
5th Division	370	0	75	46	19	510
6th Division	291	17	12	48	102	426
9th Division	524	0	45	54	83	706
Total	1,185	17	132	148	204	1,642

In total, 2nd Corps lost 1,642 men at Quatre-Bras. However, it seems two brigades, for whatever reason, were not in action. Only the 2nd Brigade of 5th Division was involved in any serious fighting, and sustained the heaviest losses overall. The corps had mustered over 18,400 men on 10 June, and so this loss represents 8.9 per cent of effective strength, and giving the corps 16,758 under arms on the morning of 18 June 1815. Scott Bowden, in his study of the campaign, states the losses of 2nd Corps at Quatre-Bras were no more than 800. Clearly, he is mistaken in this figure, for which he gives no source citation.[65] In comparison, Bijlandt's 1st Dutch-Belgian Brigade began the battle with 3,233 men, of which 420 were killed or wounded on the 16th, and 265 were reported missing—a total of 685 men. The brigade suffered comparable losses to the French 9th Division. General Pack's 9th British Brigade started the day with 2,173 men, and lost 957 dead, wounded and missing. General Kempt's 8th British Brigade mustered 2,471 men on the 16th and lost 639 men.

The Brunswick contingent lost 104 men killed and 505 wounded—some 609 losses in rank and file. These four Allied brigades lost a total of 2,890 men. The 2nd Nassau Regiment lost fourteen other ranks wounded and ninety-one killed. Thus, a partial Allied loss is some 2,995 men, almost double the casualties that the French suffered (discounting the cavalry). A number of writers present Quatre-Bras as a struggle of a valiant little band of redcoats against overwhelming numbers of French. This is simply not the case. The Allied army outnumbered the French, the Allies had on the field some 38,438 officers and men present by the evening of 16 June, compared to Ney's 18,400—Ney was outnumbered almost two-to-one. Despite his cautious approach, Ney had held off a far superior force. He could have been swept aside by Wellington, but for whatever reason, Wellington chose not to launch a large-scale assault against the French.

NOTES:

[1] Berton, p. 15.
[2] Anon, *The Journal of the Three Days of the Battle of Waterloo*, T. Chaplin, London, 1816, pp. 30-2.
[3] SHDDT: MR 7178, *Observations sur la Campagne du 1815*.
[4] Marguerite, *Fastes militaires de la France*, Paris, 1836, pp. 260-2.
[5] Heymès, p. 16
[6] SHDDT: MR 7178, Kellermann *Observations sur la Campagne du 1815*.
[7] Ensign E. Macready in *United Service Magazine*, Part I, 1845, p. 390.
[8] Booth, p. 52.
[9] John White, perssonal communication 28 June 2012.
[10] John White, perssonal communication 28 June 2012.
[11] Siborne, *Waterloo Letters*, No. 142.
[12] John White, perssonal communication 28 June 2012.
[13] *United Services Journal*, vol. II, 1834, p. 450. See also: *United Services Journal*, June 1845, pp. 292-3.
[14] Thomas Morris, *Recollections of Military Service in 1813, 1814 & 1815, through Germany, Holland and France*, J. Madden, London, 1845, pp. 196-200.
[15] SHDDT: GR 24 YC 50, *8e cuirassiers 1814-20 Juin 1815*.
[16] Marie François Joseph Raoul d'Amonville, *Les Cuirasiers du roy, le 8e cuirassiers*, A. Lahure, Paris, 1892, pp. 241-2.
[17] Mike Robinson, *The Battle of Quatre Bras 1815*, The History Press, 2010, pp. 314-5.
[18] John Franklin, perssonal communication 28 June 2012.
[19] Siborne, *Waterloo Letters*, No. 143.
[20] Martin Aaron, *2nd Battalion 69th (South Lincolnshire) Foot during the Waterloo Campaign*, The Napoleon Series, October 2007, available at http://www.napoleon-series.org/military/organization/Britain/Infantry/c_2-69Waterloo.html [accessed 22 August 2012].
[21] SHDDT: Xc 108 *8e Cuirasisers, Dossier 1815*, Lettre Colonel Garavaque, 5 Juillet 1815.
[22] SHDDT: GR 24 YC 50, *8e cuirassiers 1814-20 Juin 1815*.
[23] AN: LH/2050/6.
[24] AN: LH/2050/6.
[25] AN: LH/17779/48.
[26] AN: LH/17779/48.
[27] SHDDT: GB/2 2760, file Garavaque. See also: d'Amonville, p. 242.
[28] AN: LH/19/93.
[29] SHDDT: Succession de Tancarville.
[30] SHDDT: GR 24 YC 50, *8e cuirassiers 1814-20 Juin 1815*.
[31] SHDDT: GR 24 YC 50, *8e cuirassiers 1814-20 Juin 1815*.
[32] Raymond Balthasar Maiseau, *Vie du maréchal Ney, duc d'Elchingen, Prince de la Moskowa*, Chez Pillet, Paris, 1816, pp. 164-5.
[33] Grouchy, *Mémoires du maréchal de Grouchy*, pp. 99-102.
[34] Henckens.
[35] Delort, 'Notice sur la batailles de Fleurus et de Mont Saint Jean' in *Revue Hebdomadaire*, June 1896, p. 369.
[36] de l'Ain, p. 272.
[37] Anon, *The Journal of the Three Days of the Battle of Waterloo*, pp. 30-2.
[38] SHDDT: C15 6 *Correspondence Armée du Nord 22 Juin au 3 Juillet 1815, Dossier 16 Juin*, Kellermann to Ney.

[39] SHDDT: GR 24 YC 50.
[40] SHDDT: GR 24 YC 64.
[41] SHDDT: GR 25 YC 27, *2e artillerie à cheval Pluvose AnXI à 1815.*
[42] SHDDT: GR 24 YC 50.
[43] Joseph Louis Nicolas l'Hotte was born on 13April 1786 at Phlasbourg, Moselle. He entered the 2nd Regiment of Carabiniers on 24 September 1803. He was promoted to corporal following the Battle of Jena on 4 December 1806; promotion to sergeant followed on 21 May 1807. He passed as a sergeant to the 13th Cuirassiers (then being formed in Spain) on 21 October 1807. He entered the 8th Cuirassiers on 6 March 1811, and then (as second lieutenant) in the Grenadiers à Cheval on 9 February 1813. Following the Russian campaign, he served in 9th Company, which was part of 3rd Squadron. With the fall of Napoléon, he was taken into the Royal Corps of Cuirassiers of France on 23 July 1814, but was passed to the Royal Corps of Light Horse Lancers of France on 10 August 1814. He was admitted into the Regiment of Light Horse Lancers of the Guard on 14 April 1815. At Waterloo, he was wounded with a sabre-cut to his upper lip. He was dismissed from the regiment on 15 November 1815.
[44] General l'Hotte, *Souvenirs du Général l'Hotte*, 1925.
[45] Franklin, *Waterloo Netherlands Correspondence* (vol. 1), p. 47.
[46] Franklin, *Waterloo Netherlands Correspondence* (vol. 1), p. 48.
[47] Franklin, *Waterloo Netherlands Correspondence* (vol. 1), p. 70.
[48] Franklin, *Waterloo Netherlands Correspondence* (vol. 1), p. 108.
[49] SHDDT: GR 20 YC 166 *Régiment de chevau-légers lanciers, crée par décret du 8 avril 1815 et formé de l'ex-corps royal des lanciers de France, 8 avril 1815-22 décembre 1815 (matricules: 1 à 1,608).*
[50] AN: LH/140/81.
[51] AN: LH/790/21.
[52] Ian Smith, perssonal communication 15 July 2012.
[53] Booth, pp. lvii-lxi.
[54] *Glasgow Herald*, 19 June 1867.
[55] Author's collection.
[56] Booth, p. 33.
[57] SHDDT: 2 YB 138 *Contrôle Nominatif Officer 1ere regiment du Roi 21 Juin 1814 à 1 Septembre 1815.*
[58] Rigau, *Souvenirs des guerres de l'empire, réflexions, pensées, maximes, anecdotes, lettres diverses, testament philosophique*, A. Poilleux, Paris, 1846, pp. 108-17.
[59] GR 24 YC 158.
[60] Heymès, p. 11.
[61] SHDDT: C15 5, *dossier 16 Juin 1815*. Ney to Soult timed at 22.00. Copy of the now lost original document made on 7 April 1906.
[62] Christopher Kelly, *A Full and Circumstantial Account Of The Memorable Battle of Waterloo*, London, 1836.
[63] SHDDT: C15 22, p. 278. See also: SHDDT: C15 5, *dossier 17 Juin*. Reille to Soult.
[64] Pierre de Witt, perssonal communication citing www.waterloo-campaign.nl
[65] Scott Bowden, *Armies at Waterloo*, Empire Game Press, 1983, p. 103.

Chapter 8

Movement of 1st Corps

A well-known episode of the Battle of Quatre-Bras is the perambulation of General d'Erlon with 1st Corps along the roman road linking Gosselies with Sombreffe. Indeed, the Waterloo myth suggests that d'Erlon's 1st Corps did not take part in any fighting on 16 June, and spent the day uselessly marching between two battlefields. However, 1st Corps was in action on both battlefields, admittedly after much time-wasting. When faced with an impossible task to perform, d'Erlon divided his command, leaving his cavalry and an Infantry division at Ligny, and employed his three remaining divisions at Quatre-Bras to replace the advanced posts of 2nd Corps in the evening of the 16th.

Jean-Baptiste Drouet, born in Rheims on 29 July 1765, began his military career on 21 October 1782 with the Regiment Beaujolais. He was a capable, but not outstanding, general, but did rise to the rank of marshal. His chief-of-staff was General-de-Brigade Victor-Joseph Delcambre, Baron de Champvert.

The story goes that at about 17.00, d'Erlon got an order to march to Ligny and was then ordered to Quatre-Bras, and lastly back to Ligny. The story does not stand up to much scrutiny. Archive documents tell us that at 11.00, d'Erlon was ordered from Gosselies to Quatre-Bras, and that sometime between 16.15 and 16.45 that Delcambre had ridden ahead of Durutte's division, which formed the head of column, with the intention to meet Ney at Frasné, and inform him of the imminent arrival of 1st Corps.[1] However, before reaching Ney, d'Erlon was handed an order sent by the emperor. It was this order that sent d'Erlon to Ligny.[2] The 'who did what, why and when' is one of the great controversies of the campaign.

A number of historians like William Siborne,[3] Jean-Baptiste Charras,[4] George Hooper[5] and others all make cogent arguments that the order was carried by La Bédoyère from the emperor. The order was supposedly preserved by General-of-Artillery de la Salle. Historian Stephen Millar presents the argument that the order was a forgery made by La Bédoyère based on no shred of evidence whatsoever, thus no document could ever be found. No motivation for this act is given; this is very much pseudo-history of the worst kind.[6] However, none of these historians question the testimony of de la Salle writing decades after the event. This is a major flaw in understanding the events that took place that day. The order is said to have been:[7]

> In front of Fleurus
> Mister the Comte d'Erlon,
>   The enemy lowers his head into the trap that I intended for him. Bring at once your four divisions of infantry, your division of cavalry, all your artillery, and two divisions of heavy cavalry which I place at your disposal, carry you, say I, with all these forces the height of Saint-Amand and melt on Ligny Mister the Comte d'Erlon, you will save France and will cover yourself with glory.
>   Napoléon

The order that exists is a copy made in 1896.[8] The document de la Salle presented to the world in 1896 is now lost, so we cannot judge its authenticity. But other means of judging if the order really dates from 16 June 1815 are available to us.

Definitive proof that this order is not original can be found in the official correspondence of the French headquarters issued by Soult on 16 June; the order books list no direct order to d'Erlon. Napoléon's orders to Ney timed at 14.00 and 15.15 to 15.30, as well as a copy of the order to Lobau timed at 15.30 to march to Fleurus can be found within their pages.[9] Is this therefore case closed and proof that the 15.45 order is fake? We need to ask, though, was it possible that a key order to d'Erlon was omitted from the register as it was not sent via Soult? The answer is yes, as the emperor (as we have seen earlier) sent an order to Ney via Flahaut and not by the usual chain of command via Soult. Therefore, the fact that the order is not found within the register is not positive proof that it did not ever exist. But, if such an important order had existed, it would have made no sense, as it would have merely repeated the 15.30 order that Ney was to move to Ligny.

On balance of evidence, no order (timed at 15.45) ever existed ordering d'Erlon to Ligny; nor was there, in reality, any need for such an order.

It is highly likely however, and a point totally missed by writers who worked after the supposed order to d'Erlon was published in 1896, that the courier sending the 15.30 order to Ney would have encountered d'Erlon on his line of movement from Ligny to Quatre-Bras, before arriving with Ney. This is the line that Houssaye took, and with whom I totally agree. Thus, the courier could have passed the written order to d'Erlon before arriving with Ney. We know from Reille's own letter of around 10.30 on 16 June, cited earlier, that Flahaut carrying the order from the emperor to Ney had passed the order to Reille first. Thus, the scenario of this chain of events is backed up by known modus operandi of the French headquarters staff from indisputably authentic documents written on 16 June 1815.

It seems that the courier passed the order to d'Erlon and no doubt passed on verbal instructions about the importance of his move to Ligny. This is where the emperor's plans started to go wrong. Without acting on orders from his commander-in-chief (Ney), d'Erlon took it upon himself to move towards Napoléon, as this is exactly what the order said. General d'Erlon no doubt took the view that the order from the emperor was a direct order, and thus did not have to wait for Ney's instructions, given the emperor's orders were superior to those of Ney. The letter reads:[10]

> In front of Fleurus, June 16, between 15.15 and 15.30.
> Mister the marshal,
>   I wrote to you, one hour ago, that the emperor would make an attack on the enemy at half-past two in the position which it took between the villages of Saint-Amand and Brye; at this moment, the engagement is very marked. S. M. [His Majesty] gives me the responsibility to say to you that you must manoeuvre at once so as to envelop the right of the enemy and fall quickly on his rear; this army is lost if you act vigorously; the fate of France is in your hands. Thus, do not hesitate a moment to make the movement which the emperor orders you and directs you on the heights of Brye and Saint-Amand to contribute to a perhaps decisive victory. The enemy is taken in the act at the time when it seeks to unite with the English.
>   The marshal of empire, major-general,
>   Duc de Dalmatie.

Soult's own aide-de-camp, Baudus, adds more insight about the dispatch of the order to Ney:[11]

> At the moment when the affair was engaged all along the line, Napoléon came to me and said 'I have sent Comte d'Erlon the order to move with his entire corps on to the rear of the Prussian army's

right; you go and take a duplicate of this order to Marshal Ney which has to be communicated to him that whatever the situation he is facing it is of the greatest importance that this order is executed, that I attach no great importance to what happens to his flank today; the key is where I am, because I need to finish the Prussian army. As for him, he should, if he cannot do better, be content with containing the English army'.

About the episode of receiving the order, d'Erlon writes nearly fifteen years later that:[12]

> Towards eleven o'clock or midday, Marshal Ney sent me orders for my corps to take up arms and move towards Frasné and Quatre-Bras, where I would receive subsequent orders. My corps set off immediately, after giving the general commanding the head of column the order to move quickly. I went ahead to Quatre-Bras to see where Reille's corps was engaged.
>
> Beyond Frasné, I halted with the generals from the Guard,[13] where I was joined by General de La Bédoyère, who showed me a note in pencil which he carried to Marshal Ney, which ordered the marshal to send my corps to Ligny. General de La Bédoyère warned me that he had already given the order for this movement and the head of column had changed its direction, and he indicated to me where I could join it. I immediately took this route and sent my chief-of-staff, Delcambre, to the marshal, to warn him of the change of destination.

With clear written orders, and no doubt verbal instruction, d'Erlon headed off to Ligny and probably sent a written and verbal dispatch to Ney, via Delcambre, to inform him of his movements. For d'Erlon there was no ambiguity in the order—Ney was to hold the Allied troops in check and to wheel around towards Ligny. Ney, however, took a markedly different view.

But who did General d'Erlon meet? Soult states the order was carried by Captain Laurent, as does Ney's aide-de-camp, Heymès. Captain Chapuis, of the 85th Regiment of Line Infantry also claims Laurent carried the order,[14] as does General-de-Brigade Brue.[15] Case closed? Not really, as Colonel Forbin-Janson, an officer on the headquarters staff, claims it was he who took the order to Ney. In reading his two accounts, it becomes very clear that Forbin-Janson was sent to Ney only after two previous couriers had been sent carrying orders to him to bring d'Erlon to Ligny, and at the moment when French superiority at Ligny became apparent. He gives no time, but we suppose before the Old Guard and Milhaud's cuirassiers went into action arguably sometime around 18.00, as he arrived with Ney as Kellermann's cuirassiers were retreating around 19.00. A maximum of an hour to travel from the emperor's headquarters to Ney seems reasonable, a distance of less than ten miles on good roads if he passed from Fleurus, and thence along the rue Fleurus through Mellet, and then north up the Brussels road. Having passed on the order, Forbin-Janson tells us that for a period of roughly two and a half hours he remained with Ney. He then notes that Ney ordered him to take a British staff-officer who was made prisoner of war to Napoléon. This would make it about 21.30. Upon returning to Fleurus, he states he was sent back to Ney carrying a duplicate copy of the 15.30 order.[16] The name of the British prisoner of war has eluded identification by the author. No other eyewitness verifies this claim.

The timeline given by Forbin-Janson makes no sense tactically speaking, as by 22.00 to 22.30 the battle was over, and it means that the order he carried was of no use at all when he arrived, perhaps at midnight. But an eyewitness places Forbin-Janson arriving late at night at Quatre-Bras. Bourdon de Vatry, aide-de-camp to Prince Jérôme, says that Forbin-Janson did indeed arrive at night, once the battle had ended, and confirms that Forbin-Janson had been sent by Napoléon to get d'Erlon back to Ligny, and that he carried with him a copy of the 15.30 order. Indeed, to confirm this de Vatry presents a full transcript of the 15.30 order:[17]

> The marshal invited Jérôme to supper. The table was laid on a plank, supported on empty barrels and lit by candles stuck into bottlenecks.
>
> Night had fallen. We were just beginning our frugal meal when Comte de Forbin-Janson was brought into Ney with an order from the emperor to march on Brye. Here is the text of this order by the chief-of-staff:
>
> 'In front of Fleurus, June 16, at quarter-past three
>
> Mister the marshal,
>
> I wrote to you, one hour ago, that the emperor would make an attack on the enemy at half-past two in the position which it took between the villages of Saint-Amand and Brye; at this moment, the engagement is very marked. S. M. [His Majesty] commands me to say to you that you must manoeuvre immediately, so as to envelop the right of the enemy and fall quickly on his rear; this army is lost if you act vigorously; the fate of France is in your hands. Thus, do not hesitate a moment to make the movement which the emperor orders you and directs you on the heights of Brye and Saint-Amand

to contribute to a perhaps decisive victory. The enemy has been caught *en flagrant delit* at the time when it seeks to unite with the English.'

When Monsieur Forbin-Janson arrived, it was already dark; we were eating by candlelight. It was too late to carry out the movement indicated, and moreover 1st Corps had not yet been united. If we took one pace to the rear to support the right wing of Napoléon's army, the English troops who were posted at Quatre-Bras in considerable strength, and whom Ney, the Prince of the Moskowa, had contained, and with prodigies of valour had prevented them from aiding the Prussians, would have been on the heels on the weak corps of Reille and Kellermann.

Another eyewitness, who did not see the events as they unfolded before him, but as he is writing soon after the battle seems to have had access to men who did see Forbin-Janson, was Jean Baptiste Berton. He was a general-de-brigade commanding the 14th and 17th Dragoons, under the orders of General Chastel, whose division formed part of Excelmans's 2nd Cavalry Corps. Berton comments as follows:[18]

> Orders were sent to the left wing, and as instructed, the commander of the 1st Infantry Corps, in reserve behind Frasné to move towards Villers-Perwin, and was already quite close to the village of Brye, when he received several orders to return to the left, which he unfortunately obeyed and fell back. A sergeant of the *gendarmerie d'elite* was sent with new orders that were dispatched for the second or third time to the left wing, the same as the first, and acted as a guide to Colonel Forbin-Janson, who was responsible for carrying the order. So, that he could get there sooner, we gave him a fresh horse.

Prefect Charles Gamot, writing in 1819, states Forbin-Janson arrived with Ney at 18.00, and carried the following order:[19]

> In advance of Fleurus, 16th June, 1815. A quarter-past three o'clock.
> M. the marshal,
> I wrote to you an hour ago, to tell you that the enemy were to be attacked by the emperor at half-past two, in the position which he has occupied between St-Amand and Brye. At this moment, the engagement has assumed a determined character. His Majesty charges me to tell you that you must manoeuvre instantly, so as to surround the right of the enemy, and to fall on his rear. This part of

their force is lost if you act vigorously: the fate of France is in your hands: hesitate not a moment, therefore, to make the movement which the emperor orders, and direct your force on the heights of Brye and St-Amand, to co-operate, in all probability, in a decisive victory. The enemy will be taken in the toils at the moment that he seeks to unite his force with the English.

Signed, the major-general,
Duc de Dalmatie.

So, it seems Soult had acted wisely in sending off two couriers—Laurent and Forbin-Janson—each with copies of the same order to make sure it arrived with Ney. Soult had actually sent off three couriers; d'Erlon himself says he encountered de La Bédoyère with the order (something that Forbin-Janson confirms) and states that de La Bédoyère did indeed carry the first order (to send d'Erlon to Ligny) to Ney.[20]

So, we have orders going to Ney, sent by Laurent, de La Bédoyère and Forbin-Janson, and yet Ney never seems to have got the message that d'Erlon was to go to Ligny. Ney was being rather truculent and, perhaps in desperation at the non-arrival of d'Erlon, Soult sent his own aide-de-camp, Battalion Commander Baudus, to explain the situation to Ney![21] If all four men did take orders to Ney, he must have been in no doubt as to where the true destination of 1st Corps was to be. Baudus and Forbin-Janson both state they met the cuirassiers of Guiton streaming back from Quatre-Bras.

This would have been after 19.00 and by that time the delivery of the order they would have carried would have been of no use. Neither officer mentions the other, which seems a little odd as both men were with Ney at roughly the same time, and should have encountered one another, or even travelled together. The similarity between the two accounts is striking, one cannot help but wonder if one copied the other. Despite the problems with Baudus's account, it cannot be fully ruled out that both men were involved in missions from Imperial Headquarters to Ney. Did Baudus and Laurent take the 15.30 order along with de La Bédoyère and Forbin-Janson take a verbal order to bring d'Erlon back to Ligny? Perhaps, but we cannot be certain. The possibility exists that to ensure the order got to Ney, Soult dispatched Laurent, Forbin-Janson, Baudus and de La Bédoyère! Forbin-Janson says two orders were sent to Ney, the first carried by Laurent and then a second copy sent by de La Bédoyère fifteen minutes later, before he himself was dispatched.[22] Sending multiple copies of the 15.30 order makes perfect sense, as it ensured that a least one copy would have got through to Ney.

Into this melting pot of claim and counter-claim about who did what, why and when, history tells us that contrary to the emperor's orders, d'Erlon moved some of his corps to Quatre-Bras. But upon whose authority did he do so? Napoléon's orders and instructions would overrule all others, which, as we noted earlier, should be kept in mind on this particular subject. For d'Erlon to move towards Frasné would have been in blunt contradiction to his imperial orders. Marshal Ney himself states d'Erlon made a wrong movement:[23]

> The 1st Corps marched to Saint-Amand to join the left wing of Your Majesty, but at that critical moment the corps began to retreat to rejoin myself, thus not a single man was of use.

But was the 'wrong movement' heading to Ligny? Ney implies to some degree that it was, and that it robbed him of victory at Quatre-Bras. Ney, however, is totally silent about recalling 1st Corps and who sent the order. About this incorrect movement, Napoléon wrote the following dispatch to Ney on 16 June:[24]

If the Comte d'Erlon had carried out the movement to Saint-Amand as the emperor ordered, the Prussian army would have been totally destroyed, and we would perhaps have had 30,000 prisoners. The corps of Generals Vandamme and Gérard and also the Imperial Guard were always united; we are exposed to setbacks when detachments are compromised.

For the emperor, d'Erlon had not obeyed his orders by returning to Quatre-Bras and, therefore, for him to say this means that he cannot possibly have sent an order to d'Erlon to go back to Quatre-Bras. The finger of blame must rest on Ney. The next eyewitness writing in the immediate few hours after the blunder was Marshal Soult. Soult writes to Marshal Davout on 17 June 1815 about the movements of 1st and also 6th Corps as follows:[25]

The actions of the 6th and the 1st Corps of Comte d'Erlon were not satisfactory, and made false movements due to not carrying out the movement orders which the emperor prescribed them.

Soult describes the movements of d'Erlon as incorrect, and thus the way in which d'Erlon moved was not in accordance to Napoléon's wishes. Therefore, no order was issued from headquarters to send d'Erlon back to Quatre-Bras. The inference here is that Ney was directly responsible for ordering d'Erlon, or part of the 1st Corps, back to Quatre-Bras. In this regard, d'Erlon agrees, saying the order to move back to Quatre-Bras was from Ney directly.[26] Case closed? Perhaps.

The sequence of events of that fateful afternoon was perhaps as follows: we propose Ney met Delcambre on the field of Quatre-Bras, and was handed the 15.30 order from Imperial Headquarters regarding his new mission objective. This, we think, occurred sometime before 17.30. The meeting with the marshal must have been an unpleasant experience for Delcambre; Ney, having been unable to secure the crossroads as ordered, had been expecting the arrival of three, if not four, infantry divisions from 1st Corps to enable him to do so. Now he was being told—after the fact—that his much-needed reinforcements were now marching towards Ligny. Ney had clearly forgotten the portions of the orders from the emperor telling him that Kellermann's cuirassiers and at least a division of infantry were to be at the disposal of the emperor for service at Ligny. He totally misunderstood the situation and his mission objective. Essentially, the most probable scenario is that Ney impressed on Delcambre that the primary objective for d'Erlon's corps was the taking of Quatre-Bras, and the second objective, once the first had been achieved, was to move off to Ligny. In this scenario, Ney no doubt impressed upon Delcambre that d'Erlon had better get back to Quatre-Bras in order to carry out the emperor's orders as he (Ney) understood them to be. In this way, Ney got much needed troops, and d'Erlon could still fulfil his mission objectives. Ney had no authority to do so however. About the episode, d'Erlon writes nearly fifteen years later that:[27]

> Marshal Ney sent him [Delcambre] back to me with definitive orders to return to Quatre-Bras, where he was hard pressed, and was relying upon the co-operation of my corps. I thus decided that I was urgently required there, since the marshal took it upon himself to recall me, despite having received the note of which I spoke above.
>
> I therefore ordered my column to counter-march; but despite all the effort I put into this movement, my column only arrived at Quatre-Bras at dusk.

Ney ordered d'Erlon back to Quatre-Bras, but we need to stress that d'Erlon is as much to blame for the change of direction as much as Ney was for issuing the order. d'Erlon and Delcambre knew the emperor's orders out-ranked those of Ney, as did Ney himself, and yet Ney managed to convince Delcambre, and by inference d'Erlon, that he was to ignore an imperial order. Both men must have been convinced by Ney's line of argument to be able to convince d'Erlon to move back to Quatre-Bras against the direct orders of the emperor. De la Salle adds about this:[28]

In executing the imperial order, all the nominated forces directed their march across the plain towards Ligny. With a small escort, we went ahead of the marching columns when we came across General Delcambre, the chief-of-staff of our corps, who had been sent by Ney to demand our support.

Comte d'Erlon was unsure of what to do and hesitated; he needed advice. General-of-Engineers Garbe and I thought the emperor's order was more important, and if executed we could still fall onto the English flank later, and disengage the marshal. However, Delcambre insisted Comte d'Erlon took a middle way, which upset the plans of the general-in-chief. He sent Durutte's division, which was in the lead, Jacquinot's cavalry division and two batteries to the heights of Ligny. The remainder he moved to support Marshal Ney.

Clearly, Ney's own interpretation of the 15.30 order was somewhat different to de La Bédoyère's, and to the understanding of the order by all the other couriers.

We need to stress that the numerous orders sent to Ney during the course of the day outlined that he was to initiate a *'manoeuvres sur les derrières'* with the left wing of the army against Blücher. However, based upon the extant written orders, the general concept of the situation wasn't explained clearly to Ney. Indeed, Soult's own aide-de-camp, Baudus, claims he was tasked with making the tactical situation clear to Ney, and recalls as follows the meeting with him which he says took place after Kellermann's charge:[29]

> Soon, I found Marshal Ney at the point of most danger, in the midst of a terrible fire. I passed him the emperor's orders, but he was so agitated that I felt he was unlikely to execute them. In fact, he had a good reason to be agitated, for in his attack at Quatre-Bras, he had not hesitated to commit all three divisions of General Reille's 2nd Corps, because he was expecting the co-operation of 1st Corps commanded by Comte d'Erlon . . . the marshal was desperate at having no reinforcements to support his divisions that had only been committed because he thought he had 20,000 men in reserve.

Baudus continues, and further adds:[30]

> I insisted with the greatest force to the marshal not to oppose the emperor's orders; I thought I had succeeded; but after the events of the day as I returned to the rear, I observed that the Comte d'Erlon had returned.

This implies that meeting took place around 19.00 and cannot have lasted very long, which places the arrival of Quiot and 1st Division at 20.00, if Baudus (writing decades later) is to be believed.

Ney had sent Delcambre back to d'Erlon, perhaps at 18.00, informing him that the 1st Corps had been ordered to Quatre-Bras. Just as his corps was on the outskirts of the Ligny battlefield, Delcambre arrived with d'Erlon perhaps at 18.30. d'Erlon then halted 1st Corps while he debated the situation with his staff officers. Ney's peremptory directive reached d'Erlon just as Durutte's and Jacquinot's divisions had arrived just to the northwest of Wagnelée; the remainder of 1st corps was flung out between there and the Brussels road, according to Captain Duthlit. Duthlit also states that this was also where cavalry reserve assembled and that he witnessed the conclusion of the charge of Guiton's cuirassiers. The cavalry reserve must have been Donop and Picquet, as we shall see later. Donzelot's division did a brisk about-turn, and marched back to Quatre-Bras, where it joined the line of battle by 21.00.

D'Erlon left Durutte and Jacquinot at Ligny, in case the Prussians managed to get between Napoléon's and Ney's forces. However, d'Erlon had no specific instructions for General Durutte, other than to trust his own judgement.

Comment

How do we explain Ney's direct contradiction of the emperor's order? Rather than holding the Allies at bay, the 15.30 order had made Ney commit himself even more into the action at Quatre-Bras, as the order made it clear in that the occupation of Quatre-Bras was to be completed before he was to manoeuvre towards Ligny. Somehow, Ney could not grasp that the action at Quatre-Bras was of secondary importance and that the decisive battle was raging at Ligny, but neither did Soult make this abundantly clear to Ney in the written order. The fault here lies with the emperor, Soult and Soult's couriers for not getting the marshal to understand what the emperor wanted. But, as Baudus made clear when he was sent from Soult to Ney to make sure that Ney understood what was being asked of him, Ney seemed set on one cause of action from which he would not deviate.[31]

In defence of the emperor and Soult, Ney had not informed headquarters that he had not taken Quatre-Bras; headquarters at Fleurus assumed he had done so, based on his last dispatch. To the emperor, d'Erlon's troops were standing idly by, and were free to march in force to Ligny. As we have said before, we need to stress the importance that orders were issued in consequence of outdated information, because Ney had not kept headquarters informed of his operations. Thus, when Ney anticipated 1st Corps arriving so he could occupy Quatre-Bras, he learned instead that it had been ordered to Ligny.

Ney had no authority whatsoever to so blatantly countermand the emperor's order and, moreover, no authority to issue an order to d'Erlon to make him march back to Quatre-Bras, and both d'Erlon and Delcambre knew orders from the emperor were of more importance than from a marshal. Ney no doubt insisted that to carry out the emperor's orders, Quatre-Bras had to be taken first, as the order made out, and that d'Erlon had better get back to Quatre-Bras or face imperial wrath.

Napoléon was far from pleased with Ney for this course of action in direct contradiction of orders, and severely reprimanded him on the night of 16 June; he had shown that he could not be trusted with independent command. With Ney failing in his duties, the emperor only had one subordinate under his command that had proved to be very able—Grouchy. Ney's failure led to Grouchy being sent off in search of the Prussians, while he was recalled to headquarters in some disgrace and was placed under the direct supervision of the emperor, where his chances of making mistakes were few and far between—in theory. Grouchy was given an impossible task to catch the Prussians; a situation that Ney had directly contributed to. Ney's refusal to obey direct orders resulted in the grand plan for 16 June going awry. d'Erlon's flank attack at Brye would have made Ligny into a crushing victory rather than a damaging stalemate. This led to the French army being kept divided. If d'Erlon, the key to victory at Ligny, had arrived and the Prussians defeated, Napoléon would have never had to send off Grouchy.

Ney's mission objective for the 16th was to hold the Allies back in a secondary action, allowing 1st Corps to head to Ligny and then, on the following day, Napoléon would sweep onto Wellington's flank, who would be outnumbered and perhaps defeated, and in doing so Ney contributed greatly to the loss of the campaign and the fall of the emperor.

Durutte skirmishes at Wagnelée
With 1st Corps heading back to Quatre-Bras, d'Erlon had left a cavalry division and an infantry division at Ligny. There was still a chance that some form of flank attack be initiated and the Prussians crushed. For this to be achieved required a quick-thinking field commander, willing to take risks to exploit the situation he found himself in on the flank of the Prussians. The emperor's intention of taking the Prussians in the rear, and turning a stalemate into an out-and-out victory, was still

possible. Sadly, General Durutte was not such a general. Any other general would have jumped at the golden opportunity they found themselves in—to attack the exposed flank of the Prussian army. Where d'Erlon and Delcambre were gullible and easily swayed by a marshal of France, Ney was truculent and behaved at times like a spoiled brat with a 'teddy tantrum' over d'Erlon. The situation could still have been saved, but the man on the ground, General Durutte, was not the man to do so; he was timid and unimaginative. Hardly skills one needed in a field commander at the head of four regiments of infantry.

Napoléon's plan of operations had always been to post an infantry division at Marbais. Of the four infantry divisions in 1st Corps, Durutte's was the closest geographically to Gosselies, the 'right hand most division' (to quote Ney's 11.00 order) and, therefore, we suppose it was Durutte's division that Ney anticipated was to head to Marbais in accordance to his 11.00 orders. Yet Durutte, and all other eyewitnesses from the 4th Infantry Division seem totally ignorant of that in their writings on the campaign. Did Durutte get the order? If not, why not? If not Durutte, then who was ordered to Marbais? Certainly, it was not Quiot with 1st Division, or Marcognet with the 3rd, leaving Donzelot and Durutte as likely candidates. Given Durutte was the head of column for 1st Corps when it headed to Ligny, we assume that it was indeed Durutte who was, in theory, to have been at Marbais. So, the question is: why did Durutte not arrive at Marbais? Was his staff in such chaos that the entire division was paralysed since Gordon had deserted? It does seem so. Clearly there must have been a fundamental break down in the chain of command, or a change of order, for d'Erlon to not act on the 11.00 order, unless Ney impressed on him the importance of not sending a division to Marbais. There is no evidence to back up this statement, but something had clearly gone wrong, or orders had been changed, for a major part of the 11.00 order not to have been carried out in accordance with the emperor's wishes, or Ney's own orders. If such an order was issued, it no longer survives. It is more likely that the division's staff was in melt down, and the division was totally incapable of operations until the afternoon.

Ney never knew the truth of course, as Durutte did his best to cover up the defection of an officer who had served with him since 1807, lest guilty fingers be pointed at him. Certainly, it threw Durutte into some kind of stupor and he was rendered a mere automaton, unable to take the initiative if not directly ordered to do so. Most histories of Waterloo speak of de Bourmont almost as an afterthought in that it did not affect the outcome of the campaign. The truth is that the army was shedding officers like a tree's leaves in autumn. Not only was 14th Division paralysed, but so were 4th Division and the carabinier brigade.

Be that as it may, history tells us that the cavalry division of Jacquinot and Durutte's division remained at Villers-Perwin on the night of 16 June, with only Marcognet and Donzelot moving back to Quatre-Bras to join Quiot. According to d'Erlon himself, Durutte and Jacquinot were placed to guard against a possible Prussian attack coming between Ney and Napoléon, as Durutte's son explains:[32]

> General Durutte observed that an enemy column could emerge onto the plain which was between Brye and Delhutte Wood, and which would completely cut off the emperor's wing of the army from the command of Marshal Ney, he [General d'Erlon] concluded to leave General Durutte in this place. Besides his own division, d'Erlon placed under his command three [actually four] regiments of cavalry commanded by General Jacquinot.
>
> General Durutte, when leaving General d'Erlon, asked him if he should march on Brye. d'Erlon replied that in the circumstances he could give him no orders and that he was to rely on his own experience and judgement. General Durutte directed his cavalry towards the road running from Sombreffe to Quatre-Bras, leaving Wagnelée and Brye on his right, but still moving towards these villages. His infantry followed the same movement.
>
> General d'Erlon had told him to be cautious because things were going badly at Quatre-Bras. This resulted in General Durutte to thoroughly reconnoitre Delhutte Wood, for any retreat of Marshal Ney would place the enemy behind General Durutte.
>
> When General Jacquinot arrived a cannon-shot away from the road between Sombreffe and Quatre-Bras, he was assailed by an enemy formation, with which he began an exchange of musketry and artillery fire which lasted for three quarters of an hour. General Durutte advanced his infantry towards him in support. The enemy troops who were exchanging cannon fire with General Jacquinot retired and General Durutte, receiving no news about the left wing, marched on Brye.
>
> By the movement of our troops he presumed that we were victorious on the side of Saint-Amand. His sharpshooters engaged Prussian light troops who were still at Wagnelée. He seized the village and when the day began to end, and being assured that the enemy was in full retreat, he sent to Brye two battalions, who on arriving there found a few Prussian stragglers. During the night, General Durutte was ordered to move to Villers-Perwin.

So much for the official line of what happened. Several other eyewitnesses, including Durutte's deputy, totally disagreed with Durutte's account when it was published. Captain Chapuis, of the 85th Regiment of Line Infantry, notes:[33]

> The 85th, marching at the head of its division, was followed in its movement by the other divisions of the 1st Corps, which on the morning of 16 June, received the order of the emperor, brought by Colonel Lawrence [sic Laurent], attached to the headquarters of the army, to change our direction of march to the right. It was made when we were marching towards Quatre-Bras.
> We abandoned our movement from Marchiennes-au-Pont, and we established ourselves on the new route with celerity, the column formed by divisions was to be established behind the right of the Prussian army. The position was one of great importance.

When the column had arrived at Wagnelée, Chapuis notes an officer from Marshal Ney ordered that the column was to march back to Quatre-Bras. It was now that General Durutte began a ponderous and slow attack on Wagnelée. Battalion Commander Rullieres, of the 95th Regiment of Line Infantry, notes:[34]

> The voltigeurs of Durutte's division began to fire against Prussian scouts, it was about eight o'clock at night.

Captain Chapuis, of the 85th Regiment of Line Infantry, continues the narration:[35]

> Located a short distance from the hamlet of Wagnelée, which was close to the village of Saint-Amand, we were waiting for the order that would have us march on Wagnelée; we were all convinced 1st Corps had been called to play a great part in the struggle that was engaged … Our position at Wagnelée gave us the absolute assurance that a few minutes would suffice to place the whole of the Prussian right wing between two fires, and not one of us there, soldier or officer, who could not see that acting with vigour and promptness the safety of the enemy would be totally compromised.
> This order on which we expected to gain such favourable results arrived, but it was not executed, as General Drouet d'Erlon had left to join Marshal Ney at Quatre-Bras, under whose orders were the 1st and 2nd Corps and that General Durutte did not dare to give the

order for such a movement, refusing the responsibility as he was a divisional commander and not the commanding general of the 1st Corps. In consequence of this, he sent an officer to Quatre-Bras carrying this order and demanding instructions that others put in his situation would not have hesitated to carry out.

This can in no way be considered the strong flank attack that Napoléon desired. If d'Erlon was guilty of splitting his command, then Durutte was guilty for not attacking when he had the chance, and for not using his initiative rather than waiting for orders from d'Erlon who, at Quatre-Bras, could make no valid contribution to the action at Ligny. Surely Durutte knew this? Or was he so incapable of independent field command, as we noted before, that he was a mere automaton that had to do everything by the book? d'Erlon should have issued clearer instructions to Durutte, but Durutte should have been able to judge the situation for himself; if not, he was not fit to command the division. Both generals were at fault for the fiasco that unfolded between the battlefields of Ligny and Quatre-Bras. About the lack of action, Chapuis adroitly notes:[36]

> Whilst this position was being taken, an angrier scene was taking place between our divisional commander, Durutte, and General Brue, our brigade commander. The latter was frustrated at the caution of his superior and criticised him loudly. He shouted 'it is intolerable that we witness the retreat of a beaten army and do nothing, when everything indicates that if it was attacked it would be destroyed'.
>
> General Durutte could only offer the excuse to General Brue 'it is lucky for you that you are not responsible!' General Brue replied 'I wish to God that I was, we would already be fighting!'
>
> This episode was overheard by the senior officers of the 85th that were at the head of the regiment . . . for those that witnessed the scene and reflected upon it, that a major error had been committed in employing certain commanders, for whom the words of 'glory' and *'La Patrie'* were no longer of the same significance as to their subordinates.

Clearly, there was no trust between regimental officers and higher-ranking staff officers. General Brue, commanding the 2nd Brigade of Durutte's division (formed by the 85th and 95th Regiments of Line Infantry), notes:[37]

We were ordered to capture the village of Wangenle [sic]. This first order was transmitted to the 1st Army Corps when it debouched from Marchiennes-au-Pont by Colonel Lawrence of the artillery, attached to the staff of the emperor, or to that of the major-general.

The general adds more comments to this, as follows:[38]

> If General Durutte had attacked the defeated and retreating Prussian army at Ligny, this army would have been annihilated; all those who were not killed would have been forced to lay down their arms and would have been captured.

General Brue was perfectly correct in his assessment of the situation. For this failure, he reproached Durutte:[39]

> It is unheard of to march with shouldered arms in pursuit of a defeated army, when all indications were that we had to attack it and destroy it.

Brue further lambasted Durutte as a traitor and stated that Durutte's failures on 16 and 18 June led to the loss of the campaign—a fairly accurate summation of Durutte's catastrophic failure to seize the initiative at Ligny.[40] Napoléon's flank attack had been derailed by Ney, and then at the vital moment when the 4th Infantry Division (with Jacquinot's cavalry) could have dramatically intervened at Ligny, General Durutte seemingly panicked and did nothing. Durutte was an experienced field commander, but now in 1815 he was timid and lacked the vital spark of initiative that had driven hundreds of officers in the past. From marshal down to private, the French army of 1815 lacked something vital; it had no soul or desire to fight. The burning ambition to follow the emperor to glory had it seems, evaporated. Durutte sent word to d'Erlon at Quatre-Bras asking for orders rather than sending word to the emperor for orders. Major Pierre François Tissot, officer commanding the 92nd Regiment of Line Infantry of 2nd Corps (part of General Foy's 9th Infantry Brigade) notes, after Vandamme had spotted 1st Corps:[41]

> At half-past six, the aide-de-camp sent by Napoléon to recognise the movements of this column came to announce that it was the 1st Army Corps, commanded by General d'Erlon.

If this happened, given Tissot could never had witnessed this scene and was obviously reporting what he had been told by others, then why did the emperor not send orders to Durutte? Durutte's command could, and should, have struck a decisive blow against the Prussian army which was rapidly disintegrating. Ney made a spectacular mistake in ordering d'Erlon back to Quatre-Bras. d'Erlon compounded the error by heeding the words of Ney, and Ney's understanding of the 15.30 order. Durutte made this worse by achieving nothing significant.

3rd Chasseurs à Cheval

Both Durutte and de la Salle speak of Jacquinot's cavalry going into action on 16 June. Due to water damage, the regimental muster lists for the 3rd and 4th Lancers, as well as Marbot's 7th Hussars, are not able to be consulted at the French Army Archives. However, the returns for the 3rd Chasseurs à Cheval do exist:[42]

	Killed	Died of Wounds	Wounded	Prisoner of War	Missing
1st Squadron	0	0	0	0	1
2nd Squadron	0	0	0	0	6
3rd Squadron	0	0	0	0	1
4th Squadron	0	0	0	0	5
Suite	0	0	0	0	12
Total	0	0	0	0	25

The regiment began the campaign with twenty-nine officers and 336 other ranks. At Ligny, twenty-five men were lost and perhaps double or triple that number of horses. Presumably, the losses in the division were comparable to those of the 3rd Chasseurs à Cheval.

Donzelot attacks at Quatre-Bras

About the movement of the main column back to Quatre-Bras, Marshal-du-Camp Baron Schmitz, commanding 1st Brigade of Donzelot's 2nd Infantry Division in 1st Corps, writes as follows in his after-action report dated 25th June 1815:[43]

> The 15th ... The division was ordered to march to Marchiennes-au-Pont. Arriving at this position we passed through the town and crossed the bridge over the Sambre, and we then bivouacked in front of Jumet, on the right of the road from Charleroi to Brussels.
> The 16th ... The division leaves its positions and following the 1st and 6th Corps occupies the heights at Villers-Perwin. We were ordered to move to the right, and to advance onto the plateau located north of that village. There, we received the order to retreat

and stand on the highway from Brussels to support the 2nd Corps that was facing the enemy in the rear of Quatre-Bras. The artillery of the division only took part in the action. In the evening, the 1st Brigade relieved the outpost troops of the 2nd Corps.

Furthermore, Martinien lists that the 17th Regiment of Line Infantry lost one officer wounded in this action and the 13th Light Infantry had two officers wounded. Additionally, the 51st Regiment of Line Infantry is recorded as having an officer wounded on the 17th at Quatre-Bras, so it seems all of Donzelot's division was engaged at the battle and not just the brigade of Schmitz. The 54th Regiment of Line Infantry, part of Quiot's 1st Division, is recorded as having an officer wounded at Ligny on 16 June, namely Antoine Morio. Born 12 March 1786, he was admitted to the regiment from the 58th Regiment of Line Infantry on 6 July 1814.[44] Therefore, this indicates that contrary to the myth that 1st Corps did not fight at Quatre-Bras, at least six regiments from 1st Corps did.

Captain Pierre Charles Duthlit, aide-de-camp to General Bourgeois, commanding 2nd Brigade (part of 1st Division of 1st Corps), narrates:[45]

> On the 16th, the 1st Division was ordered to move rapidly to Marchiennes-au-Pont then move right and go to Gosselies, where we made a halt, then we were united with 1st Corps in position at Frasné, which occurred around two o'clock in the afternoon, when the gunfire was heard from Ligny. The 1st Corps could not arrive in time to take its place in the battle, and was positioned on the extreme left of the line. The 2nd Corps, commanded by Prince Jérôme, brother of the emperor and former King of Westphalia, had to give ground; the 1st Regiment of Light Infantry in which were still some of my former comrades in arms, attached to this division was employed in full, and made important service.

Louis Canler, of the 28th Regiment of Line Infantry (part of Quiot's division), notes that:[46]

> Our corps was to leave this town the next morning, the 16th, to arrive early into Fleurus, but we set off at noon, and, by a combination of circumstances, advances and counter-marches which remained inexplicable, we did not reach our destination for several hours after the engagement of the battle.
>
> My regiment was placed behind a small wood near the road to Brussels to stop the enemy cavalry which was supposed to have

debouched this side, we were ordered to form square in six rows.

We remained in that position until nine o'clock at night when we were ordered to carry us on the left side of the road to Brussels, in front of Quatre-Bras.

Summary

In summary, we admit that the conflicting orders of Ney and Napoléon judiciously affected the outcome of the battles of Quatre-Bras and Ligny, which, if d'Erlon had intervened in strength earlier at either battle, would have tipped the balance decidedly in the favour of the French. Ney blundered badly in recalling d'Erlon based on his understanding of the 15.30 order, and not what the order intended as described by de La Bédoyère and Baudus. Delcambre knew very well that the emperor's order out-ranked those of Ney, yet he was convinced by Ney's interpretation to change the mind of d'Erlon.

As it was, despite 1st Corps being split in two, Durutte could still have changed the outcome of Ligny in a more decisive victory, yet the timidity of Ney and d'Erlon seems to have been infectious, and Durutte dithered and dallied with much hand-wringing until the vital moment had gone, and then attacked ineffectively and too late. The bulk of d'Erlon's troops were uselessly tied down. The emperor had very good reasons to blame Ney and the senior officers of 1st Corps for the debacle that had unfolded, but he, too, is to blame for not making his intentions better known through more precise and clearer orders. Napoléon had appointed Ney, d'Erlon and Durutte, and in choosing these men seemingly not fit for high command, was ultimately to blame for the mistakes that took place on 16 June.

NOTES:
[1] SHDDT: C15 5, *dossier 16 Jun 1815*, d'Erlon to Duc d'Elchingen in 1829.
[2] SHDDT: C15 5, *dossier 16 Jun 1815*, d'Erlon to Duc d'Elchingen in 1829.
[3] William Siborne, *History of the war in France and Belgium, in 1815, containing minute details of the battles of Quatre-Bras, Ligny, Wavre and Waterloo*, Boone, London, 1848.
[4] Jean Baptiste Adolphe Charras, *Histoire de la campagne de 1815: Waterloo*, H. Georg, Bâle, 1863.
[5] George Hooper, *Waterloo, the Downfall of the First Napoleon*, Smith, Elder, London, 1862.
[6] Stephen Millar, *The Key to Victory: General d'Erlon's I Corps, 16 June 1815*, The Napoleon Series, November 2007, available at http://www.napoleon-series.org/military/battles/waterloo/c_waterlood'erlon.html [accessed 4 January 2017].
[7] SHDDT: C15 5, *dossier 16 Juin*, de la Salle. Copy of original order dated 1896.
[8] 'Souvenirs du général Dessales, ou de Salle' in *la Revue de Paris*, 15 January 1896.
[9] AN: AFIV 1939 *Registre d'Ordres du Major-General 13 Juin au 26 Juin 1815*, pp. 41-7.
[10] AN: AFIV 1939 *Registre d'Ordres du Major-General 13 Juin au 26 Juin 1815*, pp. 42-3.
[11] Brett-James, *Waterloo raconté par les combattants*, La palatine, 1969, p. 120.
[12] SHDDT: C15 5, *dossier 16 Juin 1815*, d'Erlon to Duc d'Elchingen on 9 February 1829.

[13] These are likely to have been Colbert and Lefèbvre-Desnoëttes.
[14] Chapuis, 'Waterloo' in *La Sentinelle de l'Armée*, 24 February 1838.
[15] J. L. Brue, *'Lettre Addresse au Colonel Chapuis'* in *La Sentinelle de l'Armée*, 1 March 1838. Letter dated Toulouse 3 November 1837.
[16] Sir Robert Wilson, Correspondence. British Library, Department of manuscripts, nr.30.147, pp. 15-18. See also: *Le Matin*, 26 March 1899, pp. 3-4.
[17] Grouchy, *Mémoires du maréchal de Grouchy* (vol. 4), pp. 99-102.
[18] Berton, p. 15.
[19] Marshal Ney, *Mémoires du Maréchal Ney, Duc d'Elchingen, Prince de la Moskowa* ed. Guillaume Gamot, H. Hournier, Paris, 1833, p. 75.
[20] Sir Robert Wilson, Correspondence. British Library, Department of manuscripts, nr.30.147, pp. 15-18. See also: *Le Matin*, 26 March 1899, pp. 3-4.
[21] Marie Élli Guillaume de Baudus, *Études sur Napoléon* (vol. 1), Debecourt, Paris, 1841, pp. 212-3.
[22] *Le Matin*, 26 March 1899, pp. 3-4.
[23] SHDDT: C15 5, *dossier 16 Juin 1815*, Ney to Soult timed at 22.00. Copy of the now lost original document made on 7 April 1906.
[24] AN: AFIV 1939 *Registre d'Ordres du Major-General 13 Juin au 26 Juin 1815*, pp. 43-5.
[25] AN: AFIV 1939 *Registre d'Ordres du Major-General 13 Juin au 26 Juin 1815*, p. 47.
[26] SHDDT: C15 5, *dossier 16 Jun 1815*, d'Erlon to Duc d'Elchingen in 1829.
[27] SHDDT: C15 5, *dossier 16 Juin 1815*, d'Erlon to Duc d'Elchingen on 9 February 1829.
[28] 'Souvenirs du général Dessales, ou de Salle' in *la Revue de Paris*, 15 January 1896.
[29] Baudus, vol. 1, p. 213.
[30] Baudus, vol. 1, pp. 212-3.
[31] Baudus, vol. 1, pp. 212-3.
[32] *La Sentinelle de l'Armée*, 4th year, no. 134, 8 March 1838.
[33] Chapuis, 'Waterloo' in *La Sentinelle de l'Armée*, 24 February 1838.
[34] SHDDT: GD 2 1135.
[35] Chapuis, *La Sentinelle de l'Armée*, 24 February 1838.
[36] Chapuis, *La Sentinelle de l'Armée*, 24 February 1838.
[37] J. L. Brue, *La Sentinelle de l'Armée*, 1 March 1838. Letter dated Toulouse 3 November 1837.
[38] Chapuis, *La Sentinelle de l'Armée*, 24 February 1838.
[39] A letter dated 3 November 1837 published in *La Sentinelle de l'Armée*, 24 February 1838.
[40] Letter of General Brue dated Tarbes 13 March 1838 published in *La Sentinelle de l'Armée*, 24 March 1838.
[41] Tissot, vol. 2, pp. 277-8.
[42] SHDDT: GR 24 YC 264.
[43] *Revue de études Napoléoniennes*, 1932, pp. 360-5.
[44] SHDDT: Xb 453 *54e de Ligne 1813-1815, dossier 1815. Situation Rapport 1 Mai 1815*.
[45] Pierre Duthlit, *Les Mémoires du Capitaine Duthlit*, Lille, 1909.
[46] Louis Canler, *Mémoires de Canler* (vol. 1), Roy, Paris, 1882, pp. 19-20.

Chapter

17 June

Written sometime between 20.00 on 16 June 5.00 on the 17th was the following dispatch from the emperor:[1]

Marshal,
General Flahaut who has arrived with us at this moment informs us that you are uncertain about the outcome of yesterday. I have informed you already of the victory the emperor has won. The Prussian army is routed. General Pajol has been sent in pursuit along the road to Namur and Liège. Already he has captured several thousand prisoners and five cannon. Our troops were well conducted. A charge by six battalions of the Guard and of the duty squadrons, supported by the division of General Delot, pierced the enemy line and carried the greatest disorder amongst their ranks, and took the position.

The emperor will move to the mill of Brye, passing the main road leading from Namur to Quatre-Bras, it will not be possible for the English to oppose you. The emperor will march directly on them on the road to Quatre-Bras, while you attack them head on with your divisions, which now must be concentrated, and this army will be destroyed. His Majesty requests that you send him details of everything that happens in front of you.

The emperor read your sentences that you failed yesterday, that the divisions acted alone and you experienced losses. This would not have happened if the corps of d'Erlon and Reille had been united, not an Englishman would have escaped. If the Comte d'Erlon had carried out the movement to Saint-Amand as the emperor ordered, the Prussian army would have been totally destroyed, and we would perhaps have had 30,000 prisoners. The corps of Generals Vandamme and Gérard and the Imperial Guard were always united; we are exposed to setbacks when detachments are compromised.

The emperor hopes and desires that your seven infantry divisions and the cavalry are concentrated and distributed over not more than one league of terrain. It is the intention of His Majesty that you will take the position of Quatre-Bras as you have been ordered; but if by any possibility this may not happen, inform His Majesty at once with a detailed account, if instead there is only a rearguard, attack them and take the position.

Today is needed to complete this operation and to re-supply munitions, and to draw in isolated bodies of troops and detachments. Give orders accordingly and make sure that the wounded are rounded up and led to the rear. Complaints have been made that the ambulances do not do their duty.

The famous partisan, Lützow, was captured and he said that the Prussian army was lost and that Blücher for a second time had exposed the Prussian monarchy.

Chances for a quick victory were still on Napoléon's side on 17 June. His plan of action detailed that Ney would tie down Wellington at the crossroads, while he would (after sending out a detachment to pursue Blücher) move against Wellington's left flank and rear for a decisive French victory at Quatre-Bras. As the sun rose, d'Erlon wrote to Ney that:[2]

Frasné 17 June,
Marshal, conforming to the orders of His Majesty, the 1st Corps is holding the line astride the Brussels road, the 1st Cavalry Division is covering its front and flanks.

I have the honour to inform Your Majesty that the 1st Cavalry Division undertook a number of successful charges and captured a number of wagons and prisoners.

Thus 1st Corps, less Durutte, was now in the front line, with 2nd Corps behind. By the morning of 17 June, General Roussel d'Herbal's command had arrived at Mellet.[3] The division had marched eighty miles in two days, and had arrived at Quatre-Bras sometime between 21.00 and 22.00, or at least Donop's brigade had. Thus, only by the morning of 17 June had all of Ney's command become concentrated.

At dawn, no doubt with the emperor's harsh words wringing in his ears, Marshal Ney attacked the Allied troops, endeavouring to establish what forces were before him. Marshal-du-Camp Baron Schmitz, commanding the 1st Brigade of Donzelot's 2nd Infantry Division in 1st Corps, writes as follows in his after-action report dated 25 June 1815:[4]

> 17th ... At daybreak, the enemy attacked the 13th and 17th Regiments who valiantly supported the attack, driving back the enemy with loss. These two regiments were, in this affair, five killed and 120 wounded.

This would have been around 4.00 to 5.00 on the morning of 17 June. This fighting is corroborated by a sergeant in the British Royal Artillery in a letter dated 22 September 1815:[5]

> We were roused on the morning of the 17th, about three o'clock, by the skirmishing of our pickets which continued till about seven, when we received orders to retire.

In the British lines, as dawn broke on 17 June, the French and Allied pickets clashed, as Captain Taylor, of the 10th Hussars, writes:[6]

> 17th ... About 2 a.m. a troop was ordered to mount to patrol with Sir A. Gordon, the Duke of Wellington's A. D. C. Captain Grey's troop went, they had twelve miles out and as many back, most of it at a smart trot as I heard, but were, I believe, unsuccessful in communicating with the Prussians. Firing commenced at daybreak between the pickets of infantry and lasted with little intermission to near twelve [midday]. Major Howard's squadron had been on picket during the night at a farm in front and to the left of Quatre-Bras, whither we all went in the morning by squadrons to water, and then returned to the brow of the hill and dismounted, and breakfasted, having a good view of the Infantry skirmishing.
> The infantry, guns and baggage commenced retiring, the pickets were withdrawn, and the firing ceased.

A number of other Allied eyewitnesses, mainly Hanoverian as the Dutch troops don't appear to have been involved in this action, also recall the action that took place in the early hours of 17 June. One such eyewitness was Friedrich von Kielmansegge, who commanded the 1st Hanoverian Brigade, which was composed of the Feldjäger, Bremen Light Infantry Battalion, Luneburg Infantry Battalion, Verden Light Infantry Battalion, Duke of York Light Infantry Battalion and the Grubenhagen Light Infantry Battalion. He writes thusly about the 17th:[7]

On the 17th at two o'clock in the morning the enemy attacked our outposts and continued these attacks of varying strength until ten o'clock, to achieve his objective. Our reserves were positioned so as to support the outposts on the 16th and 17th, and despite the superiority of the enemy force, the attacks were repelled at all points.

On both days, our jägers and sharpshooters displayed a superior level of marksmanship as well as courage, and they were able to counter the enemy's greater numbers and quick attacks. The officers also displayed the most praiseworthy example to their men, after ten o'clock in the morning the enemy attacks became weaker and the division received the order to assemble without the enemy noticing the fact.

Carl Jacobi, serving as a captain in the Luneburg Light Infantry Battalion, writes as follows about the morning of 17 June 1815 and Marshal Ney's attack:[8]

When dawn broke, the enemy advanced confidently to reconnoitre. An attack on the most advanced outposts was repulsed at all points, upon which the enemy force withdrew. However, they constantly harassed the troops occupying Piermont by sending forward small detachments so that it was impossible to stop the firing there.

Heinrich Muller, then a major with the Bremen Light Infantry Battalion (part of the Allied troops at Quatre-Bras), writes about the same events:[9]

17 June 1815.

At daybreak, firing began on the left of the Duke of York Light Infantry Battalion. The 3rd Company re-joined the battalion immediately. The enemy tried on several occasions to take the position the battalion had held on a small height behind a hedge in a marshy field, but they were thrown back repeatedly and then pursued by small detachments for three to four hundred paces, until they reached the trees standing on the heights opposite. The detachments re-joined the battalion.

Because the enemy approached to a position very close to the right wing of the battalion on a number of occasions, many officers and soldiers were wounded and several were killed. The incessant fire which lasted until nine o'clock meant our ammunition had to be replaced several times. Between nine and ten o'clock, only small enemy detachments appeared, and so the firing was not so great. At ten o'clock the firing ceased. Many of our muskets were no longer serviceable, and around eleven o'clock the author led two companies to the highroad where they made every effort to clean their muskets and make them function properly once again.

Carl von Scriba, who also served in the Bremen Light Infantry Battalion, comments on the actions of 17 June as follows:[10]

17 June.

At daybreak, the enemy forced a passage into the wood mentioned previously [noted as a quarter of an hour march on the left, in the direction of Frasné] and in strength attacked the Grubenhagen Light Infantry Battalion, which was posted there. However, after an hour of heavy skirmish fire, the enemy was repulsed. I suspect that this one isolated attack would precede a general attack on our position, and hardly had a quarter of an hour elapsed when we, too, were attacked by a significant force. The company on picket duty was withdrawn to the battalion. It was approaching four o'clock.

Our position offered us several advantages, and we were able to defend ourselves with determination and success. After three-quarters of an hour of heavy rile fire, the enemy retired, although this only occurred after he was threatened on his right flank by a detachment from the Duke of York Battalion, I believe under Lieutenant Wrede. This attack was followed by several more, interspersed by pauses, and often by forces larger than our own, several times weaker. I concluded that the enemy was trying to draw us from our position by provoking us to pursue them, which could have been greatly disadvantageous to ourselves. However, our commander only allowed small detachments to follow the enemy, going 400 to 500 paces from him.

We lost many men in these pointless attacks. Several times our ammunition, which was brought to us in small barrels, had to be replenished. Towards half-past ten in the morning a great many of our muskets had become hot and muddy and they would not work anymore.

He further notes:[11] 'With regards to the enemy we observed the column towards Frasné had increased in size.' Colonel Carl Best, commanding the 6th British Infantry Division, writes:[12]

At daybreak, we were awoken by a heavy skirmish and immediately stood to our arms. The fire became gradually more distant and stopped soon after.

Cavalié Mercer, of the Royal Horse Artillery, notes the fighting took place before daybreak:[13]

17 June ... when a popping fire of musketry, apparently close at hand, aroused me again to consciousness of my situation. At first I could not imagine where I was. I looked straight up, and the stars were twinkling over me in a clear sky. I put out a hand from beneath my cloak, and felt clods of damp earth and stalks of straw. The rattle of musketry increased, and then the consciousness of my situation came gradually over me. Although somewhat chilly, I was still drowsy, and, regardless of what might be going on, had turned on my side and began to dose again, when one of my neighbours started up with the exclamation 'I wonder what all that firing means!' This in an instant dispelled all desire to sleep; and up I got too, mechanically repeating his words, and rubbing my eyes as I began to peer about.

One of the first, and certainly the most gratifying, sights that met my inquiring gaze was Quartermaster Hall, who had arrived during the night with all his charge safe and sound. He had neither seen nor heard, however, of Mr Coates and his train of country wagons, for whom I began now to entertain serious apprehensions. From whatever the musketry might proceed, we could see nothing—not even the flashes; but the increasing light allowed me to distinguish numberless dark forms on the ground all around me, people slumbering still, regardless of the firing that had aroused me. At a little distance, numerous white discs, which were continually in motion, changing place and disappearing, to be succeeded by others, puzzled me exceedingly, and I could not even form a conjecture as to what they might be.

Watching them attentively, I was still more surprised when some of these white objects ascended from the ground and suddenly disappeared; but the mystery was soon explained by the increasing light, which gave to my view a corps of Nassau troops lying on the ground, having white tops to their shakos. Daylight now gradually unfolded to us our situation. We were on a plateau which had been covered with corn, now almost everywhere trodden down.

Four roads, as already mentioned, met a little to the right of our front, and just at that point stood a farmhouse, which, with its outbuildings, yard, etc. was enclosed by a very high wall. This was the farm of Quatre-Bras. Beyond it, looking obliquely to the right, the wood (in which the battle still lingered when we arrived last night) stretched away some distance along the roads to Nivelle and Charleroi, which last we understood lay in front, but far out of sight. Along the continuation of the Charleroi road, and in the direction of Brussels, a little in rear of our right, a few cottages scattered along it had their little gardens enclosed by banks, with here and there an elder or some such bush growing on them; and these were the only enclosures to be seen, all the rest being a wide extent of corn-land without hedge or wall. On the farther side of the road, beyond the cottages, the fields were interspersed with thickets of under wood and a few clumps of trees, which shut in the view in that direction. To the rear the country appeared perfectly naked and open.

Marshal Ney's actions, however, seems to have been limited, as Ney was ignorant of the outcome of Ligny until around 9.00 hours, due to poor communications from the emperor which, the day before, had had fatal consequences for the success of the twin battles of Ligny and Quatre-Bras. Ney could not act offensively until he knew what had happened to the Prussians and the bulk of the French army. Ney's aide-de-camp writes:[14]

> On 17 June, early in the morning, the marshal made his troops under his command take up their arms; at the same time ordered the vedettes be established at daybreak. The enemy had not quit the positions in the town; it was judged however that they were making a retrograde movement.
> The marshal did not hesitate in passing the news on to the emperor. It was not until around nine o'clock that the reconnaissance patrols, sent out earlier in the morning, reported that the army was marching on the road to Namur via Quatre-Bras; the prince arrived at about ten o'clock to where the marshal was, and there received the order to place the vedettes of the cavalry advance-guard on the road to Brussels. The troops of the 1st Corps formed the head of column and passed through Quatre-Bras in pursuit of the enemy.

Ney's troops were also exhausted having been fought to a standstill the day before. This action on the morning of the 17th has so far been overlooked by studies of the campaign, with many writers relying upon events for the French as stated by Napoléon. In reality, it seems Ney did not waste the morning of the 17th with inaction as many historians claim. The official bulletin for the day's events, no doubt written (or at least approved) by the propagandistic Napoléon, says:[15]

> On the morning of the 17th, the emperor repaired to Quatre-Bras, whence he marched to attack the English army: he drove it to the entrance of the Soignes Forest with the left wing and the reserve. The right wing advanced by Sombreffe, in pursuit of Field Marshal Blücher, who was going towards Wavre, where he appeared to wish to take a position.
>
> At ten o'clock in the evening, the English army occupied Mont-St-Jean with its centre, and was in position before the Soignes Forest: it would have required three hours to attack it; we were therefore obliged to postpone it till the next day.
>
> The headquarters of the emperor were established at the farm of Oaillon, near Planchenoit. The rain fell in torrents. Thus, on the 16th, the left wing, the right, and the reserve were equally engaged at a distance of about two leagues.

Wellington's retreat to Genappes
The night of 16 to 17 June was damp, as Cornet Bullock writes:[16]

> 17th ... It rained a little during the night, and soon after four we mounted and moved to the left, but returned again shortly after, and remained till about ten o'clock, when the infantry commenced a retreat to Mont-St-Jean; our right squadron were formed near the French and the hussar brigades on their right. We moved on to their support about half-past twelve o'clock p.m. and remained on the hill for about two hours. The French advanced about half-past two under a cannonade, which our horse artillery returned. We were soon after ordered to fall back and go by a road to the left of our position to the rear of Mont-St-Jean.

Captain A. K. Clarke Kennedy, of the 1st Royal Dragoons, writes:[17]

> It having been ascertained next morning that the Prussian army had retired during the night from Ligny, etc. the British Army commenced a similar movement on the morning of the 17th, the cavalry being drawn out and advanced to mask the infantry.
>
> My squadron was ordered to the Inn of Quatre-Bras to assist in conveying as many of the wounded men to the rear as were able to bear the motion of a horse, and considerable number were removed

in this manner to the rear of the position of Waterloo, though several that were severely wounded were left behind.

The other two squadrons, under the command of Lieutenant-Colonel Dorville and Major Radclyffe, remaining and retiring shortly afterwards towards the position where they arrived a little before dusk with the other cavalry which had been covering a slow and orderly retreat.

According to Surgeon Gibney, of the 15th Light Dragoons:[18]

> It was very late, midnight, before we reached our halting ground, and there we bivouacked, tired enough, horses and men, for we had marched from seven in the morning at least fifty miles. The place was called Quatre-Bras, from the Nivelles and Charleroi roads crossing each other at right angles.
>
> We tried hard to sleep, our lodging being the cold ground, but after the long march and small allowance of food most of us were too much knocked up to get even a wink; besides, firing was going on to our right, and that disturbed us, for we knew not how soon we might have to repel our attack.
>
> Before daybreak on the 17th we were up and in the saddle, waiting for orders in no little anxiety, as the firing to our right had become louder and more continuous; but nothing came of it. The regiment stood on the ground where they had bivouacked, ready for action, and some rations were served. Seeing hour after hour pass away, and evidently neither party very willing to try their strength, I took the opportunity of riding over the field of battle, so far as circumstances would permit.
>
> It was a painful sight, and exhibited only too distinctly the horrors of war. Dead men and horses, mixed up indiscriminately, were scattered about the field. Clotted blood in small pools, and corpses besmeared with blood, their countenances even now exhibiting in what agonies many had departed. Caps, cuirasses, swords, bayonets were strewn everywhere. Houses, fields, roads cut up and injured by artillery; drums, wagons and parts of uniforms lying about; whilst every house or cottage near was full of wounded and dying; and this was only the commencement of the war. After all, we had no really hard fighting this day, except in the wood, though towards noon a brisk cannonade on both sides commenced, and continued until we were ordered to retire, as the French were too strong for us, and for other reasons best known to the Duke of Wellington.

As Gibney alludes to, with the news that the Prussians had been fought to a bloody stalemate at Ligny, Wellington fell back north towards Waterloo as a result on 17 June. Both Allied armies retreated north. Wellington's plan of operations depended on the Prussians marching to his aid. At 10.00, Wellington issued his orders:[19]

To General Lord Hill, GCB
17 June 1815.
The 2nd Division of British infantry to march from Nivelles on Waterloo at ten o'clock.

The brigades of the 4th Division, now at Nivelles, are to march from that place on Waterloo at ten o'clock. Those brigades of the 4th Division at Braine-le-Comte, and on the road from Braine-le-Comte to Nivelles, to collect and halt at Braine-le-Comte this day.

All the baggage on the road from Braine-le-Comte to Nivelles to return immediately to Braine-le-Comte, and to proceed immediately from thence to Hal and Brussels.

The spare musket ammunition to be immediately parked behind Genappe.

The corps under the command of Prince Frederick of Orange will move from Enghien this evening, and take up a position in front of Hal, occupying Braine-le-Château with two battalions.

Colonel Erstorff will fall back with his brigade on Hal, and place himself under the orders of Prince Frederick.

To Major-General the Hon. Sir C. Colville, GCB.
17 June 1815.
The army retired this day from its position at Quatre-Bras to its present position in front of Waterloo.

The brigades of the 4th Division at Braine-le-Comte are to retire at daylight tomorrow morning upon Hal.

Major-General Colville must be guided by the intelligence he receives of the enemy's movements in his march to Hal, whether he moves by the direct route or by Enghien.

Prince Frederick of Orange is to occupy with his corps the position between Hal and Enghien, and is to defend it as long as possible.

The army will probably continue in its position in front of Waterloo tomorrow.

Lieut-Colonel Torrens will inform Lieut-General Sir C. Colville of the position and situation of the armies.

As Wellington's men withdrew north, they took up a defensive position on the slopes of the hill leading to the town of Genappes. The French cavalry did not leave Quatre-Bras for some time, as Lieutenant Henckens, of the 6th Chasseurs à Cheval, writes:[20]

> Very early on the morning of the 17th distributions were made for men and horses which we took advantage immediately, expecting to receive new orders. However, it was only two o'clock that the division of Piré was ordered to move towards Quatre-Bras to take part in the pursuit of Wellington's troops, led by Napoléon himself in the direction of Brussels.

According to an officer of the 23rd Light Dragoons, Lieutenant John Banner, the retreat began:[21]

> About two o'clock in the afternoon, when the enemy immediately afterwards emerged from the woods and pursued the Allied rearguard with the greatest enthusiasm. The rearguard had not marched half a mile from Quatre-Bras when it was overtaken by a storm of thunder and rain, the latter falling in such abundance that it rendered the roads and ground over which the troops retreated scarcely passable.
> There being only one street by which the army could pass through Genappe, the progress of the troops was consequently retarded at that village, and during this stoppage some of the cavalry regiments moved a short distance to the right of the entrance to Genappe to be ready to form and meet any attack that the French advance guard, which was rapidly approaching, might make upon our columns while they were delayed at this defile, but all our troops entered Genappe before the French came up.
> The artillery which accompanied the French advance guard to Genappe was immediately planted at the left side of the town on the bank of the river which passes through it, from which station the enemy opened a heavy and incessant fire upon our cavalry when ascending from Genappe, by which they were exceedingly galled and sustained some loss; our artillery, being all at the period considerably in front, we were without a cannon to return shot.

Captain Taylor, of the 10th Hussars, writes about the events as follows:[22]

> the cavalry forming two lines along the brow of the rising ground to the left of the road (to Namur, I believe) the heavy cavalry in second

line, we were ordered to retire and form in our place in brigade. The French cavalry then commenced its advance, the 18th Picket falling back, not by the road, but in line across the fields under us, a squadron of lancers advancing upon them, both having skirmishers out. When the enemy's cavalry were pretty thick in the opening, between the fences our brigade of horse artillery guns gave them a few rounds, apparently with effect, knocking men and horses off of the road. Both lines of cavalry were then ordered threes-about, and retired in line over the cornfields.

On our getting rather into a hollow, the enemy's guns opened upon us, throwing shells which fell over us. I saw one burst near the 18th; just then commenced a thunderstorm worthy of the tropics for the loudness of the thunder and violence of the rain. This, with the sort of ballet of war of the retiring and advancing cavalry, and the French guns firing, altogether made a picturesque and grand scene.

Our brigade then filed off into narrow roads and through a village, the 18th leading (I think), and the 10th sent on picket, the centre and the 1st G. Hussars following. I heard that their rear was attacked by the enemy just as we entered the narrow roads, but the French soon left us for the main road.

On issuing from the village there was a hollow-way with an ascent commanded by high banks, here Sir H. Vivian formed a division of the 10th on the bank, in rank entire with carbines advanced and ready to fire into the hollow-way and check pursuit, had the enemy come on, but as they did not, the division resumed its place, and the brigade marched quite unmolested through narrow roads, hearing occasional cannonade on the main road, and the shouts of the attacks that took place. Lieutenant Smith, of the 10th, was sent across to the main road, and was present at the affair between the 7th Hussars and the French lancers.

Sergeant Matthew Coglan, of the 18th Hussars, recalls the French cavalry's movements that morning, supported by horse artillery:[23]

I soon came up with the regiment my step-father was in, who gave me a welcome salutation, without dismounting, and slipped a few gold pieces into my hand, and gave me his blessing. I put spurs to the old grey, showed Manwarn the position the regiment lay in, and desired him to make all speed and report his arrival. A few minutes brought me to them, and I reported my arrival to Colonel Murray and fell in, being told off as the centre sergeant of the centre squadron, under the command of Captain Luard.

We then dismounted, and in a few minutes the enemy's cavalry made their appearance, debouching in the masterly and splendid style from a wood which bordered an adjoining field. Never have I seen movement executed in so daring and correct a manner, they formed into divisions, wheeled into line, and instantly opened a cannonade. The first shot they fired knocked over a man on my right in the squadron I belonged to, and killed him on the spot. We on our side were formed up in a similar manner, and for some time returned the fire with interest. Skirmishers were thrown out, but in a short time the retreat was ordered, and we fell back on Waterloo.

William Hay, of the 12th Light Dragoons, was also awestruck by the appearance of the French cavalry:[24]

In a moment, as if by magic, debouched from the dark foliage, which had hitherto kept them from our sight, by the three roads, the gorgeous uniforms of the French cavalry, composed of the cuirassiers, lancers, and brass-helmeted dragoons. On they came at a gallop, those from the right-hand road forming on the plain to their left, the centre to their front, and the left to their right, until three lines fronting our own were drawn up. There were now in front of us, waiting, 22,000 cavalry—double our number—and these supported by fifty guns of artillery, all ready for action.

Tomkinson, of the 16th Light Dragoons, recalls the same scene as follows:[25]

I saw the French cavalry when moving out of their bivouac, and thought from their numbers we must either bring all our force to oppose them and keep our ground, or that, if a retreat was determined on, the sooner we moved the more prudent. They advanced in very large bodies, and Lord Uxbridge soon saw that so far from having any chance afforded of charging, he had nothing left but to get his troops away without the least delay. They came out column after column, and in greater force than I ever recollect seeing together at one point.

We, in the second line, were ordered away immediately, and retired leaving Genappe to our left (in retiring). The first line got away without much loss, retiring with the heavy cavalry on Genappe, but had not the time allowed it to retire through the second line, as first intended. There was not time for the hussars to pass through our brigade, the enemy were so close upon them, and had we not got off with the least possible delay the hussars and our brigade would have been in one confused heap. We had learnt the necessity of making way for those in front, when we and they were retiring, from acting in the narrow roads of Portugal, and the retreat being ordered, we fortunately made way for the front line as we were ordered to do. The infantry being all clear, and the enemy showing so large a force of cavalry, we ought not to have waited so long. Retreat being our object, the more easily it was effected the more prudent it would have been.

At Genappe the enemy came up with the rear, pushing onto the village. Lord Uxbridge ordered the 7th Hussars to attack a regiment of French lancers. The enemy were formed across the street, and in this position were charged by the 7th.

Action at Genappe

At Genappe, the French cavalry caught up with the retreating English, as Pierre Duthlit, of the French 1st Corps, explains:[26]

> After the Battle of Quatre-Bras, at around two hours after midday, the 2nd Division of the 1st Corps started in pursuit of the enemy, whose rearguard had stopped at Genappe; half an hour later, the 1st Division followed the same movement of the 2nd, and we re-joined the emperor, at the head of his numerous staff, who saw march past him successively different regiments. He was loudly applauded by the troops who, seeing him for the first time, made the air ring with their cheers. Whilst marching, our vanguard cannonaded strongly the enemy rearguard, and we crossed Genappe where the lancers charged resolutely, tumbling back the English.

Cavalié Mercer, of the Royal Horse Artillery, notes how the fighting developed:[27]

> Meantime, the enemy's detachments began to envelop the gardens, which Lord Uxbridge observing, called to me 'Here, follow me with two of your guns' and immediately himself led the way into one of the narrow lanes between the gardens. What he intended doing, God knows, but I obeyed. The lane was very little broader than our carriages—there was not room for a horse to have passed them! The distance from the chaussee to the end of the lane, where it debouched on the open fields, could scarcely have been above one or two hundred yards at most.

His lordship and I were in front, the guns and mounted detachments following. What he meant to do I was at a loss to conceive: we could hardly come to action in the lane; to enter on the open was certain destruction. Thus we had arrived at about fifty yards from its termination when a body of chasseurs or hussars appeared there as if waiting for us. These we might have seen from the first, for nothing but a few elder bushes intercepted the view from the chaussee. The whole transaction appears to me so wild and confused that at times I can hardly believe it to have been more than a confused dream—yet true it was—the general-in-chief of the cavalry exposing himself amongst the skirmishers of his rearguard, and literally doing the duty of a cornet! 'By God! we are all prisoners' (or some such words), exclaimed Lord Uxbridge, dashing his horse at one of the garden-banks, which he cleared, and away he went, leaving us to get out of the scrape as best we could. There was no time for hesitation—one manoeuvre alone could extricate us if allowed time, and I ordered it. 'Reverse by unlimbering' was the order.

To do this the gun was to be unlimbered, then turned round, and one wheel run up the bank, which just left space for the limber to pass it. The gun is then limbered up again and ready to move to the rear. The execution, however, was not easy, for the very reversing of the limber itself in so narrow a lane, with a team of eight horses, was sufficiently difficult, and required first-rate driving. Nothing could exceed the coolness and activity of our men; the thing was done quickly and well, and we returned to the chaussee without let or hindrance. How we were permitted to do so, I am at a loss to imagine; for although I gave the order to reverse, I certainly never expected to have seen it executed.

Meantime, my own situation was anything but a pleasant one, as I sat with my back to the gentlemen at the end of the lane, whose interference I momentarily expected, casting an eye from time to time over my shoulder to ascertain whether they still kept their position. There they sat motionless, and although thankful for their inactivity, I could not but wonder at their stupidity. It seemed, however, all of a piece that day—all blunder and confusion; and this last I found pretty considerable on regaining the chaussee. His lordship we found collecting the scattered hussars together into a squadron for our rescue, for which purpose it was he had so unceremoniously left us. Heavy as the rain was and thick the weather, yet the French could not but have seen the confusion we were in, as they had closed up to the entrance of the enclosure; and yet they did not at once take advantage of it. Things could not remain long in this state. A heavy column of cavalry approached us by the chaussee, whilst another, skirting the enclosures, appeared pushing forward to cut us off. Retreat now became imperative. The order was given, and away we went, helter-skelter—guns, gun-detachments and hussars all mixed pell-mell, going like mad, and covering each other with mud, to be washed off by the rain, which, before sufficiently heavy, now came down again as it had done at first in splashes instead of drops, soaking us anew to the skin, and, what was worse, extinguishing every slow-match in the brigade. The obscurity caused by the splashing of the rain was such that at one period I could not distinguish objects more than a few yards distant.

Of course we lost sight of our pursuers altogether, and the shouts and halloos, and even laughter, they had at first sent forth were either silenced or drowned in the uproar of the elements and the noise of our too rapid retreat; for in addition to everything else the crashing and rattling of the thunder were most awful, and the glare of the lightning blinding. In this state we gained the bridge of Genappe at the moment when the thundercloud, having passed over, left us in comparative fine weather, although still raining heavily.

Attack of Colbert's lancers

As the scouts, detached from the French 1st and 2nd Regiments of Lancers, reached the outskirts of Genappe, August Petiet, of the French Imperial Staff, notes:[28]

> However, despite the bad weather and especially the precious hours of the day that were lost, the emperor continued with energy to attack the Anglo-Belgian rearguard. Our artillery force soon to accelerate his retreat, General Alphonse Colbert, commanding the 1st Brigade of Subervie's division, was ordered to move forward to reconnoitre the enemy who seems to have stopped to take up a good position behind Genappe; the brigade advanced across the field to the town at full speed. The emperor was already at the entrance to Genappe, watching the movements of the English. The rain that was falling now redoubled in its intensity. As soon as General Colbert's men arrived, Napoléon ordered him to attack the enemy. This movement took place at the gallop and soon the 1st Regiment of

Lancers, commanded by Colonel Jacquinot, was engaged with the English cavalry, which had advanced into the village to meet the French.

The pell-mell was terrible, a hand-to-hand combat lasting longer than twenty minutes and the result was glorious to our army, the English had one hundred men killed and wounded, and among the killed was Major Hodge, an officer held in much esteem, and among the prisoners were eleven officers who were led by an aide-de-camp of the Imperial Headquarters staff. General Flahaut, aide-de-camp to the emperor, translated the papers found on Major Hodge, which had been signed Wellington. At the beginning of this movement, General Alphonse Colbert had sent orders to Colonel Sourd, who commanded the 2nd Lancers, to follow the direction of the 1st Regiment, but it became separated from his column by the arrival of the 1st Corps, and especially by artillery that had been positioned too early in the rue de Genappe. Colonel Sourd, impatient of being held back, nonetheless managed to emerge from the wagons cluttering the road and reached the enemy with only a few men of his elite company. Surrounded by the English, the brave Colonel Sourd is injured in a manner so serious that the doctor, Larrey, is forced the same evening to amputate his right arm.

The effect of lances was terrible in this melee and the bravery of lancers above all praise; some beautiful horses fell into their hands … The enemy dead were covered with mud so that one could not distinguish the colour of uniforms. The loss of the French was reduced to a few wounded.

However, Lord Uxbridge prepared to avenge this defeat, but our own artillery, despite the difficult terrain, was put into battery and blasted his forces. The light cavalry division of General Domon advanced to the right of Genappe. Colonel Marbot, commander of the 7th Hussars, quickly takes advantage of his position to lead a charge on the English column, and knocked many from their horses. The British withdrew and no longer stopped our advance until they are established behind Planchenoit, on the heights covering the Soignes Forest. It was six o'clock, Ney made up his troops in battle, and Milhaud's cuirassiers executed the same movement. The emperor, impatient to arrive in Brussels and who still counts on two and a half hours of day, gives the order to move forward, but the enemy unfolds and shows that it expects the battle back against the Soignes Forest, the left extending to the village of Mont-Saint-Jean and the right resting on Hougoumont Wood.

An unknown French general, presumably of a 2nd Corps cavalry division, notes as follows about the 17th:[29]

> The 17th was occupied in pursuit of the enemy, and was remarkable for several feats of arms, and we must especially mention honourably the 1st and 2nd Regiments of Lancers under the command of General Colbert, which charged on the 7th Hussars and the English Regiment of Queen's Dragoons and made a hundred prisoners, amongst whom we noticed nine officers. We saw in this brilliant charge Colonel Sourd, of the 2nd, surrounded for a moment by one English squadron. Stubbornly refusing to surrender—though overwhelmed by the number of his enemies—and the amount of his injuries. Saved by his regiment, he was found covered with sword cuts, and especially his right arm. An hour after the amputation, the colonel was once more on horseback.
>
> At ten o'clock, the British army occupied Mont-Saint-Jean and found himself in position in front of the Soignes Forest. The Prussian army moved towards the Meuse, and Marshal Grouchy immediately received orders to pursue with the 3rd and 4th Infantry Corps and a large body of cavalry. Napoléon established his headquarters at the farm of Caillou, near Planchenoit. The rain fell in torrents.

The charge of the French 2nd Lancers developed as follows:[30]

> On this memorable day, having received the order of Comte Lobau to charge on the English infantry placed below Jemappes, in an advantageous position and supported with artillery, he immediately turned to his right and charged, overthrowing the Hanoverian hussars who came to defend the position, which were contained by one of his squadrons, while with the rest of his regiment advanced strongly against the enemy, who were on the road to Brussels. This new operation had just been commanded by General Corbineau, aide-de-camp to the emperor, but in the midst of his success, he suddenly received a counter-order which recalled him to Jemappes on the road to support the 1st Regiment of Lancers. Forced to retreat by superior forces, he crossed the town at full speed with his platoons broken into columns of four to facilitate the retreat on the left of the 1st Regiment of Lancers, and then, with the utmost promptness, he and his braves surprised the English and repelled their masses to near Waterloo.

Having then realised that his movement was not followed or supported by other regiments, he returned in good order to Jemappes, but he found the defile filled with English cavalry; he undertook a most vigorous charge. The English colonel ordered him to surrender. Colonel Sourd replied, passing his sword through his body, and all the braves who dared approach him, after ordering his troop to turn about and face them.

In the melee, Colonel Sourd, commanding the 2nd Regiment of Lancers, was seriously wounded and fell from his horse. Second-Lieutenant Jean Auguste Lapeyre, of the 2nd Regiment of Light Horse Lancers, takes up the story:[31]

> The Colonel Baron Sourd certifies and attests that I, Monsieur Lapeyre, of the 2nd Regiment of Lancers, was distinguished during his period of service with the regiment. The colonel certifies that at the affair of Genappes in 1815 I was the first officer of the regiment, which had just attacked the English, to come to the aid of the colonel who was wounded by many sabre cuts and was trapped under his horse which had been killed under him. I, M. Lapeyre, quickly dismounted and dragged him from under his horse, his own horse now having been killed. For this act of bravery, I was recommended by the colonel for the Cross of the Legion of Honour.

Lapeyre was born on 15 December 1792 at Bordeaux and had joined the 2nd Regiment of Light Horse Lancers on 28 August 1814, having served in the 7th Regiment of Lancers since 1 February 1811. He left the army on 22 September 1815. It was not until 11 June 1831 that he was awarded the Legion of Honour for his actions in saving the life of Colonel Sourd. Sourd himself, however, in July 1815, denies he served in the regiment or that he was wounded![32]

NOTES:
[1] AN: AFIV 1939 *Registre d'Ordres du Major-General 13 Juin au 26 Juin 1815*, pp. 43-5.
[2] SHDDT: C15 5, *dossier 16 Juin 1815*, d'Erlon to Duc d'Elchingen on 9 February 1829.
[3] SHDDT: C15 35 *Rapport* Roussel d'Hurbal Mellet *17 Juin 1815*.
[4] *Revue de études Napoléoniennes*, 1932, pp. 360-5.
[5] National Library of Scotland: *Caledonian Mercury*, 5 October 1815.
[6] Siborne, *Waterloo Letters*, No. 75.
[7] John Franklin, *Waterloo Hanoverian Correspondence* (vol. 1), 1815 Limited, 2010, p. 82.
[8] Franklin, *Waterloo Hanoverian Correspondence* (vol. 1), p. 15.
[9] Franklin, *Waterloo Hanoverian Correspondence* (vol. 1), p. 89.
[10] Franklin, *Waterloo Hanoverian Correspondence* (vol. 1), pp. 110-1.

[11] Franklin, *Waterloo Hanoverian Correspondence* (vol. 1), p. 110.
[12] Franklin, *Waterloo Hanoverian Correspondence* (vol. 1), pp. 162-3.
[13] Cavalié Mercer, *Journal of the Waterloo Campaign, kept throughout the Campaign of 1815* (vol. 2), W. Blackwood, Edinburgh and London, 1870, pp. 255-8.
[14] Heymès, p. 12.
[15] Booth, p. 256.
[16] 'Journal of Cornet Robert Henry Bullock' in Mandell Creighton, The *English Historical Review*, Vol. 3, July 1888, p.451.
[17] Siborne, *Waterloo Letters*, No. 34.
[18] William Gibney, *Eight Years Ago, or The Recollections of an Old Army Doctor, his Adventures on the Field of Quatre Bras and Waterloo and during the Occupation of Paris in 1815*, Bellairs & Company, London, 1896, pp. 179-81.
[19] Cited by *War Times Journal*.
[20] J. L. Henckens, *Mémoires se rapportant à son service militaire au 6e régiment de chasseurs à cheval français de février 1803 à août 1816*, M. Nijhoff, La Haie, 1910.
[21] Siborne, *Waterloo Letters*, No. 47.
[22] Siborne, *Waterloo Letters*, No. 75.
[23] Harold Esdaile Malet, *The Historical Memoirs of the XVIIIth Hussars (Princess of Wales's Own)*, Simpkin & Co, London, 1907, pp. 141-2
[24] William Hay, *Reminiscences 1808-1815 under Wellington* ed. Sarah Catherine Isabella Wood, Simpkin, Marshall, Hamilton, Kent and Co, 1901, p. 169.
[25] William Tomkinson, James Tomkinson, *The Diary of a Cavalry Officer in the Peninsular and Waterloo Campaigns 1809-1815*, S. Sonnenschein, London, 1894, pp. 284-5.
[26] Duthlit.
[27] Mercer, vol. 2, pp. 270-5.
[28] Pétiet, pp. 221-2.
[29] Marguerite, pp. 260-2.
[30] Rousselon, *Biographie du Général Baron Sourd, Commandeur se la Légion d'Honneur*, Paris, 1830, pp. 14-6.
[31] Ian Smith, perssonal communication 7 October 2012.
[32] SHDDT: Xc 181 *2e Chevau-Légers. Dossier 1815*.

Chapter 10

Charge of the 7th Hussars

The British 7th Hussars were at Genappe and had not been in action on 16 June, and were formed up to act as a rearguard waiting for the French cavalry which were approaching along the Brussels road. As a very heavy downpour of rain began, Lord Uxbridge, commander-in-chief of the British and Allied cavalry, ordered the 7th Hussars to charge the lancers; the heavy rain rendering firearms useless. An officer of the 23rd Light Dragoons, Lieutenant John Banner, writes:[1]

> The 7th Hussars being animated by the presence of their colonel [Uxbridge] rushed on the enemy with the greatest spirit and intrepidity, and drove the French advanced divisions back into the streets of Genappe upon the main body of their cavalry which occupied the town, where the most obstinate conflict commenced, each party fighting with the utmost desperation ... The conduct of this corps on this occasion was heroic in the extreme; their spirit and ardour was universally admired and acknowledged by all who witnessed the gallant affair.

Uxbridge's aide-de-camp, Thomas Wildman, recounts the charge of the 7th Hussars against the lancers as follows:[2]

> All our cavalry had arrived during the night and when the arrangement was made to retire the cavalry were ordered to cover our retreat. This movement commenced about 1 p.m. with the Infantry and artillery and lastly the cavalry moving off from the left so that the 7th, being the right regt, covered the whole. When the Infantry were all gone the French began to move and soon after advanced with an immense column of cavalry. The lancers and cuirassiers in front, three regts of each.

> We skirmished with them till we had passed the village of Gemappe [sic], when they advanced so strong that it was thought necessary to charge them; this fell to the 7th and Major Hodge moved down with his sqds and the two others. The lancers were, however, so wedged in the street of Gemappe and with so large a column in their rear that they were obliged to stand at all events and our sqd. not making an impression, was repulsed; when retiring they pursued, some men were killed and wounded. Major Hodge, Elphinstone and Myers were taken prisoners, John Wildman and Peters were also taken and stripped of their pelisses and money, but just at that moment the 1st Life Guards made a most gallant charge and drove the lancers in confusion, in which the two young gents made their escape.

John Edgcombe Daniel, attached to the 7th Hussars, writes that:[3]

> The 7th Hussars, which had been left as a kind of picket to watch their motions. No sooner, however, had the last division of our cavalry receded than the French lancers and cuirassiers began to file out of a wood in face of the 7th Hussars, upon which the regiment retreated in good order as far as Genappe, through which town passes the highroad from Quatre-Bras to Waterloo. The French being close at their heels, they had scarcely cleared the town when the enemy marched through, and our rear squadron had but just time to face about before they were charged by a mixed force of cuirassiers and lancers, against which they found it impossible to make head: the squadron was almost annihilated.
>
> Major Hodge and the adjutant of the regiment were instantaneously unhorsed and killed, and Captain Elphinstone, being severely wounded and made prisoner with a number of his men, was carried directly before the emperor, with whom he had an interesting interview and conversation; Buonaparte was standing upon a hill wrapped in his cloak and encircled by his staff: it was then raining very fast.

Standish O'Grady adds more details to the events that played out that day:[4]

> Early in the morning of the 17th, the army was drawn up to show a front, and soon afterwards the infantry began to move to the rear. When they moved off, leaving the cavalry, Sir C. Grant called the field officers together and spoke to them for some time. When Major

Hodge (who was in command of the right squadron, to which I belonged) returned, he called me aside and told me that the Prussians had been beaten and obliged to fall back, and that we must make a similar movement to prevent the two armies from being disunited; that our brigade was to retire by regiments from the left, and that the 7th had the post of honour, the main road to cover and protect, that Sir William Dornberg was to take charge of the retreat, the skirmishers of the brigade, and that our squadron was to skirmish. There was at this time no appearance on the part of the enemy of an advance, and we were to hold our ground until driven from it.

We did so and (though I cannot pretend to accuracy in point of time) I think it was twelve before their advance put us in motion. We threw out the right troop to skirmish, and Major Hodge went with them. I held the highroad with the left troop, and had from time-to-time to send them assistance, and frequently to advance to enable them to hold their ground, as their movements were difficult through ploughed fields so soft that the horses were sunk to their knees always, and sometimes to their girths. Whilst I was so employed, Sir William Dornberg joined me. Thus, we continued to dispute every inch of the ground until we came within a short distance of the town of Genappe. Here, Sir William Dornberg told me that he must leave me; that it was of the utmost importance to face the enemy boldly at this spot, as the bridge in the town of Genappe was so narrow we must pass it in file, that I should endeavour, if possible, to obtain time for the skirmishers to come in, but that I was not to compromise my troop too much.

Sir William had been riding with me some hours, when he bid me farewell he shook my hand, and I saw plainly he never expected to see me again. I then called in the skirmishers and advanced at a trot up the road. The troops opposed to me went about, and as I followed them they did not stop as soon as I did. I continued advancing and retiring alternately, until I saw all my right troop safe on the road in my rear and then I began to retire at a walk, occasionally halting any skirmishers fronting until I turned the corner of the town of Genappe. I then filed the men from the left and passed through the town at a gallop, no enemy in sight. When I arrived at Genappe at the opposite entrance to the town, I found the 7th drawn up on the road in column of divisions, and having reformed our squadron we took our place between those already formed and the town. Here, I met Sir William Dornberg, who appeared surprised to see me, and asked me how we had effected our retreat, and if we had saved any of the skirmishers, and when I told him we had not lost a man or a horse, he exclaimed 'then Buonaparte is not with them; if he were, not a man of you could have escaped'.

Here we remained drawn up about twenty minutes before any of the enemy appeared, and then only a few stragglers, some of whom rode into us and were found to be quite drunk. As well as I can guess, the cavalry column by which we were pursued, and which moved slowly, but shouting loudly along the highroad, were about fourteen squadrons. Occasionally I was able to count them, but not accurately. There might have been eighteen, and this column now showed its head within the town, the head consisted of a troop of lancers all very young men mounted on very small horses, and commanded by a fine-looking and a very brave man. For about fifteen minutes they remained in the jaws of the town, their flanks being protected by the houses; and the street not being straight, and those in the rear not knowing that the front were halted, they soon became so jammed that they could not go about.

In this state of affairs, Lord Anglesey gave us orders to charge them, which we immediately did. Of course, our charge could make no impression, but we continued cutting at them, and we did not give ground, nor did they move. Their commanding officer was cut down, and so was ours (Major Hodge), and this state of things lasted some minutes, when they brought down some light artillery, which struck the rear of the right (the charging) squadron and knocked over some men and horses, impeding the road in our rear. We then received orders to go about from Lord Anglesey, who was up with us, but not on the road during all this time. The lancers then advanced upon us, and in the melee which ensued they lost quite as many as we did, and when at last we were able to disengage ourselves they did not attempt to pursue us.

We retired through a regiment of light cavalry, and the first pass we found off the road we took, and formed in the field by the roadside. I then got the remnant of the right squadron and moved them down towards the town of Genappe to look after any of our wounded, whom it might be in our power to save. When I saw the ground upon which we had charged it was strewed with men and horses, but I saw very few fighting men of the enemy. In the meantime, the light brigade having been removed from the road where they were when we passed through them, the Life Guards came down the road and charged into the town.

I could not, of course, see what they did, but I believe they fell upon the rear of a retiring column, impeded by the narrowness of the bridge, and did their duty manfully.

Edward Cotton, who served in the 7th Hussars, adds more details to the British counter-charge of the French lancers:[5]

The first part of the day (the 17th) was sultry, not a breath of air to be felt, and the sky covered with dark, heavy clouds. Shortly after the guns came into play, it began to thunder, lighten and rain in torrents, and the ground in a short time became so soaked that it was difficult for the cavalry to move, except on the paved road: this, in some measure, checked the advance of the French cavalry, who pressed us very much.

The regiment to which I belonged covered the retreat of the main columns. As we neared Genappe, our right squadron, under Major Hodge, was skirmishing. By this time the ploughed fields were so completely saturated with rain that the horses sunk up to the knees, and at times nearly up to the girths, which made this part of the service very severe. Our other two squadrons cleared the town of Genappe, and formed on the rising ground on the Brussels side. Shortly after, the right squadron retired through the town, and drew up on the highroad in column, when a few straggling French lancers, half tipsy, came up and dashed into the head of the column; some were cut down, and some made prisoners. The head of the French column now appeared debouching from the town, and Lord Uxbridge being present, he ordered the 7th Hussars to charge.

The charge was gallantly led by the officers, and followed by the men, who cut aside the lances, and did all in their power to break the enemy: but they being chiefly lancers, backed by cuirassiers, were rather awkward customers to deal with, particularly so, as it was an arm with which we were quite unacquainted. When our charge first commenced, their lances were erect, but upon our coming within two or three horses' length of them, they lowered the points and waved the flags, which made some of our horses shy.

Upon seeing we could make no impression on them, Lord Uxbridge ordered us about: we retired, pursued by the lancers and the cuirassiers intermixed. We rode away from them, reformed and again attacked them, but with little more effect than at first. Upon this, Lord Uxbridge brought forward the 1st Life-Guards, who made a splendid charge and drove the cuirassiers and lancers pell-mell back into Genappe; the Life Guards charging downhill, with their weight of men and horses, literally rode the enemy down, cutting and thrusting at them as they were falling. In this affair my old regiment had to experience the loss of Major Hodge and Lieutenant Myer killed, Captain Elphinstone, Lieutenants Gordon and Peters wounded; and forty-two men, with thirty-seven horses, killed and wounded. We were well-nigh getting a bad name into the bargain.

Trooper Samuel Boulter, of the Scots Greys, also witnessed this scene, as he explains in a letter dated 23 June 1815:[6]

About ten o'clock, we advanced up to the wood and formed our line and stayed there some time, I suppose about two hours, when we retreated. But it was only to decoy the enemy from their position and draw them on to some advantageous situation, where we could get fair play at them.

However, they came out and the 7th Hussars attacked them, but the French outnumbering them so very much, they lost a good number and were obliged to retreat. But the Life Guards made some very pretty charges on them, but the road being so very muddy, the men were almost smothered with dirt. And as the 7th Hussars was chiefly attacked in a small village near Genappe, thus the stones were so very slippery, that I really believe they lost more men with the horses falling and being rode over.

The *Ipswich Journal* newspaper notes in its editorial of 1 July 1815 that:[7]

The great loss of officers and men in the 7th Hussars was owing to the Polish [sic] lancers having small flags at the head of their pikes, at which the horses of the 7th on their charge took so much fright as to throw that corps into great disorder, of which the enemy took so destructive advantage.

About the cuirassiers (but in Radclyffe's own testimony, the cavalry were chasseurs, as we shall see later in this chapter), Captain A. K. Clarke Kennedy, of the Royal Dragoons, writes as follows:[8]

From Genappe to Waterloo, the left squadron under Radclyffe was warmly engaged skirmishing with the enemy's advanced guard of cuirassiers, who pressed them hotly, frequently collecting with the apparent intention of charging, but never venturing to do so during the regular and orderly retreat of about five miles.

The cuirassiers may have been the 1st Cuirassiers under Colonel Ordener, who notes:[9]

> The 17th, we were sent forward to join the corps of Ney at Quatre-Bras. As soon as we had arrived, we eagerly followed the enemy in his retreat leaving the paved road to the infantry, we marched along the right side of the road. By the time we reached La Belle Alliance, the resistance of the English seemed more pronounced, we performed a movement as if we were preparing to charge and it made them expose a large battery of fifty guns. Night approached, the emperor gave orders to stop our operations.

Macready, of the British 30th Regiment of Foot, narrates how he witnessed the operations on the afternoon of 17 June:[10]

> About half-past five we came to the Charleroi chaussee as the covering division. Our jägers and the Brunswicks were busy on the flanks, the cannonade was brisk, and report said that the enemy had captured two of our guns. At this time the 7th Hussars charged some Red Lancers near Genappe, and were sadly beaten. The Life Guards then came up and fully revenged them. I saw a regiment of heavy dragoons deploy to support the Household if necessary; they had on their red cloaks, and looked like giants. Numbers of the hussars galloped by us, so covered with mud that their uniforms could not be distinguished; from counter to tail, and from spur to plume, horse and man were one cake of dirt. They must have had pretty rolling or running. The rain continued unabated, and night drew on.

Subervie's cavalry

Forming the head of column of the 5th Cavalry Division was the 1st Regiment of Lancers. At Genappes, the regiment lost the following casualties:[11]

Squadron	Killed	Died of Wounds	Wounded	Prisoner of War	Missing
1st	2	0	0	2	1
2nd	0	0	0	1	0
3rd	0	0	0	0	0
4th	0	0	0	1	3
Suite	0	0	0	0	3
Total	2	0	0	4	7

On 10 June, the regiment mustered forty officers and 375 other ranks, but lost one man at Ligny and thirteen at Genappe. Furthermore, another source states thirty men were dismounted at Ligny and fifteen at Genappe.[12] This would make a loss of forty-five other ranks.

2nd Lancers

The 2nd Lancers bore the brunt of the fighting at Genappe. Losses on the 17th are as follows:[13]

	Officers Killed	Officers Wounded	O. R. Killed	O. R. Wounded	Horses Killed	Horses Wounded
Total	0	14	1	175	0	0

On 10 June, the regiment mustered forty-one officers and 379 men. This means that at Genappe on 17 June, it had lost 45.2 per cent of its effective strength. Indeed, 34.1 per cent of the regiment's officers were wounded on the 17th. The loss of horses on average seems to be a ratio of one man for every two horses wounded, which even at a ratio of one-to-one and a half would give a loss of 264, reducing the regiment to a mere 115 men in the field on 18 June—little more than a squadron strong.

11th Chasseurs

Total losses for the 11th Chasseurs are given in the regiment's archival documentation as detailed below:[14]

	Killed	Died of Wounds	Wounded	Prisoner of War	Missing
Total	0	0	1	0	1

On 10 June, the regiment mustered 458 other ranks. Just two men were lost at Genappe.

Domon's division

The brigade comprised the 4th and 9th Chasseurs à Cheval, as well as the 12th Chasseurs à Cheval.

4th Chasseurs

On 10 June, the 4th Chasseurs mustered 306 other ranks. General Domon records six chasseurs wounded and seven troop horses killed at Ligny, and one officer's mount.[15] Casualties for the 4th Chasseurs at Genappe were as follows[16]

	Killed	Died of Wounds	Wounded	Prisoner of War	Missing
Total	2	0	0	4	4

In total, ten men were lost at Genappe, being nearly double those sustained on the 16th at Ligny.

9th Chasseurs
General Domon notes that at Ligny the 9th Chasseurs had two chasseurs mortally wounded, two wounded, three troop horses killed and one troop horse wounded.[17] The regiment's muster list records the following losses, confirming Domon's report: two men wounded in 1st Squadron, two wounded in 3rd Squadron and two men missing. Casualties for the 9th Chasseurs at Genappe were as follows, where just a single man is recorded as prisoner:[18]

	Killed	Died of Wounds	Wounded	Prisoner of War	Missing
Total	0	0	0	1	0

12th Chasseurs
Due to water damage at the French Army Archives at Vincennes, the paperwork for the regiment is not able to be consulted by the author at the timing of writing (December 2016), so we are not able to offer any comments on the losses of the regiment.

Charge of General Bruno's light cavalry brigade
The French lancers were pursued energetically back into Genappe by the Allied cavalry. General Jacquinot now approached Genappe with his cavalry division. Colonel Marbot, commanding the 7th Hussars, formed the vanguard, with the 3rd Regiment of Chasseurs à Cheval immediately behind them. The leading elements of Marbot's men now entered the village from the south, having crossed the Dyle, and they found Sourd's confused mess of lancers.

Upon assessing the situation, Colonel Marbot decided to act. Fearing the chaos that the lancers could cause by obstructing of the bridge over the Dyle, Marbot placed ordered his 1st Squadron to deploy across the road in order to block it. At the same time, he led the 2nd and 3rd Squadrons at the trot through a side-street that lead into the fields west of Genappe. Once here, he formed them into order of battle and advanced towards the British cavalry. The 3rd Regiment of Chasseurs à Cheval debouched into line of battle and advanced from Genappe itself.

Squadron Commander Victor Dupuy, who served under Marbot in the 7th Hussars, writes:[19]

> The 16th, we are directed on the road to Brussels, the 2nd Corps was in front of us, and soon we began to form line and shortly some minor skirmishes with the Hanoverian hussars and English dragoons began, in which the advantage always remained with us. Having taken position in Villers and the next day, we headed onto Jemappes.
>
> Our head of column was checked in its advance along the main street of the village by the 2nd Lancers, commanded by good and brave Colonel Sourd, who had been forced to pull back there by a strong party of British cavalry. Fearing that in their retreat the lancers would get intermingled with our regiment and later the 3rd Chasseurs who followed us, realising that the bridge we had to cross would soon be clogged and increase the disorder there, Colonel Marbot made the 1st Squadron cross the street to block it and then taking with him the 2nd and 3rd Squadrons to the left down a small lane, he debouched, trotting forward into a meadow, and formed into order of battle and then moved forward on the right flank of the British column, so that by this bold move, supported also by the 3rd Chasseurs, the British decided to retire.
>
> When we debouched from Genappe, the artillery of the Imperial Guard on the opposite side of the river, deceived by our madder red portmanteaux and trousers, we were assumed for English and they directed their fire onto us, a young quartermaster of the regiment and several hussars were victims of this unfortunate error. Our beautiful manoeuvre relieved the lancers, whose worthy chief was seriously injured at the exit of the village.

For whatever reason the Household Brigade withdrew rather than take on the French light cavalry, which was supported by Milhaud's cuirassiers and Subervie's chasseurs à cheval. In the rear of these units, Napoléon followed, being escorted by his duty squadrons. The chasseurs were seen by the 1st Royal Dragoons, as Major Radclyffe writes:[20]

> I was detached with my squadron to cover the brigade by skirmishing, and Major-General Sir William Ponsonby and the brigade generally were pleased to applaud the style in which we acquitted ourselves. It rained with greater violence than I ever witnessed before, which I found to my advantage when it was my turn to skirmish. The enemy had two squadrons of chasseurs

opposed to me, and as they could not overpower us by their fire, they huzzah'd and endeavoured to excite each other on with cries of *'Vive l'Empereur!'* and once actually charged towards my skirmishers, but they stopped short.

Jacquinot's division
The regimental muster lists for the 7th Hussars, as well as for the 3rd and 4th Lancers, housed at the French Army Archives were damaged in the 1940s and are not consultable by researchers until the year 2020, as the volumes are undergoing conservation to ensure that the books survive for future generations to use.[21] The 3rd Chasseurs lost twenty-five men on 16 June, and twenty-five men at Waterloo, but no men are recorded as being lost on the 17th.[22]

Operations of the Household Cavalry Brigade
Here at the Genappe, the Household Cavalry went into action for the first time in the war. The Life Guards had served under Wellington in Spain, but for the 1st Dragoon Guards this was the regiment's first taste of action for many years. They came into action against the French lancers.

An officer of the British Household Cavalry narrates the actions of the Life Guards at Genappes:[23]

> Next morning, our men were drawn up in a line of battle fronting the wood where the French had retired; but they would not venture to attack us. Lord Wellington by a *ruse de guerre*, however, drew them from the wood by a rapid retreat, for a few miles, towards Brussels; which brought the French exactly on the spot where he wished to fight them, and where he might bring his cavalry into play.
>
> While retreating, we were overtaken by a violent thunderstorm and heavy rain, which rendered us very uncomfortable. During the whole, no man was lost, but the Blues lost three or four; the 1st Life Guards charged some of the French lancers, and almost cut them to pieces. We were drawn up to give them a second charge, but they would not stand it. This evening, we bivouacked in a piece of boggy ground, where we were mid-leg up in mud and water.

Trooper Joseph Lord, of the 2nd Regiment of Life Guards, recalls in a letter dated 3 July 1815 that the British cavalry:[24]

> We retreated, one brigade supporting another, and forming behind each other for five to six miles. This took us two hours or better and

during this time such a storm came as I never saw in all my life of lightning, thunder and rain, the water came in such quantities that to merely say it rained would be far short of expressing it, for we had nothing dry about us in fifteen minutes. We never offered to cloak as it would have been to no purpose. After we had been retreating an hour and a half they came so fast upon us that we were called upon to arrest their progress, as the light dragoons were very near and severely cut off and not able to stand their force. Our brigade formed and the 1st Regiment of Life Guards being the nearest, they were ordered to charge them, which they did to great advantage, as they little imagined we had such strong men and horses in our army. The 1st Life Guards had some men wounded, but we got all the prisoners back, again the Blues were next, but the enemy in the meantime had got some cannon to bear on us by which the Blues had three men killed and some horses, and some men and horses wounded, but they coming in such numbers that it was not judged to charge. Accordingly, we took up position about a mile or two to the rear.

Naylor, of the King's Dragoon Guards, writes about the day as follows:[25]

At five, we began to retreat and cover the movement of our infantry. We continued to retire and form on either side of the road, as we passed through Genappe we experienced the most severe fall of rain I ever be held. A short distance from Genappe the 1st Life Guards charged a body of lancers who were pressing our rear. They charged in column of divisions on the road and we formed for the same purpose, but the enemy retiring we did not charge. We continued our retreat until we took position in front of Waterloo for the night, where we bivouacked during an incessant rain and without any refreshment or forage.

In the action by the British Household Cavalry Brigade that day, John Banner notes that:[26]

The 23rd Dragoons supported the Life Guards on this occasion, and after this successful and most brilliant charge, the 23rd Dragoons became again the last regiment in the rearguard, and continued so during the rest of the retreat.

Meantime, the Union Brigade had moved up to beyond Genappe, and had deployed west of the Brussels road, as Lieutenant A. J. Hamilton, of the Scots Greys, writes:[27]

The next morning [the 17th] we received orders to retire, and to cover the retreat of the army into the lines at Mont-St-Jean. The infantry retired by the highroad; the cavalry were formed in line; and the different brigades fronted alternately to prevent the advance of the enemy's cavalry and cannon.

Notwithstanding the torrents of rain which fell, the French continued to press us closely: their light cavalry charged ours on the road and drove them back, when Lord Uxbridge, seeing them do so, charged at the head of a regiment of the Life Guards and completely upset them, they being unable to stand against the superior weight of the men and horse of the Household troops.

About the Union Brigade, Uxbridge writes about their actions after the charge of the 7th Hussars and 1st Life Guards:[28]

Having thus checked the ardour of the enemy's advanced guard, the retreat was continued at a slow pace, and with the most perfect regularity. Assuredly this *coup ale collier* had the very best effect, for although there was much cannonading, and a constant appearance of a disposition to charge, they continued at a respectful distance.

The Royals, Inniskillings, and Greys manoeuvred beautifully, retiring by alternate squadrons, and skirmished in the very best style; but finding that all the efforts of the enemy to get upon our right flank were in vain, and that by manoeuvring upon the plain, which was amazingly deep and heavy from the violent storm of rain, it only uselessly exhausted the horses, I drew these regiments in upon the chaussee in one column, the guns falling back from position to position, and from these batteries, checking the advance of the enemy.

The French horse artillery had, it seems, also been brought up in support at the same time as the Life Guards charged, as Cavalié Mercer describes:[29]

On gaining the high ground beyond the town, we suddenly came in sight of the main body of our cavalry drawn up across the chaussee in two lines, and extending away far to the right and left of it. It would have been an imposing spectacle at any time, but just now appeared to me magnificent and I hailed it with complacency, for here I thought our fox-chase must end. 'Those superb Life Guards and Blues will soon teach our pursuers a little modesty.' Such fellows!—surely nothing can withstand them. Scarcely had these thoughts passed through my mind than an order from his lordship recalled us to the rear. On debouching from the town, seeing nothing in the country right and left of us, and fearful of impeding the retreat, whilst our hussars retired skirmishing through the street (the French having again come up), we had continued onward to gain the position occupied by our heavy cavalry, from which we were still separated by a small dip of the ground. We returned then to the end of the town, where the flight of shot and shells over us (the road was here sunk between two high banks) gave very intelligible information as to the reason of our recall.

The enemy's horse artillery, having taken up a position in the meadows near the bridge, were annoying our dragoons as they debouched from the town. The ground was heavy from the rain, and very steep, so that it was only by great exertion that we succeeded at last in getting our guns into the adjoining field. The moment we appeared the French battery bestowed on us its undivided attention, which we quickly acknowledged by an uncommonly well-directed fire of spherical case.

About the action that day, Trooper John Marshal, in the British 10th Hussars, writes on 11 July as follows:[30]

About ten in the morning of the 17th, we began to fall back, leaving us to cover their retreat. The French perceiving this, did not long remain inactive, but soon brought up their lancers to attack us; but we were not to bring them to action, but to retreat, which was accordingly done. Gen. Vivian, who commanded our brigade, conducted the retreat; in a most able and skilful manner did he complete it, covering with our brigade the retreat of the whole army, which fell back upon this point. The enemy seeing us retreat was quite delighted, and followed us with all speed, cheering and hallooing at us, thinking to alarm and frighten us; but in this they were disappointed, for we did not lose a man, although they attempted to charge us several times, but our skirmishers beat them back in spite of their boasted bravery.

Thus was our retreat completed after having fallen back about eight miles. Thus far were they to come, but no farther.

The storm breaks

Since mid-morning, the skies around Waterloo and its environs had been darkening. The clouds, leaden with rain, built up over the course of the afternoon. William Hay, of the 12th Light Dragoons, notes:[31]

> The clouds that had been gathering for some time in blackness, as striving to contrast their colour and thickness with the clouds of white dust driven upwards, suddenly burst and one of the most awful storms of thunder and lightning I ever beheld opened a battery.
>
> The enemy's lines began to close with ours, and when within a short distance, as if a sluice gate had been opened, down came such torrents of rain as quite obliterated from our view even our own advance, this continued with such violence in our teeth that our position was untenable; our horses with spurs stuck in their flanks would not keep their heads to the storm.

The storm broke around 17.00 and Trooper Samuel Boulter, of the Scots Greys, also witnessed this scene, as did many other eyewitnesses. The storm broke as the 7th Hussars charged into Genappe against the French lancers:[32]

> And at the same time a most dreadful thunder shower came on with such rapidity that we were completely wet through in the course of a few minutes and it continued to rain the whole of the night, that I can assure you we were in a most deplorable state by the morning. We had not a dry thread upon us and the horses were in the same situation for they could not lie down and had not been down then from the 15th night. We could get plenty of green forage for them, but as for ourselves we had not got anything for about forty-eight hours and could not get any provisions up.

Lieutenant A. J. Hamilton, of the Scots Greys, tells us the rain started when the Life Guards attacked:[33]

> At this moment, it rained in such a way as I never saw either before or since: it rained as if the water were tumbled out of tubs; there was also a good deal of thunder with it. Some of the hussars that were driven in upon us were so covered with mud that it was impossible to distinguish their features. The ground was so soft that at every step our horses sank halfway to the knees: and in several places, in our passing over fallow land, it had the appearance of a lake, the rain falling upon it faster than it could either be absorbed or run off.
>
> It continued to rain, and we to retire till we halted for the night in the position of Mont-St-Jean: we were placed in bivouac at the distance of 300 yards from the front of a farmhouse which lay between us and the village of Waterloo. The firing of cannon

continued till it was dark: but as it was on the other side of the hill we saw nothing of what passed, hearing merely the cannonade.

John Marshal, of the 10th Hussars, writes on 11 July as follows:[34]

> We were much hurt by a thunder-storm, which brought with it the most heavy torrents of rain that I ever beheld; nor did it abate during the night, nor till about nine next morning, and we were exposed to it all the time, for we took up our abode in a wood all night, so that we were like drowned men more than soldiers; but as many of us have long been inured to hardships and deprivations of almost all descriptions, it went off cheerfully, and none seemed to repine, for when the motives of the mind are strong for execution, all things are set aside to gain the wished-for purpose. This it is that makes us think light of misfortunes, and bear deprivations beyond conception to those who never trod this thorny path, yet with us they are borne without a murmur; but I am wandering from my subject.

The 11th Light Dragoons got a soaking during the course of 17 June, as Cornet Bullock writes how the downpour commenced just after the regiment quit Genappes:[35]

> The heaviest tempest I ever saw came on just before we left the field, and expecting to charge we none of us would cloak up. The roads were full of water, and we got to our bivouac, a muddy field situated rather high. The night proved the wettest and most uncomfortable I have ever passed. We made a large fire and by that means were not quite frozen. The right squadron returned about twelve, having charged with the hussars and Life Guards several times. Mr Moor was dangerously wounded; Captain Schrieber, Phillips, Orme, and Rotton were there.

None of the eyewitness accounts can agree on a time for when the storm broke, but both French and British accounts all agree on one thing: the deluge was of biblical proportions, and for many it was the heaviest fall of rain that they had ever experienced.

Skirmish at Waterloo
Wellington was now pulling back to Waterloo, harassed by the French. After leaving Genappes, he deployed his men on the slopes of Mont-Saint-Jean to cover the retreat. Mercer notes:[36]

Soon after, we passed a few houses by the roadside, which I afterwards found was La Belle Alliance. Hence we crossed another valley, and on rising the opposite hill I found a capital position on the top of an old gravel pit, which I occupied without loss of time. Behind the ground on which my guns were formed was a long hedge, which prevented our seeing anything beyond; and as no troops were in sight except those following us across the valley, we had then no idea that we had arrived in the position where our whole army was assembled, nor that we then stood upon ground which, by tomorrow's sun were set, would forever be celebrated throughout all generations!

We did not long remain idle, for the guns were scarcely loaded … the rear of our cavalry came crowding upon the infantry corps we had passed, and which were then only crossing the valley, the French advance skirmishing with these, whilst their squadrons occupied the heights. We waited a little until some of their larger masses were assembled, and then opened our fire with a range across the valley of about 1,200 yards. The echo of our first gun had not ceased, when, to my astonishment, a heavy cannonade, commencing in a most startling manner from behind our hedge, rolled along the rising-ground, on part of which we were posted. The truth now flashed on me; we had re-joined the army, and it is impossible to describe the pleasing sense of security I felt at having now the support of something more staunch than cavalry.

The French now brought up battery after battery, and a tremendous cannonading was kept up by both sides for some time. The effect was grand and exciting. Our position was a happy one, for all their shot which grazed short, came and struck in the perpendicular bank of our gravel pit—and only one struck amongst us, breaking the traversing handspike at one of the guns, but neither injuring man nor horse. Our fire was principally directed against their masses as we could see them, which was not always the case from the smoke that, for want of wind, hung over them; then against their smaller parties that had advanced into the valley to skirmish with the rearguard of our cavalry.

General Gourgaud, with the French Imperial Headquarters, writes as follows:[37]

At half-past six in the evening the advance guard arrived at the village of Planchenoit, opposite the entrance to the Soignes Forest; it was soon opposed by the fire of fifteen or twenty pieces of cannon; and from the manner in which these cannon were placed, there was reason to suppose that a strong rearguard had been stationed there to protect the passage to the forest. Had this rearguard amounted to no more than 15,000 men, it would have been impossible to force it from its position that evening, as night would have set in before we could have completed our preparations for the attack. The rain still continued, and it was impossible to distinguish the enemy's line. We endeavoured to impose on him by ordering Milhaud's cuirassiers with their attached horse artillery to deploy. The enemy then unmasked himself, and there was no longer a doubt that the whole of the English army was there in position. The emperor directed the different corps to establish their bivouacs, and fixed his headquarters at the Caillou Farm.

General d'Erlon adds his comments to the events of that evening:[38]

It was nearly dark. At this moment Milhaud's division of heavy cavalry came on the scene, but when it tried to get into battle order on the right of the road, and a little forward of the hillock, it was heavily shelled. The emperor said to me 'have all the troops take up positions and we will see what happens tomorrow'.

Dupuy, of the 7th Hussars, notes that Congreve rockets were also fired at the French, as they endeavoured to form line of battle and push Wellington's men deeper into the forest:[39]

I occupied until ten o'clock at night, with two squadrons, the position which the English occupied the next day. Congreve rockets were launched the whole evening, but passed over us, and due to the darkness gave a magnificent spectacle. The jokers amongst us said that the enemy had treated us to a firework display. Finally, I received orders to join up again with the rest of the brigade. The weather was awful, the rain fell in torrents, after wandering some time to find a place to bivouac, the two regiments settled on a large farm, where men and horses were neatly stabled.

General Guyot's division of the French Imperial Guard heavy cavalry saw action at Genappes and Waterloo:[40]

We marched as well in a steady rain until about four o'clock in the evening and we finally settled to Braine-le-Comte and the village of

Mont-Saint-Jean, five miles near the junction of the roads from Nivelles. The English army seems to want to hold the village of Waterloo at the entrance of the Soignes Forest, there were a few shots fired on both sides until the entrance of the night. The emperor remained in the village of Planchenoit and we spent the night in the village of Maransard, in bad weather.

The army made a great movement but it did not march in good order, it did not help that there had been no distribution of rations, so the men are tired and had had nothing to eat. This is a great pity, because they were spreading out in the surrounding fields for food, and they left their posts.

About the skirmish on the 17th at Waterloo, a sergeant with the Royal Wagon Train writes to his father as follows, in a letter dated 22 September 1815:[41]

The line being formed about six o'clock, our rear towards Brussels, the artillery in front on a small height, and the infantry closed columns behind us with the cavalry in the intervals. I had every opportunity to seeing the dispositions of both armies, having occasion to go with messages from one part of the field to another. The line of infantry was under cover of the eminence where the artillery was posted—a smart cannonading commenced on both sides, which lasted till dark. It had rained all this day and at night fell in torrents. I never saw it rain more tremendously. We had not pitched our tents.

Edward Cotton, of the 7th Hussars, notes his perspective of the skirmish that day:[42]

They opened a cannonade upon our line, but principally upon our centre behind the farm of La Haye Sainte: our guns soon answered them to their cost, and caused great havoc amongst the enemy's columns, as they arrived on the opposite heights between La Belle Alliance and the orchard of La Haye Sainte. It was now getting dusk, and orders were given to throw out pickets along the front and flanks of the army.

Our left squadron, under Captain Verner, was thrown into the valley in front of the left wing; the rest of my regiment bivouacked near where Picton fell the next day.

The mutual spirit of defiance was such that in posting the pickets there were many little cavalry affairs, which, although of no useful result to either side, were conducted with great bravery and carried to such a pitch that restraint was absolutely necessary. Captain Heyliger, of the 7th Hussars (part of our picket), with his troop made a spirited charge upon the enemy's cavalry, and when the duke sent to check him, His Grace desired to be made acquainted with the name of the officer who had shown so much gallantry. A better or more gallant officer, than Captain Heyliger, never drew a sword; but he was truly unfortunate: if there was a ball flying about, he was usually the target. I was three times engaged with the enemy, serving with the captain, and he was wounded on each of those occasions: the first time, foraging at Haspereen; next, at the Battle of Orthez; and thirdly, at Waterloo. The ball he received on the last occasion was extracted at Bruges, in 1831.

Wellington's baggage is captured

At some stage in the contest at Waterloo, elements of the Allied baggage were overrun and captured by the French. A sergeant with the Royal Artillery writes to his father as follows, in a letter dated 22 September 1815:[43]

> I was sent off with the spare division of the brigade and was appointed to go to a village called Rhode; but either through ignorance or design, the inhabitants directed us wrongly, and it was not till about four in the afternoon that we joined the brigade on the field since called Mont-Saint-Jean and Waterloo.
>
> At that time, the enemy's cavalry was following our army close up, harassing the rear. About ten minutes afterwards we had passed, the enemy cut off several detachments with the baggage, etc. that were in the rear of us.

The same incident is recorded by Thackwell, of the 15th Light Dragoons:[44]

> I commanded the rearguard. On the Nivelles road near Lillois, some squadrons of French light troops attacked, captured some baggage wagons and cattle as well as took some prisoners.

Squadron Commander Victor Dupuy, who served under Colonel Marbot in the 7th Hussars, writes:[45]

> Later, seeing a convoy defiling on a main road and taking it for artillery, we hurried towards them, it was just baggage, and as a result we captured many Scots.

Bivouacs

Following the skirmish at Waterloo, both armies began to settle down for the night and establish bivouacs as best they could in the pouring rain. That night, as the French army drew up in its positions, French General Delort notes:[46]

> The left wing and the centre of the French army encamped in front of the English on the night of the 17th. The headquarters was established at the farm of La Caillou, near Planchenoit. Rain fell in torrents all night. We had an awful time. The terrain was all mud, flooded by torrents of rain, the next day this made our movements extremely slow and difficult. The roads became almost impassable and left us little hope, that if we failed, we could not effect an orderly retreat to save our artillery and our baggage. The English, placed on high ground and in defensive positions that required little manoeuvres, were therefore in this respect, in a more favourable situation.

Around 18.00, Marshal Ney, with 2nd Corps, arrived at Waterloo. Ney's aide-de-camp again:[47]

> At six o'clock in the evening, the marshal arrived in the immediate environs of the village of Planchenoit, and arrayed his troops in line of battle in front of the village, ready to debouch and the enemy were arrayed on the heights in front of the Soignes Forest, where they had established some batteries, which caused us some losses.
>
> The emperor arrived some time later, and he ordered that we were to advance, but we were not able to shake them from their positions, the enemy deployed ready for battle in front of the Soignes Forest, the right was fixed at the wood and chateau of Hougoumont, the centre was held by the cavalry on the main road covered by a farm, which had been fortified, and the left on the village of Mont-Saint-Jean. The emperor then ordered the troops to retire and take up position for the night.

Louis-Etienne Saint-Denis, otherwise known as the Mameluck Ali, narrates that:[48]

> The emperor, who arrived by a road which joins the highroad to Brussels, went a quarter, or half, a league farther in advance, and we soon found ourselves on high ground which commands the large basin bounded on the north by the curtain of the Soignes Forest. The horizon, which was grey, did not permit the naked eye to see

distinctly; we only saw on our left an English rearguard followed by some French troops, where they fired from time-to-time cannon shots whose smoke we could see. It was near the end of the day.

A little while after the emperor had finished examining the whole plain with his glass, an immense line of fire shone in our eyes. It was the English artillery, which showed the immense front of its army in line of battle. There was only a single volley; then nothing more was heard, but a few shots fired on the left, both by our advanced guard and by the enemy's rearguard, which was retiring.

It was night, or nearly that, when the emperor reached the Caillou Farm; he fixed his headquarters there. As his room was not yet ready, they made a bivouac fire near the buildings (these were to the right of the road), and there, lying on a bundle of straw, he waited while his room was being put in order to receive him. When he had taken possession of the little hovel in which he was to pass the night he had his boots taken off, and we had trouble in doing it, as they had been wet all day, and after undressing he went to bed, where he dined. That night he slept little, being disturbed every minute by people coming and going; one came to report, another to receive orders, etc.

Adjutant-Commandant Toussaint-Jean Trefcon writes:[49]

17 June, we remained in our positions all day. In the evening, we received orders to occupy Genappe. In this town was already the corps of General Comte Lobau and the cavalry division of General Comte de Valmy. Our division bivouacked outside the town. There had fallen in the afternoon and at night a terrible storm of rain which had soaked the roads, filling them with a thick mud that we were all covered with from head to toe. The convoy of rations did not arrive until late at night, which meant that many soldiers slept without eating. I worked at length with General Bachelu in a barn.

We received reports from colonels and generals the actual situations and took our detailed provisions for the battle which was to deliver the next day. After dining on a very brief meal, we divided a bundle of straw between the general and I. In the night, General Husson, who had nowhere to stay, soon joined us and I shared with him the little straw I had left. The soldiers were no less tired than us, they went to sleep where they could, most simply slept in the mud.

NOTES:
[1] Siborne, *Waterloo Letters*, No. 47.
[2] The National Army Museum: 1981-12-53-557. Transcript provided by John Franklin.

[3] John Edgecombe Daniel, *Journal of an Officer in the Commissariat Department of the Army*, Porter and King, 1820, p. 387.
[4] Siborne, *Waterloo Letters*, No. 65.
[5] Edward Cotton, *A Voice from Waterloo*, Mont-St-Jean, Belgium, 1877, p. 21.
[6] The National Army Museum: 9501-118.
[7] *Ipswich Journal*, 1 July 1815.
[8] Siborne, *Waterloo Letters*, No. 34.
[9] Henri Lot, *Les deux généraux Ordener*, R. Roger et F. Chernoviz, Paris, 1910.
[10] Carole Divall, perssonal communication 7 October 2012.
[11] SHDDT: 24 YC 96.
[12] Jérôme Croyet, '*Le 1e Chevau-Leger-Lancier*' in *Traditions Magazine*, Vol. 3, August 2015, pp.26-32. Dr J. Croyet citing documentation in the *Musée l'Empéri*.
[13] Dr J. Croyet citing documentation in the *Musée l'Empéri*.
[14] SHDDT: GR 24 YC 309.
[15] SHDDT: C15 5, *dossier 16 Juin,* Domon to Soult.
[16] SHDDT: GR 24 YC 274.
[17] SHDDT: C15 5, *dossier 17 Juin*.
[18] SHDDT: GR 24 YC 299.
[19] Victor Dupuy, *Mémoires Militaire 1794-1816*, Librairie des deux Empirés, 2001.
[20] Charles P. de Ainslie, *Historical Record of the First or the Royal Regiment of Dragoons*, Chapman and Hall, London, 1887, pp. 150-1.
[21] Discussion with the staff at Vincennes, 19 January 2016.
[22] SHDDT: GR 24 YC 264.
[23] Booth, p. 62.
[24] Oldham Local Studies and Archives: 2006-046.
[25] Courtesy of Queen's Dragoon Guards.
[26] Siborne, *Waterloo Letters*, No. 47.
[27] Edward Almack, *The History of the Second Dragoons: 'Royal Scots Greys'*, London, 1908, pp. 64-6.
[28] Siborne, *Waterloo Letters*, No. 4.
[29] Mercer, vol. 2, pp. 276-80.
[30] *United Services Journal*, Part 1, 1831, p. 313.
[31] Hay, p. 170.
[32] The National Army Museum: 9501-118.
[33] Almack, pp. 64-6.
[34] *United Services Journal*, Part 1, 1831, p. 313.
[35] 'Journal of Cornet Robert Henry Bullock' in Mandell Creighton, The *English Historical Review,* Vol. 3, July 1888, p.451.
[36] Mercer, vol. 2, pp. 282-5.
[37] Gaspard Gourgaud, *La campagne de 1815,* P. Mongie, Paris, 1818, p. 82.
[38] Jean-Baptiste Drouët, *Le maréchal Drouet, comte d'Erlon: Vie militaire écrit par lui même*, Guvatve, Paris, 1844.
[39] Dupuy.
[40] Claude Etienne Guyot, *Carnets de campagnes (1792-1815)* ed. Jean-Hugues de Font-Réaulx, Teissèdre, Paris, 1999.
[41] National Library of Scotland: *Caledonian Mercury*, 5 October 1815.
[42] Cotton, p. 24.
[43] National Library of Scotland: *Caledonian Mercury*, 5 October 1815.
[44] Harold Carmichael Wylly, *XVth (The King's) Hussars 1759-1913*, Caxton Publishing Company, 1914, p. 242.
[45] Dupuy.
[46] Delort, '*Notice sur la batailles de Fleurus et de Mont Saint Jean*' in *Revue Hebdomadaire*, June 1896, pp. 375.
[47] Heymès, p.13.
[48] Mameluck Ali, *Souvenirs sur l'empereur Napoléon*, Ed. Christophe Bourachot, Arléa, Paris, 2000.
[49] Trefcon.

Chapter 11

Waterloo

On Sunday 18 June 1815, the sun rose at 04.00 hours. The French army was strung out along the road from Genappe to Waterloo. They had advanced along a single road, and as a result the road had become congested, and many regiments were still many miles away from the battlefield as the dawn emerged. Only the leading elements, mostly 2nd Corps, Milhaud's cuirassiers, Domon's cavalry and elements of 1st Corps had been at Waterloo since the 17th. All of 6th Corps, Kellermann's cavalry corps and the Imperial Guard were between Genappe and what was to be the field of battle. Napoléon's army mustered perhaps 74,000 men with 256 guns. The 2nd Corps formed the left wing and 1st Corps the right. The reserve was formed from 6th Corps and the two cavalry corps of Milhaud and Kellermann. The Guard was deployed flanking the Brussels road.

At 10.00, Napoléon established his field headquarters and wrote an order to Marshal Grouchy. An hour later, he dictated the following order to Marshal Soult, addressed to Marshal Ney:[1]

> Mont-St-Jean, on June 18 at 11.00 hours.
> Orders dictated by the emperor.
>   Once the army is in battle array, at about one o'clock in the afternoon, when the emperor will give the order to Marshal Ney, the attack will begin to seize the village of Mont-Saint-Jean, where the intersection of the roads is. To this end, the 12-pounder batteries of the 2nd Corps will meet in the sixth that of the 1st Corps. These twenty-four guns will fire against the troops of Mont-St-Jean, and the Comte d'Erlon will begin the attack, carrying forward his left division and support, according to circumstances, by the divisions of the 1st Corps.

The 2nd Corps is able to advance to keep the height of the Comte d'Erlon. The companies of sappers of the 1st Corps will be ready to barricade themselves on the field in Mont-Saint-Jean.

The key to attacking the Allied centre was the farm of La Haye Sainte, which had to be taken if the French were to stand any success of breaking the Allied lines. General Gaspard Gourgaud, of the Imperial Staff, writes about the same event from his viewpoint with Milhaud's cuirassiers:[2]

> At midday, the emperor ordered me to carry the order to Marshal Ney, who commanded the right wing, to attack with energy the enemy, which was to be proceeded by an artillery barrage. This battery was formed in front of the corps of d'Erlon and had sixty-four guns, of which thirty were 12-pounders, and began a vigorous cannonade. The enemy greatly suffered from this.
>
> Our sharpshooters advanced to Mont-Saint-Jean. Marshal Ney ordered the line to advance, the artillery quit their good position to support the advance. Ney ordered four squadrons of cuirassiers to charge along the left side of the road. Three or four hundred Brunswickers were ambushed on Mont-Saint-Jean and were captured. Arriving on the plateau, we suffered from a strong fusillade and the fire from the English artillery. During this movement, three or four hundred English Guards charged our sharpshooters on the highway, and debouched on Mont-Saint-Jean behind us. The remaining squadrons of Milhaud's cuirassiers charged to the front. The English Guards could no longer advance and were repulsed. I shout to ask them to surrender, when suddenly they jumped the ditches beside the road and threw themselves in disorder onto d'Erlon's infantry, we followed them. Quiot's infantry brigade was disordered and they were trying to take away the artillery, fortunately, the English thought to flee from our sabres and soon order was restored.
>
> I killed in this melee four English Guards with my sabre, and an officer with a shot from my pistol. My horse had its neck pierced by a sword thrust.

Michel Ordener, commanding the 1st Regiment of Cuirassiers, recounts what happened that day:[3]

> It was then that the furious Battle of La Haye Sainte began. Impatient of the losses suffered by our troops, and of the delay which the

enemy resistance on this point brought to the movement of the corps, Ney gave me orders to take an English battery placed near the farm of Mont-St-Jean, whose fire was the greatest evil in our lines. I made my regiment advance at the trot. I then formed my regiment into column by squadron with large intervals.

The Hanoverian battalion of Luneburg and the 2nd Light Infantry of the King's German Legion were placed in our way, and I fell on them with the corps. I killed under my hand three officers, their flag is in our possession, we address in the same breath the English battery and we captured the twenty-four guns and limbers that composed the battery and had the guns spiked, and I continued the charge that carried us to the edge of the Soignes Forest. I approached to within ten feet of a square, when one face opened a murderous fire on us, my horse was killed, I am struck by a bullet to the neck, protected by my armour, I can free myself, I leave my horse, and returned with my men to our lines where, after some first aid, I mounted a fresh horse and resumed my command.

The question, therefore, is: when Ney had left the cuirassiers, what did he do? General Bachelu comments that 'Ney constantly stood between the French and British lines, often alone, whilst those around him were killed or wounded, he alone was spared:[4]

While d'Erlon was attacking the Allied left, General Reille began his assault on Hougoumont. Eyewitnesses only speak of Ney's involvement here, directing the action only from late afternoon. The actions of the marshal are not clear from late morning to early afternoon. He seems absent during the counter-attack against the Union and Household Brigades. Following the Allied cavalry charge against 1st Corps, the French cavalry again became heavily involved in the operations following this attack.

It was around 15.30 that Marshal Ney perceived activity in the Allied lines. Now began the famous mass-charges of Waterloo. What Marshal Ney observed, and what the corps commanders could also witness, were the advanced Allied light infantry companies at the bottom of the slope leading to the plateau of Mont-Saint-Jean. These troops, a large body of some four battalions, moved back up the slope close to 15.00. It is the retreat of these troops which appears to have been taken by the French as a major retreat by the British infantry line, but Wellington was simply bringing his infantry back behind the ridge; Ney mistook it for a retrograde movement, which of course was a logical conclusion to make.

This is indeed commented upon by French eyewitnesses as the general understanding of what was happening on the field—a retreat by the British. When the British had retreated to the reverse slope, the infantry could no longer be seen from the French position. Having ridden over the ground, it becomes clearly apparent that the steepness of the slope, and boggy nature of the ground on the day, would have slowed the French advance to a trot. It was not until the French cavalry crested the slope that the cavalry could see where to attack. The charges could not be directed against specific targets—the cavalry was attacking blindly. A charge is best executed by cavalry when the target of the charge can be clearly seen and the squadrons of the attacking force can attack the target in line, in successive waves. Not being able to see the target greatly reduces the effect of the charge. As a result, the attacks were haphazard and piecemeal. Rather than hitting squares in solid waves of horsemen, the attacks faltered as the cavalry crested the hill to be met by close-range volley fire from the infantry squares. Colonel Heymès, aide-de-camp to Marshal Ney, tries to exonerate the action of the cavalry and the marshal in ordering these mass-cavalry charges:[5]

> It was at this moment that the marshal, seeing the importance of occupying the position of the centre which had been abandoned by the enemy, and having no infantry at his disposition, applied for a brigade of cavalry. This brigade executed its movement at a trot; but we know not through what infatuation (*par quelle vertige*), it was followed by all the reserves, not excepting those of the Guard, which, as is known, never obey any other than its own officers, or the orders of the emperor, who used them sparingly.
>
> All this cavalry, to the number of 15,000 horses, charged on without order, and their ranks were reciprocally incommoded; the first regiments were on the summit of the position that had been occupied by the enemy, the others on the slope of the plateau. Some charges were executed with tolerable success, but the most advanced soon received the direct and flank fire of the English infantry, who had established themselves in perfect order, backed by the Soignes Forest, in order to procure shelter from the deadly fire of our artillery.

The bulk of the French cavalry, which had so far not been engaged, were itching for a fight, as General Lhéritier explains:[6]

> They had been placed in a position so exposed, and had been so dreadfully galled by the fire of their infantry and guns, that the impetuosity of the French character would no longer be restrained within bounds, especially as the suddenness of their reorganisation

after Napoléon's return had, of necessity, somewhat deranged their discipline; and there arose such a dangerous clamour in the ranks, and such earnest demands to be led forward, and in their own words, that the officers were compelled to lay aside their better discretion, and at once bring them into action at all hazards.

Horses were reluctant to go straight into a solid infantry wall, outwardly protected by kneeling infantrymen with raised bayonets. French officer Pontécoulant, of the Imperial Guard horse artillery, narrates that:[7]

> The sudden appearance on the plateau of Mont-St-Jean of the 12,000 cavalry, led by the intrepid Marshal Ney, who seemed invincible in the midst of bullets and shells, first produced an irresistible effect. The ground seemed to tremble under their weight . . . all gave way before this human avalanche, the enemy's cavalry, hastened to oppose their passage, was overthrown and almost crushed by their terrible shock.

The French cavalry repeatedly charged at, and were repelled by, the infantry squares, aided by fire of British artillery and the counter-charges of the Allied light cavalry regiments, the Dutch heavy cavalry and some of the few remaining effective units of the British heavy cavalry.

Ney, at some stage, appeared on the French left during a lull in the massed cavalry charges. He desperately needed infantry support to move up behind the cavalry. What lay as yet uncommitted was part of Foy's division and all of Bachelu's. It was not until around 18.00, according to General Trefcon, that the divisions of Foy and Bachelu were fully committed to the attack in the wake of the cavalry. Captain Robinaux, of the 2nd Regiment of Line Infantry, narrates that:[8]

> At six o'clock, Marshal Ney came to our position and he cried with a loud voice: 'Courage, the French army is victorious, the enemy is defeated on all points!'
>
> The emperor, seeing an army corps that emerged into the plain, immediately announced the arrival of General Grouchy, he ordered the commander of the cavalry to attack immediately the plateau of Mont-Saint-Jean, occupied by the British under the command of General-in-Chief Commander of the Combined Armies Lord Wellington, and there he found a strong resistance and numerous artillery lying in wait, which vomited fire and flames on all sides.

Bachelu's command had seen comparatively little action, and headed the French attack columns. Thus, some twenty French battalions (perhaps 6,000 men after the losses of Quatre-Bras and earlier in the day) marched forward to break the Allied line. Also involved was the 3rd Regiment of Line Infantry which, according to Major Beaux, of the 1st Regiment of Line Infantry, was stationed on the right of the orchard of Hougoumont. Major Beaux also hints his regiment was involved in this action. These two regiments would add perhaps another 1,000 to 1,500 bayonets to the French infantry assault. This attack has been written out of the story of Waterloo. Perhaps because it was against primarily non-British troops that most British or Anglophone authors have been ignorant of the attack; perhaps because it has been often been assumed 2nd Corps, by this time, had been bled dry at Hougoumont and could not mount an attack, and finally that the myth created by the French that Ney demanded infantry and Napoléon replied that he had none to spare has been openly taken as hard fact.

These two competing myths have overshadowed the part played by the French infantry on the French left in mounting a large attack on the Allied right. Indeed, Siborne is ignorant of this attack, and even ascribes actions undertaken by the Imperial Guard or 2nd Corps to elements of 1st Corps, which, by tradition, was annihilated by the Union Brigade! The truth is that neither force was annihilated and were spent combating forces in the evening of 18 June. Napoléon was not yet running out of men. The failure of Ney's infantry assault was the last roll of the dice, which forced Napoléon to commit the Imperial Guard to action.

It was perhaps too little too late. The corps of Milhaud, and most of Kellermann's, were exhausted. If Ney had perhaps not been so hot-headed riding at the head of the cavalry, he could, and should, have been able to take into appreciation the events unfolding on the battlefield, rather than become mission-blind in leading the cavalry to glory and mutilation by cannon and musket ball for two hours. Ney to have had no other vision of the field of battle other than the immediacy of the cavalry squadron he rode with. Why Napoléon as commander-in-chief did nothing to stop Ney is not known. Surely here, Ney and Napoléon are equally guilty of inaction in not supporting the cavalry earlier when infantry support was available, contrary to the myth of Waterloo?

In order to extricate 2nd Corps from its attack against the Allied troops to the immediate north of Hougoumont, Marshal Ney ordered the cavalry reserve, comprising the carabinier brigade and the heavy cavalry brigade of the Imperial Guard, to attack. Many authors from the period, and in more modern works, say this attack was never ordered. In a letter addressed to General Pelet dated 27 April 1835, Guyot says the following about the charge he and the carabiniers were ordered to undertake:[9]

> At six o'clock the emperor, wanting to force the centre of the enemy line, gave the order to the Duc de Valmy to charge. This division was brought up to my left. I received the order at the same time to bring my division forward and act under the orders of Marshal Ney. He made me immediately execute a charge on a few squadrons which masked the artillery and our approach to the squares behind.
>
> The retrograde movement made by the cavalry exposed me to artillery fire and to the fire from the squares that protected it and made us suffer great losses. Our two divisions alternately charged on this line of artillery, and failed every time to capture it and we were always obliged to retire precipitately, because we only had our swords to use against the volley-fire from the squares and the grapeshot from the artillery, which greeted us as we arrived on the plateaux. The enemy cavalry took advantage of each disorder the bullets and grapeshot had put into our ranks to pursue our dishevelled squadrons, but since we did not allow him long-term success as we had earlier repulsed his major means of defence.

After successive charges, Napoléon massed the infantry of the Guard to move up in the wake of the Guard heavy cavalry. The battle had raged for six hours, with no one side having any degree of certainty about who the victor was. By this time, La Haye Sainte was in French hands, but the Prussians were now attacking Papelotte, La Haye Sainte and Planchenoit, and had forced Napoléon to commit the Young Guard, 6th Corps, parts of 2nd Corps, battalions from the Old Guard and a proportion of his cavalry force that had not yet seen action to defend his right flank.

In order to try and break Wellington and turn what forces he had remaining to him on the Prussians, Napoléon committed the Old Guard to the attack. The stage was now set for Napoléon's last gamble, as he ordered the Old Guard to make preparations to attack Planchenoit and the Allied centre, in a last attempt to snatch victory from the impending jaws of inevitable defeat. Marshal Ney writes about the attack as follows:[10]

> I observed the arrival of four regiments of Middle Guard, led by the emperor in person, who wished to renew the attack with these

troops, in order to penetrate the enemy's centre. He ordered me to march at their head with General Friant. Generals, officers, soldiers all displayed the greatest intrepidity. But this corps was too weak to resist for any length of time the forces which the enemy opposed to it, and we had soon to renounce the hope which this attack for a few moments. General Friant was struck by a ball at my side. I had my horse killed, and was thrown down under him.

Now, amidst the musket balls and cannon shot, Ney was once more the redoubtable sergeant-major, fighting in the front rank. Ignorant of what was happening around him, Ney was now only concerned with what he could observe. With the designated commander of the French left wing in effect absent, any chance of co-ordinating the attack of the Guard infantry with the remaining cavalry was impossible. With Napoléon having moved to just south of La Haye Sainte to observe the attack, no field commander for the French right wing existed to co-ordinate the defence against the Prussian onslaught. Generals Mouton and Pelet were left, in essence, abandoned to their fate while Napoléon concentrated his efforts on the French left. Indeed, Napoléon seems to have been ignorant of the operations undertaken by Lobau on the French right. Only too late, when the Prussians broke through Lobau's meagre defences and attacked La Haye Sainte, did Napoléon perhaps realise that his last gamble had totally failed. Sergeant-Major Jean Michel Chevalier, of the chasseurs à cheval of the Imperial Guard, which he had joined in 1808, confirms the sequence of events:[11]

> the invincible battalions marched in close column, despite a hail of bullets and shrapnel that fell upon them, and supported by their artillery, they remained steadfast like walls of iron and continued to advance, sweeping aside everything in their path. Across the action the carnage was awful, for a moment victory was definitely with us, and we 60,000 men had beaten 125,000.
>
> Everything was going well. But suddenly, a cry of alarm is heard. Blücher had taken possession of La Haye Sainte. This move cut our army in two.

Senior aide-de-camp to Marshal Ney, Colonel Pierre Heymès, writes in 1820 about the end of the battle as follows:[12]

> Night was falling, disorder began to spread in our ranks, all of our troops were forced back, the Guard does not even resist, she followed the torrent and the road was covered with fugitives. The

enemy took over the embattled farm and, having restored the batteries on the plateau that he had abandoned in the morning, and loosed his cavalry, putting the finishing touch to our disaster. The emperor was mingled in this dreadful disorder; the rout was complete. Marshal Ney, who had five horses killed under him on that fatal day on foot, at the head of the remains of four battalions of the Guard, was the last to leave the field of carnage. An officer of the chasseurs à cheval of the Imperial Guard passed his horse to him, and he re-joined the road and arrived at Marchiennes-au-Pont. From there he took a coach to Paris.

With the Guard repulsed, and Planchenoit in Prussian hands, by 22.00 the battle was effectively lost. The attack of the Guard infantry had been repulsed and Prussian troops were arriving onto the battlefield in large numbers. At this stage, as part of the general advance ordered by the Duke of Wellington, the Dutch-Belgian 6th Hussars and the dragoons of Vandaleur again came into contact with what remained of the grenadiers à cheval and Empress Dragoons. Both the latter regiments had been in near-constant action for four hours, horses and men were exhausted, but it did not stop the regiment from collapsing and fleeing the field of battle.[13]

About the chaos of the rout, Marshal Ney recounts on 26 June 1815 that:[14]

> As for myself, constantly in the rearguard, which I followed on foot, having all my horses killed, worn out with fatigue, covered with contusions, and having no longer the strength to march, I owe my life to a corporal who supported me on the road and did not abandon me during the retreat. At eleven at night I found Lieutenant-General Lefèbvre-Desnoëttes, and one of his officers, Major Schmidt, had the generosity to give me the only horse which remained to him.
>
> In this manner, I arrived at Marchienne-au-Pont at four o'clock in the morning, alone, without any officers of my staff, ignorant of what had become of the emperor, who before the end of the battle had entirely disappeared, and who I was allowed to believe might be either killed or taken prisoner. General Pamphile Lacroix, chief-of-staff of the 2nd Corps, whom I found in this city, having told me that the emperor was at Charleroi, I was led to suppose that His Majesty was going to put himself at the head of Marshal Grouchy's corps to cover the Sambre, and to facilitate to the troops the means of rallying towards Avesnes, and with this persuasion I went to

Beaumont; but parties of cavalry following us too near, and having already intercepted the roads of Maubeuge and Philippeville, I became sensible of the impossibility of arresting a single soldier on that point to oppose the progress of the victorious enemy. I continued my march upon Avesnes, where I could obtain no intelligence of what had become of the emperor.

In this state of matters, having no knowledge of His Majesty nor of the major-general, confusion increasing every moment, and with the exception of some fragments of regiments of the Guard and of the Line, everyone following his own inclination, I determined immediately to go to Paris by St. Quentin, to disclose as quickly as possible the true state of affairs to the Minister of War; that he might send to the army some fresh troops, and take the measures which circumstances rendered necessary. At my arrival at Bourget, three leagues from Paris, I learned that the emperor had passed there at nine o'clock in the morning.

Death

Ney had fought in his last battle and arrived in Paris on 21 June; the Empire was starting to rapidly unravel. On the following day, he spoke to the Chamber of Representatives. By now he knew the game was up, and denounced Marshals Soult and Davout.[15] Napoléon was forced to abdicate on 22 June 1815, the French army capitulated on 3 July 1815 and the Bourbon Monarchy was restored. Wanting vengeance against the army and the instigators of the 'rebellion', on 24 July 1815 some fifty-seven individuals were condemned to death for participating in a conspiracy without equal against the French king. Of these men, nineteen were army officers:

> At the Chateau of Tuileries, 24 July 1815.
> Louis, by the grace of God, king of France and of Navarre,
> Wanted, for the crime of an attack without precedent, but in degrees of punishment and limiting the number of perpetrators to reconcile the interest of our people and the dignity of our Crown and the tranquillity of Europe, for which we need justice and the complete security of all other citizens without distinctions, we have declared and do declare the following:
> Article 1. The generals and officers who betrayed the king before 23 March, or who attacked France and the government with weapons, and those who by violence have seized power, will be arrested and taken before the qualified councils of war in their respective divisions, namely:

Ney, Grouchy, La Bédoyère, Clauzel, the two brothers Lallemand (Henri and François), Delaborde, Drouet d'Erlon, Debelle, Lefèbvre-Desnoëttes, Bertrand, Ameil, Drouot, Brayer, Cambronne, Gilly, Lavalette, Mouton-Duvernet, Rovigo.

Article 2. The individuals whose names follow, namely:

Soult, Dejean the son, Allix, Garrau, Excelmans, Réal, Bassano, Bouvier-Dumolard, Marbot, Merlin (de Douai), Felix Lepeletier, Durbach, Boulay (de la Meurthe), Dirat, Méhée, Defermon, Fressinet, Bory-Saint-Vincent, Thibaudeau, Félix Desportes, Carnot, Garnier de Saintes, Vandamme, Mellinet, Lamarque (the general), Hulin, Lobau, Cluys, Harel, Piré, Courtin, Barrère, Forbin-Janson the oldest son, Arnault, Le Lorgne-Dideville, Pommereul, Regnaud (de Saint-Jean-d'Angely), Arrighi (de Padua) will leave the city of Paris within three days, and retire to the interior of France to the places that our Minister of Police indicates to them, and where they will remain under surveillance, while waiting for the Chambers to rule on those that will leave the kingdom versus those that will be handled by the courts.

Those who would not go to the place assigned to them by our Minister of Police will be arrested on the spot.

Article 3. The individuals who are condemned to leave the kingdom will be allowed to sell their goods and properties, dispose of them, or transport them out of France within the period of one year, and can receive income from foreign countries during this time, as long as they provide evidence of their obedience to this order.

Article 4. The list of all the individuals to which Articles 1 and 2 may be applicable, are and shall remain set by the initial designations included in these articles, and they cannot be extended to include others, under whatever pretext may be, other than in the manner and following the constitutional laws which are expressly waived for this case only.

Given at Paris, at the Chateau of Tuileries, 24 July of the year of His Grace 1815, and the twenty-first of our reign.

Signed by Louis the king and the Minister of State and Police, the Duc de Otranto

Of the men named in Article 1 of the list, Ney, de La Bédoyère and Mouton-Duvernet were to be executed. De La Bédoyère was executed, but Mouton-Duvernet managed to escape. Marshal Brune was murdered by the mob. Ney was arrested on 3 August 1815. He asked to be tried by court-martial, but the court ruled it did not have the jurisdiction to do so. He was tried instead on 4 December 1815 for treason by the Chamber of Peers.

To the restored Bourbons, Ney was the arch-traitor. He had sworn to stop Napoléon and bring him back to the king in a supposed iron cage. Neither Bonapartist nor royalist had much love for Ney. For the new government, examples had to be made.

Ney was shot on 7 December 1815. It was reported that:[16]

> During his execution, Ney refused to wear a blindfold and insisted upon giving the order to fire himself. His final words were reportedly:
> 'Soldiers, when I give the command to fire, fire straight at my heart. Wait for the order. It will be my last to you. I protest against my condemnation. I have fought a hundred battles for France, and not one against her ... Soldiers Fire!

The Times newspaper of 13 December 1815 noted, regarding the execution of Ney, that:[17]

> The French papers to the 10th instant, which have at length arrived, bring the interesting news of the condemnation and execution of Marshal Ney. This circumstance is of importance, in as much as it establishes the fact, that the laws are still superior to private and particular influence in France. The existence of Ney, a known and notorious traitor, furnished a problem, whether the established authorities were yet strong enough to execute justice on those who braved their powers. The Chamber of Peers has decided on the side of law and justice; and the executive power has followed up that decision by a speedy execution of justice.
>
> Ney was shot on the Avenue de la Observatoire, at nine in the morning of 7 December. He desired to be attended in his last moments by a minister of religion. He was so; and at a signal given by himself, he fell dead. Thus perished a traitor, in whose crime ingratitude was a feature no less prominent than folly. This person, sprung from the lowest class of society, and raised to a lofty height by the favour of the despot whom he served, was maintained in his high rank by the (perhaps injudicious) liberality of the king; and in return for such benevolence, he engaged in a rebellion, calculated to shake his country to its centre, and to affect Europe in its most essential interests. When we see a man so selfish in his views, so little affected by the extensive consequences of his actions to

mankind, we cannot regret his fate, if the course of his crimes is overtaken by justice.

Fell a man who would have been honoured for his valour in the field, had he possessed what is equally essential to the character of a soldier—devotion and fidelity to his sovereign.

There were 160 Peers who were present. One hundred and thirty-nine voted for the punishment of death; seventeen for banishment (deportation), and four refused to vote at all: three on the principle that it is not lawful for one man to decide upon the life of another, and one (the Duc de Choiseul) said, that having himself been more than once condemned to death during the Revolution, the horror of that situation was so strong upon his mind, he could not bring himself to place any other human being in a similar one.

Publicly, the execution of Ney seems to have made no particular impression in regard to conversation.

NOTES:
[1] Napoleon I, *Correspondance de Napoleon 1er*, vol.28, H. Plon, J. Dumaine, Paris, 1858. Order No. 22060, *18 June 1815 timed at 1.00*. However, this order does not appear in the correspondence register of Marshal Soult, or that of General Reille.
[2] *'Bataille de Waterloo 18 Juin 1815: relation d'un Officier General Francaise'* in *Nouvel Revue Rétrospective*, January 1896.
[3] Lot.
[4] Erwin Muilwijck, perssonal communication 6 June 2016.
[5] Heymès.
[6] *United Services Magazine*, Part II, 1831, p. 526.
[7] Gustave de Pontécoulant, *Mémoires*, Paris, 1866, p. 310.
[8] Robinaux.
[9] Guyot.
[10] *The Times*, 13 July 1815.
[11] Lieutenant Chevalier, *Souvenirs des Guerres Napoleoniennes* ed. Jean Mistler and Helene Michaud, Hachette, Paris, 1970, p. 325.
[12] Heymès, pp. 26-7.
[13] André Dellevoet, *The Dutch-Belgian Cavalry at Waterloo*, André Dellevoet, The Hague, 2008, p. 217.
[14] *The Times*, 13 July 1815.
[15] John Cam Hobhouse Broughton, *The Substance of some Letters*, Ridgways, London, 1816, pp. 250-1.
[16] Anon, Aspire Auctions, available at https://www.aspireauctions.com/#!/catalog/357/1928/lot/86217 [accessed 28 February 2017].
[17] *The Times*, 13 December 1815.

Chapter 12

Conclusion

What do we make of Ney's actions from 15 to 19 June? We do not seek to analyse his actions in 1814, nor review in detail his arrest and trial. We seek merely to look at his military operations in 1815.

Ney only joined the army on 15 June, and he is made out to be a scapegoat, along with Grouchy, for the loss of the Hundred Days campaign. The bungling of the orders sent to 1st Corps were perhaps due to faulty staff work by Soult, and also a lack of clarity on behalf of Napoléon in his orders and making his intentions clear to his subordinates.

However, while Napoléon was indeed at fault for making many errors during the campaign, the failure to win a clear victory by Ney lies solely with him. He had been ordered to take Quatre-Bras. He advanced as far as Frasné, where his outposts reported the position occupied, but rather than attack, he chose to withdraw. Perhaps this was in part due to his forces not yet being concentrated under his command, as 2nd Corps was, on the evening of 15 June, strung out along the road to Frasné. However, as soon as Reille's men had arrived, Ney could, and should, have attacked. He displayed uncharacteristic caution both on 15 and 16 June.

In the early hours of 17 June, Ney attacked the Allied troops soon after daybreak. Given that by now he was outnumbered, and having no clear information about the strength of the Allied forces, he chose not to commit to a full-scale action. During 16 June, the Allies had been constantly reinforced throughout the course of the day, whereas Ney only had a single infantry corps to face down what may have been the entire Anglo-Dutch army. The strength of the Allied force in front of him no doubt dampened his desire to attack. General Reille, who had faced Wellington in Spain, knew only too well how Wellington fought: concealing his reserves and showing only a small percentage of his troops in the front line. A full-scale attack by three Infantry divisions (Bachelu, Jérôme and Foy) against what may have been all of Wellington's troops would have been suicidal.

Ney's caution once battle was joined was no doubt due to a lack of reconnaissance reports about the strength of the forces under Wellington marching to aid the Dutch-Belgians.

An attack early on 16 June would have brushed the Dutch-Belgian forces aside, the crossroads would have been occupied and Wellington's men would have been faced with Ney blocking the Allied line of advance, and Wellington would have been forced to retreat north. The fact remains, however, that until 15.00 on 16 June, the only Allied troops opposing the French left wing at Quatre-Bras were the 7,900 men and sixteen guns of Perponcher's 2nd Netherlands Division. Later, between 15.00 and 15.30, Picton's 5th Division arrived. Picton's arrival was the first of much-needed reinforcements; Jérôme's division arriving at the same time.

Why did Ney not press his advantage on 15 or 16 June? Several factors now contributed to delay the advance of 1st Corps towards Quatre-Bras, not least of which was the immense congestion created by almost 50,000 men on the single main road. Both Ney and Reille displayed caution. Ney failed to concentrate his forces on the morning of 16 June. Napoléon knew the importance of this, as did Ney. Ney. By leaving the divisions of Foy and Jérôme at Gosselies, rather than ordering them to march to Frasné at daybreak on the 16th, Ney let an easy victory slip through his fingers. But with Durutte's division at Jumet, Quiot, Donzelot and Marcognet's divisions were still further behind at Marchienne-au-Pont by poor marching discipline and congested roads, for which poor planning by the staff was to blame in marching two army corps on one road, Ney seems to have waited until 11.00 to issue orders—was this because Reille counselled Ney to attack only when all of 2nd Corps arrived? By not concentrating his forces at, or soon after, daybreak, leaving 1st Corps and Kellermann far behind rather than waiting, he made a sudden occupation of Quatre-Bras impossible, in contradiction to his orders. He knew well enough the way in which Napoléon waged war.

In defence of Ney, Soult's orders from Napoléon were vague, but we only have the written portion of the orders, as no doubt the orders carried a verbal portion which is lost to history. In the first orders issued on 16 June, Napoléon desired that Ney was to take a position at Quatre-Bras and at the same time make provisions to wheel around behind the Prussians in a *'manoeuvre sur les derrières'*. In all the orders sent to Ney prior to the 15.30 order, his initial task was to take up a position at Quatre-Bras as a stage towards a march towards Brussels. This changed in the 15.30 order, as the occupation of Quatre-Bras became an objective to be achieved before Ney began the *manoeuvre sur les derrières*.

It is understandable, therefore, why Ney, once he got the 15.30 order, was so fixated on taking Quatre-Bras, but it does not explain his lack of action in the early hours of 16 June, or why he became so mission-blind and fixated on Quatre-Bras. Indeed, when we read Ney's report of the battle, written on the evening of 16 June, it does seem that he disregarded the primary and the secondary objectives set out by the emperor. He had totally misunderstood his orders, both written and verbal. Orders were transmitted with a verbal portion to ensure that the courier thoroughly knew what the order meant, could explain the order to the officer receiving the order, and crucially, where necessary elaborate on the written portion to detail exactly what was required of the party which had received the order. Ney's understanding of the 15.30 order that Quatre-Bras was to be occupied before he commenced his wheel was clearly at odds to the verbal portion of the orders, which Baudus states was to send 1st Corps to Ligny and fulfil its role as outlined in earlier chapters. Why Ney acted as he did we cannot say.

When we look at Napoléon's own report of 17 June, it is very clear that had planned to conduct a *manoeuvre sur les derrières* to get between Wellington and Brussels. The plan relied on the fact that he would have defeated the Prussians, due to 1st Corps, and by not having to have dispatched Grouchy in pursuit, would have been able to concentrate his forces and crush Wellington at Quatre-Bras by wheeling the 1st, 3rd and 4th Corps from Ligny to Quatre-Bras. Ney, d'Erlon, Delcambre and Durutte are all culpable in preventing this from happening.

The very simple explanation that d'Erlon's absence at Quatre-Bras lost Ney the battle, however, does not actually fit the realities of the situation. Ney lost the battle not due to a lack of troops, but from a total lack of initiative in the early hours of 16 June, coupled with a breakdown of communications. In this regard, more than just Ney was to blame:

Soult—his orders were vague, but we do not have the verbal portion of orders, which were no doubt a lot clearer. Soult sent multiple copies of orders, via different couriers, to ensure that orders got to where they were intended.

Kellermann—as we have seen earlier, for whatever reason Kellermann did not keep his immediate commander-in-chief, Marshal Grouchy, or the emperor, informed about his actions on 15 or 16 June. He did not tell any officer beyond his immediate staff of the problems he had faced with the carabinier brigade, nor does he actually mention this in his own writings on the campaign.

d'Erlon—rather than reporting to his immediate commander-in-chief, Ney, he reported to Soult about the location of 1st Corps. Furthermore, d'Erlon did not achieve his objectives for 15 June, thus his corps was nowhere near where it should have been.

Delcambre—he knew very well that an Imperial order out-ranked an order from a marshal, and yet he allowed himself to be convinced to the contrary.

Ney—Ney didn't report back to Napoléon at all about his situation and intentions, which is a grave omission and which could only make matters worse. In fact, Soult asked Ney in his orders sent at daybreak, and again at 14.00, for a report for the emperor about the situation at his front. Ney sent no such report until after 11.00. We know he sent one with General Flahaut, as Napoléon mentions this in his letter to Ney, by which time (sometime well after 21.00) the news was too late for any action to be taken. Soult and Napoléon thus had no idea as to what Ney was doing at Quatre-Bras.

Napoléon—he sent orders outside the normal chain of command, often with slightly different mission objectives to those sent via Soult. He acknowledged the headquarters courier system of Soult was defective, but did nothing about it. Yet, at no stage did Soult's couriers fail on 16, 17 or 18 June. As commander-in-chief, the ultimate blame lies with him; he was in charge—the book, as they say, stops with him. Ney had no staff with him, a situation that Napoléon knew about from 15 June. Ney's command and control on 15 to 17 June was compromised, but little was done to rectify the situation beyond allowing officers and men of the Red Lancers to fill this vacuum.

The inevitable conclusion is that the absence of mutual communication from Ney to Napoléon, clear instructions from Napoléon to Ney, and from corps commanders to either Ney or Soult paralysed the movements of 1st Corps. Communication, then as now, was the key to success.

At Waterloo, Ney acted with his usual bravado and courage; and as was all too predictable with Ney, he lost sight of the larger tactical picture, loosing focus on any considerations above the fighting that was taking place around him. At Waterloo, he led the cavalry to the attack at the head of the cuirassiers, he led forward the 3rd and 4th Grenadiers and was again found amongst the front ranks of the Guard. Had he remained away from the front ranks, and able to process the scene of fighting as it developed in front of him in an objective manner, maybe the fighting at Waterloo could have had a different outcome. Ney repeatedly lost his sense of judgement and presence of mind, so critical in an army commander, who needed to take objective decisions and issue clear orders based on a far wider tactical awareness beyond the front line, where Ney had been so fond of being. But where was he on 16 June? At Quatre-Bras, he was not to be found among the front rank of his army. The command and control of 2nd Corps seems to have devolved directly onto Reille, with Piré and Kellermann acting reactively to the situation with their cavalry corps. About the way that Ney himself actually handled the action, there is almost no information available, except that which derives from anecdotes which are repeated over and over again. What we do know, however, is that he had the direct command over the divisions of Piré and Jérôme Bonaparte, though they formally fell under Reille. What may have been the reason for this division in command is unknown. Jérôme seems to have acted independently on the left of the French positions. Countless memoirs of soldiers at Waterloo recall Ney being the fighting marshal, up front and personal in hand-to-hand fighting. He is noticeably absent in the recollections of Quatre-Bras. He was undoubtedly at Quatre-Bras, but why was he so lethargic, why does he seem to have taken so little a part in the action and devolved command to others? On the 17th, Ney should have taken control of the situation at Genappe, and given clear instructions, yet the action at Genappe was one of reaction by both sides. Colonel Sourd's charge down the Brussels road through Genappe was a hare-brained suicide mission. Ney seems totally missing from any command and control of his army corps on 17 June.

The Ney of the rearguard of the Russian campaign was at Waterloo, but at Quatre-Bras his character seems to be the polar opposite: cautious, timid, not wanting to take command. He seems to not have become fully committed to the campaign until the 18th. At Waterloo, he fought like a man possessed, always in the front rank of the attacking troops and was totally incapable, therefore, of acting as a field commander for the left wing of the army.

Ney, at Waterloo, it seems, was incapable of carrying out the duties as field commander. Napoléon was well aware of his tendencies to shirk command and instead try and command his army from the front rank in the thick of the fighting. Ney was a fighting marshal—by his sheer force of personality he inspired his men to great feats of arms, but this was a different thing to thinking clearly and tactically about how best to attack the enemy with the troops at hand. One cannot fight bravely in the midst of his men and be an effective corps or army commander.

How far did Ney and Soult's animosity affect the outcome of the campaign? Ney and Soult had served together in Spain, where Ney's hot-headedness, truculence and ego resulted in a duel being fought between the two men. He managed to get sacked from field command by Masséna for his insubordination. In 1815, did Ney, who in previous campaigns had taken direct orders from Napoléon, become, when out of sight of the emperor, the truculent schoolboy of Spain? Whereby he obeyed Soult's orders to the letter and did not question orders even if they were vague, and not show any initiative simply because he had not been ordered to do so? This is a distinct possibility. Napoléon was well aware of the personal dislike between Ney and Soult. Divide and rule had been one of Napoléon's methods of controlling his marshals, yet playing this game was foolhardy in 1815. Napoléon had a lack of senior field officers; Mortier had resigned his command days before the campaign opened. This left Davout, Soult, Grouchy, Brun, Masséna and Suchet. Perhaps this is why Ney was recalled. Yet, Napoléon never replaced Mortier as commander of the Guard. When Grouchy was detached on the 17th, Napoléon did not replace the commander of the reserve cavalry. Milhaud and Kellermann had no superiors other than Ney or Napoléon. The lack of a chain of command became very apparent at Waterloo—the lack of a senior officer to take stock of the situation of the battlefield during the cavalry charges, and the attack on the French right perhaps cost the French the battle. The blame for that, however, lies directly with Napoléon.

Ney started the campaign with a major disadvantage—he did not know his corps or divisional commanders, nor did he know his troops; nor did his senior officers know Ney. Ney had turned his coat three times in eighteen months, as had many army officers. Indeed, the defection of de Bourmont on the 15th and Colonel Gordon on the 16th as well as officers from the carabiniers on the 16th and 18th, and from the 5th Line Lancers and 1st Chasseurs à Cheval on the 18th clearly showed that the loyalty of officers and men of the army were dubious. Ney himself must have been under suspicion. He had led the coup of the marshals in 1814 against the emperor, and yet here he was being welcomed back into the bosom of the Imperial state. Could he be trusted? What were his true loyalties? Napoléon, the great politician, in appointing Ney once more, was endeavouring to 'forgive and forget'. But, with the defection of de Bourmont, Gordon, and no doubt others, Ney was looked upon with some degree of suspicion. Is this why Grouchy was sent off after Blücher, as he had a very recent track record of success, whereas Ney had shown himself to be timid and not suited for independent command? Did Ney act with caution as he was hedging his bets? It was not only Ney who acted with caution and prudence in 1815. Ney only joining the army on the 15th also resulted in another major handicap: as no commander of the left wing had been considered before the campaign opened, Ney had no staff and headquarters. His staff had to be improvised—perhaps we should forgive Ney for not concentrating his forces on the 16th in the light of the fact; with no staff officers and orderlies, he had no way of getting orders to and from divisional commanders with ease, or being able to effectively command his army. Colonel Heymès was required to act as chief-of-staff, and had to assign mounted officers to the cobbled-together staff to act as orderlies. Thrust into the role of independent commander, a role history has shown Ney was ill-suited for, once the campaign opened, with little or no understanding of the emperor's plans and intentions for military strategy, he had to 'play catch up'. He certainly seems to have been distracted on 15 to 17 June—perhaps he was preoccupied by his fate if the campaign was lost. Certainly, this was on the mind of other officers. Ney had stopped Wellington linking with Blücher, which must be considered a great success given the size of the army available to him. His failure on the morning of 16 June from first light to concentrate his forces and to send out more reconnaissance patrols to clarify the strength of the force in front of him (as he had been ordered to on the 15th) is unforgivable. Ney's caution in waiting for orders from Napoléon is reminiscent of earlier campaigns, where he showed no initiative unless ordered by Napoléon.

Ney, therefore, in 1815, presents a man of two halves. When under the direct supervision of the emperor, he was a man possessed, fighting in the front ranks, not caring that he commanded half of the army at Waterloo and needed to see the bigger picture of the events of that day, to the cautious and perhaps truculent Ney, not acting until ordered to do so. Ney, who, though undoubtedly brave, was not a master of strategy, but had held off a far superior force on 16 June. He, like Grouchy, has been damned for the loss of the Hundred Days. Napoléon and Ney's bungling over 1st Corps resulted in the battles of the 16th being a stalemate. Lack of clear orders from Napoléon on the 15th and 16th, Napoléon's spur of the moment decision to add a marshal to the command of the left wing, with no supporting organisation, crippled Ney's field command from the start. His appointment was perhaps a spur of the moment, reactionary decision by Napoléon. Ney was unsuited to independent command, as his actions in 1813 and 1814 had shown. Hampered by no staff and perhaps wracked with self-doubt about the outcome of the campaign, perhaps fighting for a cause he no longer believed in, Ney's timid actions and limited generalship still held off Wellington for two days, which should be considered a great achievement when we remember he was outnumbered two-to-one.

Appendix

D'Erlon's Communication of 15 June

Communication between headquarters and field commanders was not always as efficient as could be hoped for. For example, d'Erlon sent the following dispatch to Soult at 16.30. As we saw, d'Erlon did not get any orders about his troops at Thuin until very late on 15 June, and could only issue recall orders in the early hours of the 16th, very nearly twelve hours after he had requested orders. The slow rate of communication from headquarters to officers in the field was to have a major impact on the operations on 16th June. D'Erlon's letter reads:

> Your Highness
>
> I received two dispatches which your Excellency had the honour to write to me. The first was received at Montigny-le-Tigneux and I just received the second at Marchienne, my present location. Under yesterday's orders, I left a brigade of cavalry in Solre and Bienne-sous-Thuin, and my infantry divisions are at Thuin, Lobbes and the Abbey of Aulnes.
>
> My other troops are arriving at Marchienne at this moment. As soon as the last elements of the 2nd Corps have past, I will have my men cross the Sambre. I will establish a brigade on the Mons road, and another will remain in front of Marchienne, I will march with the two other infantry divisions to Gosselies.
>
> I reconnoitred the position at Thuin, it is a very strong one, but given the countryside around the place, we cannot establish a bridge head. I ask Your Excellency to let me know if I should still leave troops at Thuin, Solre and immediate area.

Reference: SHDDT C15 5 Dossier 15 June, d'Eron to Soult, 16.30 hours

Bibliography

The bulk of this work is based primarily on archive sources held in the Archives Nationales and Service Historique du Armée du Terre, both institutions being in Paris.

Archives Nationales:
AN AFIV 1170 Garde Impériale et Garde des Consuls
AN AFIV 1171 Garde Impériale
AN AFIV 1172 Garde Impériale
AN AFIV 1173 Garde Impériale 1813
AN AFIV 1940 Garde Impériale 1815
AN AFIV 1939
AN LH/19/93
AN LH/64/22
AN LH/134/23
AN LH/140/81
AN LH/165/53
AN LH/166/3
AN LH/486/75
AN LH/555/16
AN LH/601/4
AN LH/790/21
AN LH/1091/33
AN LH/1168/88
AN LH/1285/74
AN LH/1298/59
AN LH/2050/6
AN LH/2704/63
AN LH/17779/48

Service Historique Armée du Terre:
C15 3 Rapport 26 Mai 1815
C15 4 Correspondence Armée du Nord 1 au 10 Juin 1815
C15 5 Correspondence Armée du Nord 11 Juin au 21 Juin 1815
C15 6 Correspondence Armée du Nord 22 Juin au 3 Juillet 1815
C15 20 registre d'ordres du 2e regiment des Chasseurs à Pied de la Garde Impériale 22 Avril au 27 Aout 1815

C15 22 registre correspondence 2e corps observation Armée du Nord
C15 34
C15 35 Situations Armée du Nord 1815
C16 20 Correspondence Militaire General 1 Juin au 7 Juin 1815
C16 21 Correspondence Militaire General 8 Juin au 18 Juin 1815
C16 22 Correspondence Militaire General 19 Juin au 25 Juin 1815
C16 23 Correspondence Militaire General 26 Juin au 6 Juillet 1815
C37 15 Correspondence Ministre de Guerre
Xb 342 1e de Ligne 1791-1808
Xb 343 1e de Ligne 1808-1815
Xb 345 2e de Ligne 1813-1815
Xb 348 3e de Ligne 1808-1815
Xb 366 11e de Ligne 1791-1815
Xb 382 17e de Ligne 1813-1815
Xb 387 19e de Ligne 1791-1815
Xb 392 21e de Ligne 1791-1815
Xb 406 28e de Ligne 1791-1815
Xb 436 45e de Ligne 1791-1815
Xb 447 51e de Ligne 1791-1815
Xb 453 54e de Ligne 1813-1815
Xb 455 55e de Ligne 1791-1815
Xb 469 61e de Ligne 1791-1815
Xb 488 72e de Ligne 1791-1815
Xb 502 85e de Ligne 1813-1815
Xb 508 92e de Ligne
Xb 511 93e de Ligne
Xb 519 100e de Ligne 1791-1815
Xb 528 105e de Ligne 1791-1815
Xb 533 108e de Ligne 1813-1815
Xb 565 1e Legere
Xb 567 2e Legere
Xb 572 4e Legere
Xc 91 1e Carabiniers
Xc 93 2e Carabiniers
Xc 95 1e Cuirassiers
Xc 97 2e Cuirassers
Xc 99 3e Cuirassiers
Xc 101 4e Cuirassiers
Xc 104 6e Cuirassiers
Xc 106 7e Cuirassiers
Xc 108 8e Cuirasisers
Xc 110 9e Cuirassiers
Xc 112 10e Curassiers
Xc 114 11e Cuirassiers
Xc 116 12e Cuirassiers
Xc 135 2e Dragons
Xc 144 7e Dragons
Xc 180 1e Lanciers

BIBLIOGRAPHY

Xc 181 2e Lanciers
Xc 182 3e et 4e Chevau-Légers
Xc 183 5e et 6e Chevau-Légers
Xc 186 1e Chasseurs à Cheval
Xc 190 3e Chasseurs à Cheval
Xc 192 4e Chasseurs à Cheval
Xc 196 6e Chasseurs à Cheval
Xc 202 9e Chasseurs à Cheval
Xc 206 11e Chasseurs à Cheval
Xc 208 12e Chasseurs à Cheval
Xc 249 7e Hussard 1791-1815
Xc 250 7e Hussard 1813-1815
Xc 264 Cavalerie Generalities
Xd 10 2e Artillerie à Pied
Xd 43 3e Artillerie à Cheval
Xd 360 Artillerie Armée du Nord
GB/2 2760
GD 2 1135
GR 20 YC 13
GR 20 YC 14
GR 20 YC 18
GR 20 YC 19
GR 20 YC 44
GR 20 YC 45
GR 20 YC 46
GR 20 YC 55
GR 20 YC 56
GR 20 YC 137
GR 20 YC 154 registre matricule Dragons Garde Impériale
GR 20 YC 166 Régiment de chevau-légers lanciers, crée par décret du 8 avril 1815 et formé de l'ex-corps royal des lanciers de France, 8 avril 1815-22 décembre 1815 (matricules: 1 à 1,608)
GR 21 YC 8 1er régiment d'infanterie de ligne dit régiment du Roi, 1 mai 1814-6 décembre 1814 (matricules 1 à 3,000)
GR 21 YC 9 1er régiment d'infanterie de ligne dit régiment du Roi, 6 décembre 1814-3 juillet 1815 (matricules 3,001 à 4,386)
GR 21 YC 19 2e regiment d'infanterie de ligne dit regiment de la Reine, 20 mai 1814-21 août 1814 (matricules 1 à 2,997)
GR 21 YC 31 3e régiment d'infanterie de ligne dit régiment du Dauphin, 16 juillet 1814-17 décembre 1814 (matricules 1 à 1,800)
GR 21 YC 32 3e régiment d'infanterie de ligne dit régiment du Dauphin, 17 décembre 1814-1 juillet 1815 (matricules 1,801 à 2,135)
GR 21 YC 40 GR 21 YC 40 4er régiment d'infanterie Legere, 1814 à 1815
GR 21 YC 49 5e régiment d'infanterie de ligne dit régiment d'Angoulême, 6 septembre 1814-23 décembre 1814 (matricules 1 à 1,800)
GR 21 YC 50 5e régiment d'infanterie de ligne dit régiment d'Angoulême, 23 décembre 1814-25 août 1815 (matricules 1,800 à 2,208)
GR 21 YC 74 8e régiment d'infanterie de Ligne dit régiment de Condé, 30 août 1814-11 mai

BIBLIOGRAPHY

1815 (matricules 1 à 1,800)

GR 21 YC 75 8e régiment d'infanterie de ligne dit régiment de Condé, 14 mai 1815-10 juillet 1815 (matricules 1,801 à 2,379)

GR 21 YC 92 10e régiment d'infanterie de ligne dit régiment Colonel-Général, 1 septembre 1814-6 mai 1815 (matricules 1 à 1,800)

GR 21 YC 93 10e régiment d'infanterie de ligne dit régiment Colonel-Général, 6 mai 1815-22 juillet 1815 (matricules 1,801 à 1,943)

GR 21 YC 100 11e régiment d'infanterie de ligne, 9 septembre 1814-4 février 1815 (matricules 1 à 1,800)

GR 21 YC 101 11e régiment d'infanterie de ligne, 4 février 1815-23 août 1815 (matricules 1,801 à 2,690)

GR 21 YC 158 17e régiment d'infanterie de ligne, Octobre 1814-22 juin 1815 (matricules 1 à 2,593)

GR 21 YC 178 19e régiment d'infanterie de ligne, 18 août 1814-26 avril 1815 (matricules 1 à 1,800)

GR 21 YC 179 19e régiment d'infanterie de ligne, 26 avril 1815-16 juillet 1815 (matricules 1,801 à 2,598)

GR 21 YC 197 21e régiment d'infanterie de ligne, 18-20 mai 1815 (matricules 1 à 1,800)

GR 21 YC 198 21e régiment d'infanterie de ligne, 29 avril 1815-16 juin 1815 (matricules 1,801 à 1,817

GR 21 YC 202e régiment d'infanterie de ligne dit régiment de la Reine, 9 septembre 1814-6 juin 1815 (matricules 3,000 à 4,723))

GR 21 YC 255 27e régiment d'infanterie de ligne, 1 août 1814 (matricules 1 à 1,800)

GR 21 YC 256 27e régiment d'infanterie de ligne, 1 juillet 1814-19 juillet 1815 (matricules 1,801 à 2,778)

GR 21 YC 264 28e régiment d'infanterie de ligne, 6 juillet 1808-23 juin 1815 (matricules 1 à 1,762)

GR 21 YC 271 29e régiment d'infanterie de ligne, 21 juillet 1814-24 décembre 1814 (matricules 1 à 1,800)

GR 21 YC 272 29e régiment d'infanterie de ligne, 24 décembre 1814-21 juillet 1815 (matricules 1,801 à 2,226)

GR 21 YC 391 42e régiment d'infanterie de ligne (ex 45e régiment d'infanterie de ligne), 1 août 1814-4 juin 1815 (matricules 1 à 1,800)

GR 21 YC 400 43e régiment d'infanterie de ligne (ex 46e régiment d'infanterie de ligne), 1 août 1814-31 mai 1815 (matricules 1 à 1,800)

GR 21 YC 401 43e régiment d'infanterie de ligne (ex 46e régiment d'infanterie de ligne), 31 mai 1815-30 juillet 1815 (matricules 1,801 à 2,075)

GR 21 YC 456 50e régiment d'infanterie de ligne (ex 54e régiment d'infanterie de ligne), 21 juillet 1814-10 mai 1815 (matricules 1 à 1,660)

GR 21 YC 463 51e régiment d'infanterie de ligne (ex 55e régiment d'infanterie de ligne), 1 août 1814-3 août 1815 (matricules 1 à 2,049)

GR 21 YC 516 57e régiment d'infanterie de ligne (ex 61e régiment d'infanterie de ligne), 1 août 1814-14 juin 1815 (matricules 1 à 1,800)

GR 21 YC 599 66e régiment d'infanterie de ligne (ex 72e régiment d'infanterie de ligne), 11 août 1814-27 février 1815 (matricules 1 à 1,800)

GR 21 YC 600 66e régiment d'infanterie de ligne (ex 72e régiment d'infanterie de ligne), 21 février 1815-4 août 1815 (matricules 1,801 à 2,092)

GR 21 YC 653 72e régiment d'infanterie de ligne (ex 84e régiment d'infanterie de ligne), 1 août 1814-4 février 1815 (matricules 1 à 1,800)

BIBLIOGRAPHY

GR 21 YC 655 72e régiment d'infanterie de ligne (ex 84e régiment d'infanterie de ligne), 20 janvier 1815-24 juillet 1815 (matricules 1,801 à 2,756)
GR 21 YC 665 73e régiment d'infanterie de ligne (ex 85e régiment d'infanterie de ligne), 16 septembre 1814-29 juillet 1815 (matricules 1 à 1,285)
GR 21 YC 690 76e regiment d'infanterie de ligne (ex 92e regiment d'infanterie de ligne), 4 septembre 1814-28 mars 1815 (matricules 1 à 1,512)
GR 21 YC 691 76e régiment d'infanterie de ligne (ex 92e régiment d'infanterie de ligne), 25 avril 1815-27 juin 1815 (matricules 1,513 à 1,728)
GR 21 YC 701 77e regiment d'infanterie de ligne (ex 93e régiment d'infanterie de ligne), 13 août 1814-22 décembre 1814 (matricules 1 à 1,800)
GR 21 YC 702 77e regiment d'infanterie de ligne (ex 93e régiment d'infanterie de ligne), 22 décembre 1814-8 août 1815 (matricules 1,801 à 3,108)
GR 21 YC 717 79e régiment d'infanterie de ligne (ex 95e régiment d'infanterie de ligne), 26 août 1814-25 mai 1815 (matricules 1 à 1,800)
GR 21 YC 734 81e régiment d'infanterie de ligne (ex 100e régiment d'infanterie de ligne), 24 septembre 1814-1er mai 1815 (matricules 1 à 1,800)
GR 21 YC 735 100e régiment d'infanterie de ligne, 1 mai 1815-16 août 1815 (matricules 1,801 à 2,248)
GR 21 YC 771 86e régiment d'infanterie de ligne (ex 105e régiment d'infanterie de ligne), 13 août 1814-21 février 1815 (matricules 1 à 1,800)
GR 21 YC 772 86e régiment d'infanterie de ligne (ex 105e régiment d'infanterie de ligne), 24 février 1815-10 août 1815 (matricules 1,801 à 1,881)
GR 21 YC 781 88e régiment d'infanterie de ligne (ex 107e régiment d'infanterie de ligne), 21 juillet 1814-6 juillet 1815 (matricules 1 à 1,396)
GR 21 YC 790 89e régiment d'infanterie de ligne (ex 108e régiment d'infanterie de ligne), 9 septembre 1814-7 juin 1815 (matricules 1 à 1,800)
GR 22 YC 19 2er régiment d'infanterie Legere 1814 à 1815
GR 22 YC 40 4er régiment d'infanterie Legere 1814 à 1815
GR 22 YC 47
GR22 YC 48
GR 22 YC 116 13er régiment d'infanterie Legere 1806 à 1815
GR 24 YC 9
GR 24 YC 21 Regiment de Reine organisation 1814-29 Juillett 1815
GR 24 YC 26 Regiment du Dauphin organisation 1814-Juin 1815
GR 24 YC 41
GR 24 YC 46 Controle Nominiatif Troupe 7e Cuirassiers 9 Aout 1814-6 Aout 1815
GR 24 YC 50
GR 24 YC 55
GR 24 YC 60 Controle Nominiatif Troupe 10e Cuirassiers 15 Avril 1815-27 Juillet 1815 organisation 1814
GR 24 YC 64
GR 24 YC 96
GR 24 YC 158
GR 24 YC 254
GR 24 YC 264
GR 24 YC 274
GR 24 YC 282
GR 24 YC 299

GR 24 YC 309
GR 25 YC 14 1e Artillerie à Cheval
GR 25 YC 21 2e Artillerie à Pied
GR 25 YC 27
GR 25 YC 40 3e Artillerie à Cheval
M59
MR 7178
276 138
Succesion de Tancarville

PRINTED WORKS
Winand Aerts, *Waterloo, opérations de l'armée prussienne du Bas-Rhin pendant la campagne de Belgique en 1815, depuis, la bataille de Ligny jusqu'a l'entrée en France des troupes prussiennes*, Spineux, Brussels, 1908
Maurice Girod de l'Ain, *Vie militaire du Géneral* Foy, E. Plon, Nourrit et Cie, Paris, 1900
Charles P. de Ainslie, *Historical Record of the First or the Royal Regiment of Dragoons*, Chapman and Hall, London, 1887
Mameluck Ali, *Souvenirs sur l'empereur Napoléon,* Ed. Christophe Bourachot, Arléa, Paris, 2000
Edward Almack, *The History of the Second Dragoons: 'Royal Scots Greys'*, London, 1908
Marie François Joseph Raoul d'Amonville, *Les Cuirassiers du roy, le 8e cuirassiers*, A. Lahure, Paris, 1892
Anon, *Almanach royal pour les années M.DCCC.XIV et M.DCCC.XV*, Asnard et Pochin, Paris, 1814
_____, *Memoires pour servir a l'Histoire de France*, Richard Phillips & Co, London, 1820
_____, *Tales of War*, William Mark Clarke, London, 1836
_____, *The Journal of the Three Days of the Battle of Waterloo*, T. Chaplin, London, 1816
Thomas Joseph Aubry, *Mémoires d'un capitaine de chasseurs à cheval*, Jourdan, Paris, 2011
Paul Avers, *Historique du 82e Régiment d'Infanterie de Ligne et du 7e Régiment d'Infanterie Légère, 1684-1876*, Lahure, Paris, 1876
Robert Batty, *An Historical Account of the Campaign of Waterloo*, Rodwell and Martin and Co, London, 1820
Marie Élli Guillaume de Baudus, *Études sur Napoléon* (two volumes), Debecourt, Paris, 1841
Charles Paris Nicholas Beauvais, *Victoires, conquêtes, désastres, revers et guerres civils des Français, de 1792 à 1815*, C. L. F. Panckoucke, Paris, 1821
Pierre Berthezène, *Souvenirs militaires de la republique et de l'empire*, J. Dumaine, Paris, 1855
Jean Baptiste Berton, *Précis historique, militaire et critique des batailles de Fleurus et de Waterloo, dans la campagne de Flandres, en juin 1815*, J. S. Wallez, La Haye, 1818
John Booth, *The Battle of Waterloo*, Booth, Egerton, London, 1816
Scott Bowden, *Armies at Waterloo*, Empire Game Press, 1983
Brett-James, *Waterloo raconte par les combattants*, La palatine, 1969
General Bro, *Mémoires, 1796-1844*, Librairie des deux Empires, 2001
John Cam Hobhouse Broughton, *The Substance of some Letters*, Ridgways, London, 1816
Albert Burow, *Geschichte des Könglich Preussischen 18 Infanterie-Regiments von 1813 bis*

BIBLIOGRAPHY

1847 ed. Rudolph von Wedell, Posen, 1848

Louis Canler, *Mémoires de Canler* (two volumes), Roy, Paris, 1882

Jean Baptiste Adolphe Charras, *Histoire de la campagne de 1815: Waterloo*, H. Georg, Bâle, 1863

Lieutenant Chevalier, *Souvenirs des Guerres Napoleoniennes* ed. Jean Mistler and Helene Michaud, Hachette, Paris, 1970

Silvain Larreguy de Civrieux, *Souvenirs d'un cadet, 1813-1823*, Hachette, Paris, 1912

John Coates, *The Hour Between Dog and Wolf*, Fourth Estate, London, 2012

Jean-Roch Coignet, *The Narrative of Captain Coignet Soldier of the Empire, 1776-1850*, Chatto & Windus, London, 1897

Combes-Brassard, *Notice sur la bataille de Mont-Saint-Jean* in *Souvenirs et Correspondance sur la bataille de Waterloo*, Librairie historique Teissèdre, Paris, 2000

Emile von Conrady, *Geschichte des Könglich preussischen sechsten Infaterie-regiments*, Glogau, 1857

Edward Cotton, *A Voice from Waterloo*, Mont-St-Jean, Belgium, 1877

Alexandre Coudreux, Gustave Léon Schlumberger, *Lettres du commandant Coudreux à son frère, 1804-1815*, Plon-Nourrit, Paris, 1908

Karl von Damitz, *Geschichte des Feldzuges von 1815 in den Niederlanden und Frankreich* (two volumes), E. S. Mittler, Berlin, 1838

John Edgecombe Daniel, *Journal of an Officer in the Commissariat Department of the Army*, Porter and King, 1820

François-Thomas Delbare, *Relation circonstanciée de la dernière campagne de Buonaparte, terminée par le bataille de Mont-Saint-Jean, dite de Waterloo ou de la Belle-Alliance*, J. G. Dentu, Paris, 1816

André Dellevoet, *The Dutch-Belgian Cavalry at Waterloo*, André Dellevoet, The Hague, 2008

J.B.J. van Doren, *Strategisch verhaal van de veldslagen tusschen het Fransche leger en dat der Gealliéerden op 15, 16, 17 en 18 Junij 1815, Mont-Saint-Jean*, Amsterdam, 1865

Jean-Baptiste Drouët, *Le maréchal Drouet, comte d'Erlon: Vie militaire écrit par lui même*, Guvatve, Paris, 1844

Jacques-Antoine Dulaure, *1814-1830 Historie des Cent-jours,* Paris, 1834

Victor Dupuy, *Mémoires Militaire 1794-*1816, Librairie des deux Empirés, 2001

Pierre Duthlit, *Les Mémoires du Capitaine Duthlit,* Lille, 1909

J.B. Duvergier, *Collection complète des lois, décrets, ordonnances, règlements et avis du Conseil d'état, (De 1788 à 1836 inclusivement, par ordre chronologique), publiée sur les éditions officielles, Continuée depuis 1836, et formant un volume chaque année,* A. Guyot et Scribe, Paris, 1827

John Robert Elting, *Swords Around a Throne,* Phoenix Giant, 1996

Théo Fleischmen, *L'Armée impériale racontée par la Grande Armée,* Librairie Académique Perrin, Paris, 1964

Fernand Fleuret, *Description des passages de Dominique Fleuret*, Firmin-Didot et Cie, Paris, 1929

Maurice Fleury, *Souvenirs anecdotiques et militaires du colonel Biot*, Henri Vivien, Paris, 1901

France Ministère de la guerre, *Annuaire officiel des officiers de l'armée active*, 1822

Hilarion François marie de Forsanz, *Le 3e régiment de chasseurs d'Afrique*, Nancy, Berger-Levrault et Cie, Paris, 1898

Charles François, *Journal du capitane François (dit le Dromadaire d'Égypte) 1792-1830*,

BIBLIOGRAPHY

publié d'après le manuscrit original par Charles Grolleau, C. Carrington, Paris, 1904
John Franklin, *Waterloo Hanoverian Correspondence,* 1815 Limited, 2010
_____, *Waterloo Netherlands Correspondence,* 1815 Limited, 2010
Paul Fussell, *The Great War and Modern Memory,* Oxford University Press, Oxford, 1975
John G. Gallaher, *Napoleon's Enfant Terrible: General Dominique Vandamme,* University of Oklahoma Press, Norman, 2008
Jean-Jacques-Basilin de Gassendi, *Aide-mémoire à l'Usage des Officiers d'Artillerie de France Attachés au Service de Terre,* Magimel Anselin et Pochard, Paris, 1819
Etienne-Maurice Gérard, *Dernières observations sur les opérations de l'aile droite de l'armée française à la bataille de Waterloo,* Mesner, Paris, 1830
_____, *Quelques documents sur la bataille de Waterloo,* Paris, 1829
Philippe Gerbet, *Souvenirs d'un officier sur la campagne de Belgique en 1815,* Émile Javal, Arbois, 1866
William Gibney, *Eight Years Ago, or The Recollections of an Old Army Doctor, his Adventures on the Field of Quatre Bras and Waterloo and during the Occupation of Paris in 1815,* Bellairs & Company, London, 1896
Pierre Giraud, *Précis des Journées de 15, 16, 17 et 18 Juin 1815,* Alexis Eymery, Paris, 1815
Gaspard Gourgaud, *La campagne de 1815,* P. Mongie, Paris, 1818
Anna Green, Kathleen Troup, *The Houses of History,* Manchester University Press, 1999
Emmanuel Grouchy, George Grouchy, *Mémoires du maréchal de Grouchy,* E. Dentu, 1873
_____, *Relation de la campagne de 1815,* n.d.
_____, *Relation succincte de la campagne de 1815 en Belgique,* Delanchy, Paris, 1843
Guverich, *The French Historical Revolution: The Annales School,* in Hodder et al, *Interpreting Archaeology,* Routledge, London, 1995
Claude Etienne Guyot, *Carnets de campagnes (1792-1815)* ed. Jean-Hugues de Font-Réaulx, Teissèdre, Paris, 1999
William Hay, *Reminiscences 1808-1815 under Wellington* ed. Sarah Catherine Isabella Wood, Simpkin, Marshall, Hamilton, Kent and Co, 1901
J.L. Henckens, *Mémoires se rapportant à son service militaire au 6e régiment de chasseurs à cheval français de février 1803 à août 1816,* M. Nijhoff, La Haie, 1910
Jean-Baptiste d'Héralde, *Mémoires d'un chirurgien de la grande armée,* Teissèdre, Paris, 2002
Émile Herbillon, *Quelques pages d'un vieux cahier: souvenirs du Général Herbillon (1794-1866),* Berger-Levrault, Paris, 1928
Colonel Heymès, *Relation de la campagne de 1815, dite de Waterloo,* Gaultier-Laguionie, Paris, 1829
Peter Hofschröer, *Waterloo 1815 Quatre Bras and Ligny,* Pen & Sword, Barnsley, 2006
George Hooper, *Waterloo, the Downfall of the First Napoleon,* Smith, Elder, London, 1862
James Hope, *Letters from Portugal, Spain, and France, during the memorable campaigns of 1811, 1812 and 1813 and from Belgium and France in the year 1815,* Michael Anderson, Edinburgh, 1819
General l'Hotte, *Souvenirs du Général l'Hotte,* 1925
Henry Houssaye, *1815 Waterloo,* Paris, 1903
François Hue, *Jean-Louis de Crabbé, colonel d'empire,* Canonnier, Nantes, 2006
E.F. Janin, *Campagne de Waterloo,* Chaumerot Jeune, Paris, 1820
Christopher Kelly, *A Full and Circumstantial Account Of The Memorable Battle of Waterloo,* London, 1836

BIBLIOGRAPHY

W.J. Knoop, *Quatre-Bras en Waterloo*, Roelants, Schiedam, 1855

Henry Lachouque, *Le General Tommelin,* Tournai, n.d.

Jonathan Leach, *Rough Sketches of the Life of an Old Soldier*, Longmans, Rees, Orme, Brown and Green, London, 1831

Lefol, *Souvenirs sur le prytanée de Saint-Cyr sur la campagne de 1814, le retour de l'empereur Napoléon de l'île d'Elbe, et la campagne de 1815, pendant les Cent-jours,* Montalant-Bougleux, Versailles, 1854

Jean Baptiste Lemonnier-Delafosse, *Campagnes de 1810 à 1815: souvenirs militaires faisant suite a ceux première et deuxième campagnes se St-Domingue de 1801 a 1809*, Alph. Lemale, Havre, 1850

Octave Levavasseur, *Souvenirs militaires 1800-1815*, Librairie des Deux Empirés, 2001

Henri Lot, *Les deux généraux Ordener*, R. Roger et F. Chernoviz, Paris, 1910

Mackenzie MacBride, *With Napoleon at Waterloo*, J. B. Lippincott & Co, Philadelphia, 1911

Raymond Balthasar Maiseau, *Vie du maréchal Ney, duc d'Elchingen, Prince de la Moskowa*, Chez Pillet, Paris, 1816

Harold Esdaile Malet, *The Historical Memoirs of the XVIIIth Hussars (Princess of Wales's Own)*, Simpkin & Co, London, 1907

Roland-Marchot, *Notice biographique sur le général-major Édouard de Mercx de Corbais*, Namur, 1855

Marguerite, *Fastes militaires de la France*, Paris, 1836

Jacques François Martin, *Souvenirs d'un ex-officier 1812-1815*, Paris, 1867

Hippolyte de Mauduit, *Les derniers jours de la Grande Armée* (two volumes), Paris, 1848

William Hamilton Maxwell, *Stories of Waterloo*, Henry Colburn and Richard Bentley, London, 1833

Cavalié Mercer, *Journal of the Waterloo Campaign, kept throughout the Campaign of 1815*, W. Blackwood, Edinburgh and London, 1870

Hubert Miot-Putigny, *Putigny, grognard d'empire*, Gallimard, Paris, 1950

Thomas Morris, *Recollections of Military Service in 1813, 1814 & 1815, through Germany, Holland and France*, J. Madden, London, 1845

Napoleon I, *Correspondance de Napoleon 1er*, vol.28, H. Plon, J. Dumaine, Paris, 1858

Wilhelm Neff, *Geschichte des Infanterie-Regiments von Goeben (2. Rheinischen) Nr. 28*, Ernst Siegfried Mittler und Sohn, Berlin, 1890

Marshal Ney, *Mémoires du Maréchal Ney, Duc d'Elchingen, Prince de la Moskowa* ed. Guillaume Gamot, H. Hournier, Paris, 1833

Michel Louis Felix Ney, *Documents inédits sur la campagne de 1815*, Anselin, Paris, 1840

Antoine Noguès, André Maricourt, *Mémoires du général Noguès (1777-1853) sur les guerres de l'Empire*, A. Lemerre, Paris, 1922

Louis Florimond Fantin des Odoards, *Journal du général Fantin des Odoards*, E. Plon, Nourrit et Cie, Paris, 1895

Auguste-Louis Pétiet, *Souvenirs militaires de l'histoire contemporaine*, Dumaine, Paris, 1844

Julius von Pflugk-Harttung, *Vorgeschichte der Schlacht bei Belle-Alliance, Wellington*, R. Schröder, Berlin, 1903

Gustave de Pontécoulant, *Mémoires,* Paris, 1866

Colonel du Génie Répécaud, *Napoléon à Ligny et le Maréchal Ney à Quatre-Bras*, Degeorge, Arras, 1847

Rigau, *Souvenirs des guerres de l'empire, réflexions, pensées, maximes, anecdotes, lettres diverses, testament philosophique*, A. Poilleux, Paris, 1846

BIBLIOGRAPHY

Pierre Robinaux, Gustave Léon Schlumberger, *Journal de route du Capitaine Robinaux 1803-1832*, Plon-Nourrit, Paris, 1908
Mike Robinson, *The Battle of Quatre Bras 1815*, The History Press, 2010
Louis-Jacques Romand, *Mémoires de ma vie militaire, 1809-1815*, F. Barthelet, Besançon, 1981
Rousselon, *Biographie du Général Baron Sourd, Commandeur se la Légion d'Honneur*, Paris, 1830
Marie Théodore de Gueilly Rumigny, *Souvenirs du général comte de Rumigny, aide de camp du roi Louis-Philippe, 1789-1860*, Émile-Paul frères, Paris, 1921
Sénécal, *General le Sénécal campagne de Waterloo*, Philadelphia, 1818
C.W. Serjeant, Joseph Butterworth, *Some particulars of the battle at Waterloo*, J. & T. Clarke, London, 1816
Michael Shanks, Ian Hodder, *Processual, postprocessual and interpretive archaeologies* in Hodder et al, *Interpreting Archaeology*, Routledge, London, 1995
William Siborne, *History of the war in France and Belgium, in 1815, containing minute details of the battles of Quatre-Bras, Ligny, Wavre and Waterloo*, Boone, London, 1848
_____, *The Waterloo Campaign 1815*, A. Constable, 1900
_____, *Waterloo Letters* ed. H. T. Siborne, Greenhill Books, 1993
Pierre François Tissot, *Histoire de Napoléon, rédigée d'après les papiers d'État, les documents officiels, les mémoires et les notes secrètes de ses contemporains, suivie d'un précis sur la famille Bonaparte* (two volumes), Delange-Taffin, Paris, 1833
William Tomkinson, James Tomkinson, *The Diary of a Cavalry Officer in the Peninsular and Waterloo Campaigns 1809-1815*, S. Sonnenschein, London, 1894
Jean-Phillipe Tondeur, Patrice Courcelle, Jean Jacques Patyn, Paul Megnak, *Carnets de la Campagne No. 1—Hougoumont*, Tondeur Diffusion, Brussels, 1999
Toussaint-Jean Trefcon, *Carnet de la campagne du colonel Trefcon, 1793-1815*, E. Dubois, Paris, 1914
Achille de Vaulabelle, *Campagne et bataille de Waterloo*, Perrotin, Paris, 1845
August Wagner, *Plane der Schlachten und Treffen, welche von der Preussischen Armee in den Feldzügen der Jahre 1813, 14 und 15 geliefert worden*, Reimer, Berlin, 1825
Hans Wellmann, *Geschichte des Infanterie-Regiments von Horn (3-tes Rheinisches) N. 29*, Lintzcher Verlag, Trier, 1894
Harold Carmichael Wylly, *XVth (The King's) Hussars 1759-1913*, Caxton Publishing Company, 1914

ONLINE SOURCES

Martin Aaron, *2nd Battalion 69th (South Lincolnshire) Foot during the Waterloo Campaign*, The Napoleon Series, October 2007, available at http://www.napoleon-series.org/military/organization/Britain/Infantry/c_2-69Waterloo.html [accessed 22 August 2012]
Anon, Aspire Auctions, available at https://www.aspireauctions.com/#!/catalog/357/1928/lot/86217 [accessed 28 February 2017]
Paul L. Dawson, *Memoires: Fact or Fiction? The Campaign of 1814*, The Napoleon Series, December 2013, available at http://www.napoleon-series.org/research/eyewitness/c_memoires.html [accessed 28 February 2017]
Stephen Millar, *The Key to Victory: General d'Erlon's I Corps, 16 June 1815*, The Napoleon Series, November 2007, available at http://www.napoleon-series.org/military/battles/waterloo/c_waterlood'erlon.html [accessed 4 January 2017]

Index

Adjutant-Commandant Durosnel, 25
Adjutant-Commandant Jeanin, 27,28, 44,45,98, 99, 150
Adjutant-Commandant Nillis, 30
Adjutant-Commandant Toussaint-Jean Trefcon, 18, 58, 216
Alten, 86, 92
　division of, 93

Baron Galbois, 96
Baron Soye, 114
Battalion Commander Baudus, 160
Battalion Commander Claude François Marie Répécaud, 63
Battalion Commander Gaugler, 33
Battalion Commander Rullieres, 168
Battle of Ligny, 34, 68, 99
Battle of Quatre-Bras, x, 133, 154, 173, 188, 248
Baudus, 156, 160, 163–64, 173–74, 244
Bédoyère, 35, 155, 157, 160, 163, 173, 228
Belgian army, 19
Belgian Battalion, 17, 112
Belgian cavalry, 92, 97, 146
Belgian Light Dragoons, 143
Belgian regiment of hussars, 146
Belgium, 16, 24, 105, 173, 217, 245–46, 248
Bonaparte Jérôme, 49, 103, 105, 107, 115, 119, 158, 232, 235
　King, 142
　Prince, 67, 70, 107–8, 114, 116, 123, 147, 150, 158, 172
　division of, 100, 107, 109, 111, 117, 118–19, 232
Bonaparte, Napoléon, 26–32, 34, 36–37, 39–49, 106, 148–50, 154–56, 158–59, 161–62, 164–66, 170–73, 175–76, 181–82, 190–92, 215–16,217, 226–27, 244, 247
Bossu Wood, 19, 50, 61–62, 67–68, 77, 81, 86, 91–93, 107, 109–11, 115–16, 127, 138, 141–42
Bourmont, 15, 29, 31, 103, 166, 236
Braine-le-Comte, 19, 51, 112, 144, 184, 212
Bremen Light Infantry Battalion, 177–79
Brevet-Major Leach, 85
British Army, 36, 69, 122, 157, 182, 212–13
British Division, 84, 86
British Guards, 141
British Household Cavalry, 205, 206
British infantry, 57, 94, 123, 179, 184
Brue, 170, 174
Brunswick, 84–87, 90–93, 107, 113, 123, 146, 151, 201
Brunswick battalions, 93
Brunswick cavalry, 79, 88, 129
Brunswick corps, 92, 94
Brunswick division, 91
Brunswickers, 53, 83–84, 86–88, 127, 129
Brunswick hussars, 92, 146
Brunswick infantry, 85, 93, 129
Brunswick infantry battalions, 87
Brunswick Light Battalion, 89

INDEX

Brunswick troops, 87, 111
Brussels, 17–18, 35–36, 38, 44, 55–57, 81, 89–90, 104, 108, 150, 171–73, 181, 184–85, 191–92, 204–5
Brussels road, 26, 34, 36–37, 48–49, 55–57, 77, 104, 122, 127, 151, 158, 164, 176, 195, 206
Brye, 98, 104, 156, 158–59, 165, 167, 175
  heights of, 156, 158, 160
Bülow, 89

Cabaret la Baraque, 57
Captain-Adjutant-Major Louis Charles Joseph Beissac, 115
Captain Arnaud, 60
Captain Bertrand, 134
Captain Bijleveld, 78–80, 105
Captain Bisson, 134
Captain Charles-François Durousseau-Lagrange, 113
Captain Claude Joseph Giro, 118
Captain Pierre Charles Duthlit, 133, 164, 172, 174, 188, 194, 245
Captain Elphinstone, 196, 200
Captain Geij, 78–80
Captain Grey, 177
Captain Hay, 128
Captain Henry Royen, 80
Captain Henry Scheltens, 111
Captain Jacques Philibert Rene Guillaume, 96
Captain Jean Jacques Lemonnier, 115
Captain Laurent, 157
Captain Louis Alexandre Druez, 108
Captain Luard, 186
Captain Mathey, 32
Capatin Cavalié Mercer, 180, 188, 194, 207, 247
Captain Pigeau, 96
Captain Robinaux, 114, 222
Captain Schrieber, 210
Captain Sijbers, 110
Captains Pierre Cesar Bunel, 115
Captain Stevenaar, 78, 80
Captain Taylor, 177, 185
Captain Verner, 213
Captain Werneck, 61, 142

Chapuis, 33, 54, 168–69, 174
Charleroi, 14–18, 21, 24, 26–29, 31, 36, 43, 45, 74, 79, 81–82, 92–93, 101–2, 121, 128
Charleroi road, 71, 76, 86, 181, 183
Claude Etienne Guyot, 217, 246
Claude Frederic Donop, 143
Claude Joseph Girot, 119
Colonel Auguste Louis Petiet, 16
Colonel Baron Pieter Hendrik, 50, 142
Colonel Biot, 22, 245
Colonel Boreel, 77, 79
Colonel Carl Best, 179
Colonel Chapuis, 174
Colonel Crabbé, 246
Colonel Deschamps, 31
Colonel Despans des Cubières, 119
Colonel Dick, 94
Colonel Edouard, 18
Colonel Faudoas, 76
Colonel Forbin-Janson,157–60, 228
Colonel Garavaque, 131, 135–36, 140
Colonel Gordon, 33, 236
Colonel Pierre-Agathe Heymès, 17, 22, 24, 41–42, 49, 53–55, 119, 115, 124, 147, 152–53, 157, 194, 217, 221, 225, 230, 237, 246
Colonel Higonet, 59–60, 66
Colonel Jacquinot, 191
Colonel Jean Baptiste Lemonnier-Delafosse, 17
Colonel Jeanin, 27
Colonel Jean Marie Tissot, 72
Colonel Lawrence, 168, 170
Colonel Lord Somerset, 110
Colonel Louis Bro, 31
Colonel Macara, 94
Colonel Marcelin Marbot, 171, 191, 203–4, 214, 228
Colonel Mercx, 79
Colonel Merlin, 130
Colonel Murray, 186
Colonel Nicolas Marie Mathurin, 96
Colonel Ordener, 201
Colonel Prince Bernhard, 91
Colonel Talhouet, 76
Colonel Tancarville, 27, 136

238

INDEX

Colonel Trefcon, 22, 248
Colonel Tripe, 119
Combes-Brassard, 245
Comte Lobau, 26, 43, 192
Corporal Borgnes, 132, 136
Cuirassier Henry, 132
Cuirassiers, 86–87, 92, 95, 108, 121, 123–27, 129–41, 143, 145–47, 152–53, 195–96, 199–201, 219–20, 240, 243–44

Delhutte Woods, 150, 167
Duke of Brunswick, 85–87, 92–93, 107, 123, 146
Duke of Wellington, vii, 14, 83–84, 86, 90–92, 111, 113, 146, 183, 226
Duke of York Battalion, 179
Duke of York Light Infantry Battalion, 177–78
Dutch-Belgian Cavalry, 81, 230, 245
Dutch heavy cavalry, 222
Dutch horse artillery, 112
Dutch hussars, 82, 143
Dutch jägers, 71, 112
Dutch militia, see Militia Battalions
Dutch troops, 58, 115, 177
Dyle, 203

Empress Dragoons, 226

Farm of Quatre-Bras, 57, 61, 64, 79, 84, 87, 112, 122, 124, 137, 142, 181
Field Marshal Gebhard Leberecht von Blücher, 13–14, 46, 52, 98–99, 115, 146, 163, 176, 182, 225, 236–37
Fleurus, 17, 19–22, 31, 35, 38, 46–47, 67–69, 96, 98, 135, 144, 147, 152, 155–56, 158–59
Fleurus road, 26
François Napoléon Charonnet, 131
Frasné, 16–19, 21–22, 41–46, 48–50, 55–56, 62, 67, 108–9, 112, 121–22, 138–40, 147–48, 157, 179, 231–32
 heights of, 122, 139
 village of, 27, 57–58
Frederick, Prince, 184
French army, 13–14, 82, 97, 165, 170, 181, 215, 218, 222, 227

French infantry, 79, 83, 84, 87, 91, 92, 143, 145, 223
French lancers, 94–95, 97, 186, 188, 199, 203, 205, 209

Galbois, 96
Gembloux, 35–38, 68
Gémioncourt, 58, 62–63, 69, 71, 73, 76–77, 86, 91–93, 149
 advanced post of, 69, 149
 front of, 70, 149
Gémioncourt Farm, 67, 71, 76–77, 105
Genappe, 36–37, 43, 45–47, 53, 55, 89–90, 182, 184–85, 187–88, 190–91, 193, 195–206, 216, 218, 235
General Antoine Noguès, 26, 53, 247
General Bachelu, 15, 18, 20, 22, 46, 49–50, 52, 57–58, 67–64, 70, 71, 75, 81, 86, 103, 105, 137, 149, 216, 220, 222, 232
Général Baron Sourd, 191, 193, 194, 235, 248
General Bourgeois, 172
General Bro, 244
General Brue, 169–70, 174
General Chastel, 46, 159
General Colbert, see Marshal-du-Camp Colbert
General Corbineau, 192
General-de-Brigade Brue, 157
General-de-Brigade Cyrille Simon Picquet, see Marshal-du-Camp Picquet
General-de-Brigade Guiton, 116
General-de-Brigade Jean Baptiste Berton, 121,136, 152, 159, 174121
General-de-Brigade Pelletier, 114
General-de-Brigade Victor-Joseph Delcambre, 102, 154, 157, 162–66, 173, 233–34
General D'Erlon, 15, 17, 24–28, 45, 47–48, 53, 55, 99–100, 102–4, 147–48, 154–58, 160–71, 173–76, 217–20, 233–34
 corps of, 137, 162
 flank attack, 165
 infantry, 219
 troops, 100, 164, 173

239

INDEX

General Roussel d'Hurbal, 29–30, 100, 123, 176
General Decaen, 13
General Delort, 138, 175
General Dominique Vandamme, 246
General Domon, 46, 191, 202–3, 217
  cavalry of, 15, 218
General Donop, 140, 143, 164
  brigade of, 143, 147, 176
General Donzelot, 26, 48, 101, 103, 167, 171, 177, 232
  division of, 164, 172
General Durutte, 33, 47–48, 56, 100–102, 164, 166–71, 173, 176, 233
  division of, 56, 100–101, 154, 163, 166–69, 232
General Flahaut, 38–42, 47, 49–50, 155-156 175, 191, 234
General Comte Foy, 16, 22, 46, 49-50 51–52, 54, 57, 58, 62, 64, 67–69,71, 73, 75 86, 92, 105, 115, 138, 149, 170,222, 244
General Friant, 225
General Gaspard Gourgaud, 219
General Gauthier, 72
General Gérard, 32, 35
General Girard,36, 44, 47–49, 55–56, 67
 division of, 21, 32, 35, 103, 148
General Gourgaud, 211
General Guilleminot, 70, 108
General Halkett, 93
Général Herbillon, 246
General Husson, 18, 216
General Jacquinot, 39, 46–47, 56, 101, 103, 121, 164, 167, 203
  division of, 163, 164, 170–71, 205
General Jamin, 70, 149
General Jean Rapp, 13
General Kellermann, 26-33 29, 38–39, 42, 48, 50, 55-56, 100, 102-4, 116,121, 124, 131, 139, 140–41, 232–33, 235–36
  cavalry corps of , 32, 34, 101, 137, 141, 218
  cuirassiers of, 41, 138–39, 158, 162
General Lamarque, 13
General Lecourbe, 13
General Lefèbvre-Desnoëttes, 18, 19, 21, 22, 26, 36, 38, 43, 49, 51, 174, 228
General Lhéritier,29–30, 67, 115, 116, 123, 124, 140, 147, 221
  division of, 123, 147
General de Bourmont, 32
General Lord Hill, 184
General Maitland, 144
General Noguès, 25, 247
General Pack, 151
General Pamphile Lacroix, 226
General Pelet, 224
General Piré, 18, 22, 43, 49, 55, 59, 62, 67, 92, 96–97, 147, 149–50
General Reille, viii, 15, 17, 20, 22, 24, 39, 41, 43,45, 47, 48, 49, 51, 64, 66–67, 69, 147–48, 230–31, 102–4, 151, 153, 156, 159, 231–32, 235
  corps of, 102, 157
General Quiot, 101–3, 164, 166–67, 172, 232
General Roussard, 139
General Samuel François Lhéritier, 116
General Tommelin, 247
General Trefcon, 222
General Vandamme, 15, 30, 35, 161, 175
General van Merle, 51
General van Merlen, 78–81
General Zeithen, 22
Gilly, 14, 31, 228
Gosselies, 16–22, 24–27, 29, 32, 34, 36, 49, 53, 55–56, 98, 100–103, 122, 148, 154, 166
  occupied, 22
Grouchy, viii, 27, 29, 31, 34, 36–41, 46–47, 53–54, 100, 152, 165, 174, 228, 231, 236–37
  Emmanuel, 54, 118, 246
Grubenhagen Light Infantry Battalion, 177, 179

Hamburg, 119
Hanoverian battalion of Luneburg, 220
Hanoverian Brigade, 84, 177
Hanoverian hussars, 192, 204
Hanoverian jägers, 125
Hautain-le-Val, 113
Hautam-Leval, 111
Haye Sainte, 213, 219, 224–25
Heppignies, 21–22, 46
Household Brigades, 204, 220

INDEX

Household Cavalry, 205
Household Cavalry Brigade, 205

Imperial Guard, 14–15, 18, 26, 36, 43–44, 46, 49–51, 61–62, 67, 69, 75, 142–43, 218, 222–23, 225–26
Imperial Guard cavalry, 33, 41, 51, 53, 67
Imperial Guard infantry, 225–26
Imperial Guard light cavalry, 17, 18, 34, 52
Inniskillings, 207

Jäger Battalion, 62, 78, 109, 142–43
Jemappes, 67, 192–93, 204

Lanciers, 153, 240–41
Laon, 14
Leib Battalion, 92–93
Leipzig, vii
Lemale, 22, 247
Lemonnier-Delafosse, 22, 54, 74
Liberchies, 43, 55, 57
Lieutenant Antoine Amelot33, 118
Lieutenant Armand Noel, 96
Lieutenant Carondal, 112
Lieutenant Claude Glorget, 117
Lieutenant-Colonel Dorville, 183
Lieutenant-Colonel Edouard, 82
Lieutenant Deebetz, 75, 105
Lieutenant-general aide-de-camp, 27
Lieutenant-General Collaert, 80
Lieutenant Grand, 73
Lieutenant Henckens, 76, 138, 185
Lieutenant Honoré Bel, 115
Lieutenant Irwin, 95
Lieutenant John, 185
Lieutenant John Banner, 195
Lieutenant Myer, 200
Lieutenant Noel, 97
Lieutenant Pattison, 128
Lieutenant Paul Esteve, 20
Lieutenant Pigot, 133
Lieutenant Riddick, 97
Lieutenant Simon Cottan, 115
Lieutenant Smith, 186
Lieutenant Vandenzande, 83
Lieutenant Wassenaar, 78, 105
Lieutenant William Thain, 87

Lieutenant Wintsinger, 78
Lieutenant Wrede, 179
Lieutenant Wynoldie, 78
Life Guards, 196, 198, 200–201, 205–7, 209–10
Ligny, 32, 37, 44–45, 66, 99–100, 104–5, 114, 121, 142, 154–58, 160–66, 169–73, 181–82, 202–3, 246–48
Ligny battlefield, 137, 164
Lobbes, 15, 20, 25
Lombrie Wood, 20
Lombue Wood, 21
London, x, 54, 105, 152–53, 173, 194, 217, 230, 244–48
Lord Anglesey, 198
Lord Uxbridge, 187–88, 191, 195, 199, 207
Lord Wellington, 19, 123–24, 137, 149, 205
Luneburg Infantry Battalion, 177
Luneburg Light Infantry Battalion, 178
Lützow, 176
Lyon, 135

Major Alexander Rigny, 32
Major Amerongen, 109
Major Beaux, 223
Major-General Bylandt, 91
Major-General Colville, 184
Major-General Count Bylandt, 91
Major-General Sir Colin Halket, 130
Major-General Sir William Ponsonby, 204
Major-General van Marle, 111
Major Howard, 177
Major Lebeau, 119
Major Radclyffe, 183, 200, 204
Major Rauschenplatt, 89
Major Schmidt, 226
Major Villoutreys, 32
Maransard, 213
Marbais, 33–34, 36–39, 41–43, 55–56, 98–100, 166
Marchienne-au-Pont, 15–17, 24–26, 101, 226, 232
Marchiennes, 15–16, 18, 20–21, 25, 121
Marchiennes-au-Pont, 50, 168, 170–72, 226

241

INDEX

Marcognet, 101–2, 166–67
Marengo, 14, 124
Marshal Brune, 13, 228
Marshal Davout, 13, 30, 161
Marshal-du-Camp Colbert, 18–19, 23, 46, 49, 150, 174 190, 191, 192
Marshal-du-Camp Baron Picquet, 116, 134, 135, 140–41, 143, 164
  dragoon brigade of, 124, 140
Marshal-du-Camp Baron Schmitz, 171, 176
Marshal Grouchy, vii, 13, 31, 36–37, 40, 43, 46, 69, 98, 192, 218, 226, 233
Marshal Mortier, 17
Marshal Ney, vii, 66, 152, 174, 247, 256
Marshal Soult, vii, 20, 22, 161, 218, 230
Marshal Suchet, 13
Materne Brook, 105
Materne Pond, 71
Mellet, 18, 21–22, 57–58, 148, 158, 176
Mellinet, 228
Metz, 66
Meurthe, 228
Meuse, 192
Milhaud's cuirassier division, 15, 158, 191, 204, 218–19, 212
Militia Battalion, 39, 49, 50, 51, 59, 61–62, 65-66, 71, 77, 93, 97, 100, 101, 104,113, 116
Moncaux Wood, 21
Monceaux Wood, 16
Mons, 19, 25, 27, 44–45, 48, 104, 150
Mons road, 27
Mont Saint Jean, 152, 217
Mont-Saint-Jean, 56, 105, 114, 182, 207, 210, 213–14, 217-219, 222, 245
  plateau of, 220, 222
Moselle, 153
Moulaux Wood, 20

Namur, 14, 46, 50, 62–63, 69, 75–76, 81, 92, 105, 115–16, 146, 175, 181, 185, 247
Namur roads, 47, 56–57, 59, 63, 94, 99–100, 149
Nancy, 106, 245
Nantes, 246

Nassau Battalion, 18, 51, 61, 109–10, 142
Nassau Regiment, 151
Nassau troops, 19, 90, 107, 112, 142, 180
National Militia Battalions, 61, 109
Netherlands Division, 27, 232
Netherlands Infantry Division, 50, 142
Netherlands Militia Battalion, 77
Nivelles, 19, 51, 76, 80–81, 86, 99, 108–9, 112, 130, 144, 146, 150, 181, 183–84, 213

Octave Levavasseur, 247
Old Guard, 119, 158, 224
Orange-Nassau battalion, 109
Orange-Nassau Regiment, 61–62

Perponcher, 102, 104, 150, 232
Phlasbourg, 153
Pierrepoint Farm, 113
Piraumont, 58–59, 89, 92
Piraumont Farm, 64
Pirémont, 149
Piré's cavalry, 34, 86
Planchenoit, 182, 191–92, 215, 224, 226
  village of, 211, 213, 215
Private William Hemmingway, 129
Prussian army, 36, 43, 68–69, 112, 156–57, 161, 166, 168, 171, 175–76, 182, 192
Prussian rearguard, 21
Prussians, vii, 14–16, 18, 33–37, 44, 52, 99, 111–12, 114, 134, 137, 164–65, 168, 224–26, 232–33
Prussian Uhlans, 18

Quatre Bras, 14, 16, 18, 20, 22, 26, 28, 30, 32, 34, 36, 37, 38, 40, 42, 55–62, 64-68, 71–73, 81–84, 92–94, 102, 111-14, 120–25, 135–38, 141–44, 152,156–65, 167–73, 181–85, 231–35

Red Lancers, 34, 75, 141–43, 201, 234
  famed, 18
Regiment of Hussars, 20–21, 34, 36, 79, 81, 92–93
Regiment of Foot
  1st, 130

INDEX

3rd, 73
28th, 83-84
30th, 113-14, 118, 189
33rd, 75, 81, 85, 115-17, 118
42nd, 75, 82
44th, 75, 84, 85
69th, 85, 115, 118, 120-22, 124, 138
73rd, 118
92nd, 72, 73, 75, 80, 81
95th, 73, 74
1st regiment of Foot Guards, 133
Regiment of Line Infantry,
   1st, 21, 102, 105, 211
   2nd, 102, 105, 210-11,
   3rd, 97, 105, 211
   11th, 20
   17th, 160
   28th, 160-61
   45th, 3, 9
   51st, 160
   54th, 160
   61st, 52, 53
   72nd, 48, 51, 52, 53, 138
   85th, 21, 145, 156-57,
   92nd, 56, 60, 158
   95th, 156
   93rd, 36, 56, 60
   100th, 56, 57, 58, 61, 137
   108th, 47, 48, 54, 58, 137
Regiment of Light Infantry
   1st, 58, 96-97, 104-105
   2nd, 4, 8, 40, 41, 51, 52
   4th, 56, 58, 60, 61, 138
Regiment of Carabiniers
   1st, 16-18
Regiment of Cuirassiers,
   1st, 189, 207-08,
   3rd, 131
   8th, 111, 119-20, 122-23, 124, 128, 129
   11th, 111, 119-20, 127, 128-29
Regiment of Dragoons
   2nd, 104, 135
   7th, 104, 135
Regiment of Chasseurs a Cheval
   1st, 8, 21
   3rd, 159, 191, 193
   4th, 190-91,

6th, 64-65, 71, 173
9th, 191
11th, 21, 190
12th, 191
Regiment of Hussars,
   1st, 9, 22, 24
   7th, 159, 180, 191, 192, 193
Regiment of Lancers,
   1st, 178-79, 180, 189, 190
   2nd, 178-79, 180, 181, 190
   3rd, 193
   4th, 193
   5th, 21,46
   6th, 18, 21,46, 84-85
   7th, 181
Regiment of Foot Artillery
   2nd, 106
Regiment of Horse Artillery,
   2nd, 129
Répécaud, 63, 66
River Sambre, 15, 121–22
Roman road, 38, 42, 47, 56

Saint-Amand, 41, 48, 137, 147, 156, 158, 161, 167, 175
   villages of, 156, 158, 168
Sambre, 15–16, 18, 25, 171, 226
Scots Greys, 200, 206, 209
Second Lieutenant Carel Emilius, 78
Second Lieutenant Desbuisserets, 31
Second-Lieutenant Jean Auguste Lapeyre, 193
Sergeant Graumann, 90
Sergeant Jacques Aubert, 96
Sergeant Julien Chaboudy, 46
Sergeant-Major Silvain Larreguy, 68
Sergeant Massiet, 134
Sergeant Matthew Coglan, 186
Sergeant Pessler, 90
Sergeant Winsinger, 112
Sir Colin Halket, 127–28
Sir Henry Hardinge, 146
Sir James Kempt, 86, 95–96, 126, 151
Sir Robert Wilson, 174
Sir Thomas Picton, 80, 85,92, 125, 128
Sir William Dornberg, 197
Smith, Ian, 29, 53, 106, 153, 194

INDEX

Soignes Forest, 182, 191–92, 211, 213, 215, 220–21
Solre-sur-Sambre, 15, 101
Sombreffe, 34–38, 44, 46, 98, 114, 154, 167, 182
Soult, 20, 22–28, 31–32, 34, 36, 39–43, 45–46, 53–54, 99–100, 102–3, 153, 155–56, 160–61, 163–64, 233–36
Squadron Commander Victor Dupuy, 204, 214, 217, 245
St-Amand, 122, 148, 159–60
Sub-Lieutenant Dominique Botto, 117
Sub-Lieutenant Nicolas Bouchard, 73
Sub-Lieutenant Simon Charles Herlobig, 115
Sub-Lieutenant Victor Baudinet, 143
Surgeon Gibney, 183

Tancarville, 45, 136, 152, 244
Tancarville's information, 150
town of Genappe, 185, 197–99
Trois-Bras, ix, 34, 36, 42–43, 45, 55–56, 121, 148
　position of, 36, 69, 149
Trooper John Marshal, 208
Trooper Joseph Lord, 205
Trooper Samuel Boulter, 200, 209
Trumpeter Jean-Baptiste François Charonnet, 130
Trumpet-Major Jean Joachim Baston, 96

Valmy, 26–27, 34–38, 43, 45, 50, 55, 140, 147, 216, 224
van Balveren, 105
van Bronkhorst, 79
van Corswarem, 82
Vandaleur, 226
Vandamme, 15, 31, 35, 47, 170, 228
van Doren, 81, 105, 245
van Hogendorp, 109
van Limburg Stirum, 80
van Loeben Sels, 105
van Merlen, 75, 81
van Nyevelt, 50, 61–62, 142
van Opstall, 78
van Pittius, 78
van Remoorter, 82
van Stirum, 110
van St Pancras, 78, 105
van Westenberg, 51
van Zuijlen, 50, 142
Vatry, 107, 137, 158
Villers-Perwin, 62, 159, 167, 171

Wagnelée, 56, 100, 164–65, 167–68
Waterloo, village of, 209, 213
Wellington's army, 44, 104
Westphalian Landwehr Regiment, 15

York Light Infantry Battalion, 177–78